Dromkeen:
A Journey into Children's Literature

Court and Joyce Oldmeadow, the founders of the Dromkeen Collection.

Dromkeen:
A Journey into Children's Literature

Jeffrey Prentice and Bettina Bird

Henry Holt and Company
New York

First published in the United States in 1988 by
Henry Holt and Company, Inc., 115 West 18th Street,
New York, New York 10011.
Published in Canada by Fitzhenry & Whiteside Limited,
195 Allstate Parkway, Markham, Ontario L3R 4T8.
Originally published in Australia by J. M. Dent Pty Limited.

Library of Congress Card Catalog Number: 87-46073
Library of Congress Cataloging in Publication Data is available.

ISBN 0-8050-0773-3

First American Edition

Designed and typeset by Q-Mark Design Pty Ltd
Photography by Dennis Wisken
Produced by Island Graphics Pty Ltd
Printed in Singapore
10 9 8 7 6 5 4 3 2 1

ACKNOWLEDGEMENTS

The authors are indebted to the following people for
supplying information or for providing secretarial assistance
in compiling this book: John Arnold, Joyce Badgery, Derek
Cadsky, Nance Donkin, Michael Dugan, Margaret East,
Hank Ebes, Brian Harris, Julie Hedderman, John Holroyd,
Margaret Ingham, Eleanor Kauffmann, A. M. Morris,
Maureen O'Sullivan, Darren Ryan, Richard Sands, Dr Neil
Shand and Marian Shand, the late Noreen Shelley, Joan
Short, Albert Ullin, John Ward and Pegi Williams.

ISBN 0-8050-0773-3

CONTENTS

Foreword

I shall never forget my first visit to Dromkeen in 1979. Albert Ullin, the well known children's bookseller, who was to receive the Dromkeen Medal 'for services to children's literature' in 1987, drove me through a grove of thick pines to the front entrance of a charming homestead. On this occasion, as part of the programme for those attending the second Pacific Rim Conference on Children's Literature, the house was thronged with guests. Some were quietly dipping into books; others were delightedly examining original artwork; some were hunting autographs from Pixie O'Harris and the other prominent authors present. Groups of school children were listening with rapt attention to stories, calling out spontaneously at dramatic moments, or drinking in the details of how a book is created. I can remember the author-artist, Ted Greenwood, sitting in the 'English' room in earnest conversation with a visitor from overseas. Later, there was a book launching, followed, as always at Dromkeen, by refreshments.

Dromkeen is a house — a home — with an all-pervading ambience: the grounds, the gardens, the nineteenth century weatherboard building are unmistakeably, but not aggressively, Australian: there are the carpets over which so many feet have wandered; the patina of antique furniture and the gleam of silver; hand-painted china and ornaments placed with seeming casualness; artwork that catches the breath — a relief collage, a pen and ink sketch, a series of water colours; and rare, first edition books. All these elements, harmoniously blended, manifest a unique expression of an ideal: an ideal which inspired Joyce Oldmeadow and her late husband Court to create 'Dromkeen' that so many have experienced and enjoyed.

On one face of the Dromkeen Medal is shown, in relief, the homestead with a crescent moon framed by acacias; on the reverse side an open book above the recipient's name is surrounded by the legend, 'Dromkeen Medal/Children's Books'. This symbolically captures the essence of Dromkeen: a meeting place of minds, children and books.

Children's books have always reflected the attitudes and values of the society that produced them. As our present society grows more complex we are warned that childhood is in danger of being swept away. Certainly, the demands on children, if not greater than ever before, are increasingly threatening. All the more need to present them with positive images to delight the senses, stir the emotions, nourish the mind and inspire the soul.

Dromkeen does all this and more. Through its collection of historical books, illustrations, memorabilia and records, it provides access to the history of Australian children's literature, to the writers, illustrators, editors, publishers and booksellers who gave us a tradition and heritage. It also puts Australian children's books in an international context. And it goes further. It helps children to become keen, discerning and enthusiastic readers: an invaluable service to our young and to our nation.

Speaking in Sydney at the opening of Australian Children's Book Week in 1976, I expressed my dream of 'a national collection of children's books'. In my speech, I said, 'Apart from enthusiasm, foresight and enterprise, what is needed is the nucleus of a collection and a fitting place to house it . . . I leave with you the thought that this country now needs a permanent exhibition of its children's books so that this aspect of our history will be preserved to inspire both readers and writers in the years to come'.

In the years that have passed since 1976, the Dromkeen Collection has become known nationally and internationally; the Lu Rees Archives collection of books, manuscripts, articles, notes and records at the Canberra College of Advanced Education has been opened to scholars and visitors; and the James Hardie Collection of rare books, illustrations and memorabilia in Sydney has welcomed researchers and held exhibitions for the general public around Australia. Since then, too, courses in children's literature in Australia have proliferated at both the under-graduate and post-graduate level. Doctoral theses on Australian children's literature are now being written.

There is currently an urgent need to document, for scholarly research, the holdings of children's literature and artwork around Australia. Dromkeen still stands unique, but there are complementary collections and liaison between them is essential. This book about the Dromkeen Collection is not only a tribute but also a record and, I believe, the formative link in a network of information vital to research.

Australian children's literature has come of age. In 1986, Patricia Wrightson, who was the third recipient of the Dromkeen Medal and who delivered the fourth Courtney Oldmeadow Memorial Lecture, was awarded the Hans Christian Andersen Medal for authorship — the only truly international award in children's literature. At the same ceremony, Robert Ingpen, an Honorary Governor of the Courtney Oldmeadow Children's Literature Foundation, received the Hans Christian Andersen Medal for illustration. A significant linkage of people, place and books.

Maurice Saxby
1987

6

Preface

Dromkeen: A Journey Into Children's Literature is concerned with the Dromkeen Collection, which is preserved in the nineteenth century homestead, Dromkeen, in Victoria.

When writing this book, we had several purposes in mind: to put forward the philosophy underlying the concept of the Dromkeen Collection of children's literature, originated and put into practice by its founders, Joyce and Court Oldmeadow; to present an overview of the Collection and its associated activities; and to provide some insight into the development of Australian children's literature from colonial times to the present day, using representative examples of rare and contemporary books, and manuscripts, artwork and other pre-publication material in the Dromkeen Collection.

We have not attempted a critical work, rather we have endeavoured to present an appreciation of the creative works of the many authors and illustrators of children's books who are represented by material in the Collection.

We are indebted to Rosemary Wighton, Maurice Saxby, Walter McVitty, Hugh Anderson, Marcie Muir and Brenda Niall for their valuable works in the field of Australian children's literature. We are indebted also to the many authors, illustrators and people with a background knowledge of Australian printing and publishing houses, and the book trade, who have granted interviews or entered into correspondence in order that information could be compiled for this work.

Because the Dromkeen Collection is a 'living' collection, displays of artwork, manuscripts and other pre-publication material at Dromkeen are changing constantly. Therefore it was necessary to establish a date beyond which no new material arriving at Dromkeen could be included in this book. The designated date was 1 January 1985. The only exceptions are the reference to the exhibition of artwork by Beatrix Potter, which was held at Dromkeen homestead, February — April 1985, and the award of the Dromkeen Medal in 1986.

We wish to express our gratitude to Joyce Oldmeadow and her son, John. Without their continual encouragement, and appraisal of factual information regarding the founding of the Dromkeen Collection and its subsequent development, this book could not have been written.

Jeffrey Prentice
Bettina Bird

Interior view of the Green Room at Dromkeen Homestead.

Dromkeen at dusk: mid-winter 1984.

Cover design for Joan Phipson's historical work, Bennelong. (Original artwork)

Chapter 1
Dromkeen - The Realisation of a Dream

Dromkeen homestead lies north-west of Melbourne, close to the township of Riddells Creek, where gently rolling pastoral country gives way to the timbered foothills of the Great Dividing Range.

The mellowed, nineteenth century homestead is positioned comfortably on the brow of a hill. Its tall windows are shielded from the glare of the afternoon sun by a long verandah and command wide views of the green and gold countryside below. Secluded from the road by surrounding lawns, trees and gardens, Dromkeen provides an ideal setting for a world-renowned collection of children's literature, the Courtney Oldmeadow Children's Literature Foundation.

The Foundation is generally referred to as the 'Dromkeen Collection', and comprises numerous pieces of artwork, which are mainly the original drawings and paintings for illustrated children's books, together with preliminary sketches, manuscripts, photographs, pre-publication production material, tapes, correspondence and other documents, and a comprehensive library of children's literature.

A Brief History of the Dromkeen Collection

Woven through the early history of the Dromkeen Collection is the story of a dream, a vision shared by its founders, Joyce and Court Oldmeadow. They dreamed of gathering a small collection of artwork from which illustrations for children's books had been reproduced and of displaying these treasures so that children could enjoy them.

As booksellers, Joyce and Court Oldmeadow had often been shown new artwork for children's books on their book-buying visits to publishing companies, and they were amazed and delighted by the freshness and vitality of the paintings and drawings. When looking at these illustrations later in the

9

printed book, they had frequently felt a sense of disappointment because the illustrations seemed to have lost some of their liveliness and crispness in the printing process. Convinced that the vibrancy and feeling of immediacy of original paintings and drawings would give children pleasure, the Oldmeadows nurtured their dream of commencing a collection of artwork and of forming a permanent exhibition that children could visit. They both felt certain that if children could see drawings and paintings which had been created especially to illustrate children's books, 'their own kind of books', then books would become more meaningful and real for them — and that this intimate experience, in turn, would help to further a love of books and reading.

For years, the Oldmeadows' dream seemed unattainable. Then, in 1973, they purchased Dromkeen homestead and it was there that the opportunity to commence a collection at last became a possibility, for there was ample space to set up a modest display. Moreover, there was also the opportunity to create a truly 'living' collection which would allow children to become more actively involved in the creative processes inherent in the production of a book.

The first few pieces of artwork that formed the nucleus of the Collection were acquired early in 1974 and exhibited in one of the front rooms of the homestead. Named the Dromkeen Collection of Australian Children's Literature, it was officially opened on 12 October 1974, at a barbecue lunch held on the lawns surrounding the homestead. The large audience comprised authors and illustrators of children's books, editors, publishers, academics, teachers, librarians and interested members of the public.

Bennelong was not at the meeting place when the Governor's boat arrived the next day but he came up in his canoe soon afterwards. The first thing he did was to lift his arms to show he was not holding any weapons. He did not want his 'father' to think there was anything to fear from him. He was delighted to see the Governor again and, as usual when he was pleased, talked a lot. He told Governor Phillip the name of the man who had wounded him and that he and Colbee had already administered the punishment.

More cheerful subjects now occupied them, for Governor Phillip had brought many presents with him and these were distributed. Fishing lines and hatchets were followed by a petticoat and other small things for Barrangaroo. Bennelong wanted to take them to her immediately, but Phillip persuaded him it would be better if Barrangaroo came to take them for herself. He was eager for Barrangaroo to lose her distrust of the white men.

She came willingly for her presents and Bennelong was very pleased they had remembered her especially. He was even more delighted when the Governor gave him the red jacket with silver epaulettes which he had been accustomed to wear at Government House.   35

No 31

BOT

Collins Bennelong   ONE 12 Baskerville 2 pt. leaded

1. Boy Bennelong

Bennelong dropped his basket of fish by the ashes of last night's fire and rubbed his arms. It had been a good catch and it was a heavy load for a boy of six. The other children dropped theirs, too. Behind them, chattering as they always did, came their mothers, aunts and grandmothers. They carried the fishing gear and treated it more carefully than the children treated the fish, for good tools meant more food. One of the women bent over the ashes and began carefully to revive the glowing coals buried beneath them.

It was a crisp autumn morning. A faint breeze blowing off the water made the patches of sunlight that fell through the leaves dance and caper over the ground. Below their camp at the bottom of the rocky slope the waters of the harbour sparkled. Through the eucalyptus trunks they could see the canoes far out on the water. The men were out there spearing bigger fish than the women and children could catch in the nets. Behind the camp the scrub-covered hills rolled endlessly; peaceful, sun-drenched hills that were the familiar surroundings of home to Bennelong. About them round the shores of the harbour and farther back in the hills lived other groups of his tribe. All were dependent on that wide, tranquil stretch of water for their daily food. The tide, flowing twice a day through the narrow gap of the Heads, brought all the fish they needed. They caught and ate other food as well; duck, wallaby, possum, bush rat, lizard, snake and the bigger and more succulent grubs. But most of these came and went with the seasons. The fish were always there. There was no need for the tribe to move far afield in search of food. The harbour kept them safe, and its shores were home.

It was a day early in May in the year 1770. About noon when most of the men had returned from fishing and canoes were drawn up on the rocks below, they were visited by some men from a different group of the tribe. This group lived about the shores of another stretch of water just south of their harbour. Although none of them knew it that stretch of water had, in the last few days, been named Botany Bay.

The philosophy and aims underlying the Collection were
outlined to those present in an address by Court Oldmeadow.
The aims were twofold. The first involved the conservation of
all manner of material associated with Australian children's
literature, and in his address, Court stressed the urgent need to
collect and preserve pre-publication material as well as first and
early editions of children's books. He explained that once a
book was on the market, the manuscript, the drawings and
paintings for the illustrations, and much of the other material to
do with production, were usually placed in the publisher's
warehouse where they were frequently lost as later pre-
publication material accumulated, and even destroyed in a
general clean-up of the warehouse. He pointed out that these
irreplaceable materials, the result of so much creativity and
expertise, formed as vital a part of our cultural heritage as the
published books, something which was only just beginning to be
appreciated in this country.

The second aim outlined by Court Oldmeadow was extremely
unusual, and so were the means suggested for achieving it. The
audience was informed that the Dromkeen Collection was not
intended to be static, shut away from public view and shown
only on request, as are many collections. It was to be a *living*
collection, displayed and always available for children to enjoy,
to examine and discuss, and that its purpose could be summed
up in a phrase often used by Joyce, namely, 'to bring children
and books together in a more intimate way'.

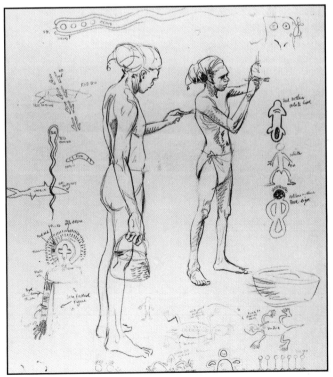

Court Oldmeadow addressing the audience at the official opening of the Dromkeen Collection.

Illustration by Quentin Hole for the William Collins edition of The Man from Ironbark. (Original artwork)

Expanding on this theme, Court Oldmeadow explained that most children had no idea how a book came into existence, no understanding of the creative forces that prompted an author to write a story and an artist to illustrate it, nor any realisation of how a publisher caused the material to be printed and made into a book. This lack of knowledge resulted in many children regarding books as remote, unreal and lacking in meaning for them, and so an emotional gap developed between these children and the world of books.

One reason why the Dromkeen Collection was to be a 'living' collection was to help as many children as possible to bridge this gap. Another was to extend the interest of children who had already developed a love of books. It was anticipated that as a consequence of experiencing displays of artwork glowing with colour and vitality, seeing an illustrator's preparatory sketches, and an author's manuscript with the editor's comments written in the margins, together with other pre-publication material, all children visiting Dromkeen would come to understand that books were created by *real* people who had an equally *real* audience in mind. Inherent in the concept of the Dromkeen Collection as a 'living' collection was also the intention of inviting children's authors and illustrators to visit the homestead and conduct workshops with groups of children.

At the conclusion of Court Oldmeadow's address, Anne Ingram, the editor of children's books for William Collins, Australia, launched four new books published by that company. One, *The Man From Ironbark*, a rollicking Australian ballad written last century by A. B. Paterson, was first published in the Sydney *Bulletin* in 1892. The Collins edition was illustrated by Quentin Hole, and the artist donated a piece of his artwork for the book to the new collection at Dromkeen.

In general, the response to the official opening of the Dromkeen Collection was positive. In a short time, offers of material for display, either donated or on loan, were flowing in from authors, illustrators, publishers and interested members of the public. With this encouragement and the help of close friends whose interest had been aroused, the Oldmeadows continued to develop the Collection at the homestead, and to put their philosophy concerning its use into practice.

Authors and illustrators of children's books, many from interstate and overseas, began to visit Dromkeen where they spent a few days in the guest quarters, sometimes to recover from the exhausting effects of a lecture tour, at others to conduct a workshop for children or adults.

The workshops were lively affairs. Children entered enthusiastically into discussions about stories, or about the materials and methods used to obtain a particular effect in a piece of artwork. At one workshop, the British author William Mayne made up stories incorporating the ideas of the school children in the group. At another workshop, visiting British illustrators of children's books, Helen Oxenbury and John Burningham, worked with primary-school children to create a giant mural which has been preserved at Dromkeen. In other activities, children investigated the various stages in the production of a book, using as examples edited manuscripts, galley proofs and other pre-publication material in the Collection. It soon became

obvious that workshops and activities such as these were of tremendous help in bringing books to life for children.

Through media coverage and the recommendations of teachers and librarians who had visited Dromkeen, interest in the Dromkeen Collection and its underlying educational philosophy spread rapidly, and the number of school groups and adults visiting the homestead escalated.

In 1976, only two years after the Dromkeen Collection had been officially opened, Joyce and Court Oldmeadow were presented with the prestigious Eleanor Farjeon Award in recognition of their contribution to children's literature. This United Kingdom award 'for distinguished services to children's books' is presented annually by the Children's Book Circle, a group of British editors of books for children. It was the first time the Eleanor Farjeon Award had been given to anyone outside the United Kingdom, or to booksellers. With its presentation to Joyce and Court Oldmeadow, the importance of the Dromkeen Collection to children's literature became recognised internationally.

Oldmeadow Booksellers

The course of events that led to Joyce and Court Oldmeadow's vision of a home for children's literature and its realisation in the living collection at Dromkeen, stretch back over the years to their youth. In order to gain some understanding of this development, it is necessary to glance briefly at their lives, both before and after their marriage, including the gradual expansion of their bookselling business in Melbourne.

Joyce and Court Oldmeadow's backgrounds were different in many ways, and so, therefore, were the skills and emphasis that each brought to bear in the course of building up their retail business, Oldmeadow Booksellers. It was their determination to direct their separate skills and aptitudes towards a common purpose that resulted in the success of their bookshop. This, in turn, made the Dromkeen Collection possible.

Joyce Oldmeadow

Joyce Oldmeadow's early life was probably the perfect prelude to her involvement in a bookshop that specialised in various kinds of books for children. Her own love of books, encouraged during her childhood by her mother, was given fresh impetus when, in the late 1930s, she became a student at the Kindergarten Teacher's Training College in Kew, a Melbourne suburb. There, the enthusiasm of a lecturer in children's literature had an immense effect on her.

The lecturer had a genuine talent for story-telling. Her dramatisation of characters, incidents and action held her audience entranced, and she expected a similar standard of story-telling from her students. Each student had to choose a book suitable for kindergarten children, memorise the story and then relate it to the rest of the student group. The story-teller had to capture the mood and vitality of the original narrative; pictures in the book could be shown only when the story-telling was over.

Joyce recalls memorising *The Tale of Peter Rabbit* by repeating it over and over again as she walked to college. She remembers another story she learned, too, a longer one — *The Story About Ping*. Ping was a yellow duckling who lived on a boat on the Yangtze River in China with his mother and father, two sisters and three brothers, eleven aunts, seven uncles and forty-two cousins.

The college lecturer kindled an interest in children's literature, and developed an understanding of the delight young children take in a story well told, that were to remain with Joyce Oldmeadow throughout the years to come.

The Tale of Peter Rabbit, by Beatrix Potter, and *The Story About Ping*, by Marjorie Flack, were British publications. Very few books for pre-school children were being published in Australia during the 1930s. In order to develop an appreciation of the creative effort underlying the production of a picture-story book, student teachers at the college had to write and illustrate their own stories for pre-school children.

There can be no doubt that the type of activities allied to books for young children in which Joyce Oldmeadow was involved during her student years had a great deal to do with the gradual formation of the dream that was eventually realised at Dromkeen. In interviews, she has frequently stressed the important role that stories, picture-story books and games of make-believe play in the life of a young child.

To take Joyce Oldmeadow's point further — young children often demand a favourite story over and over again until the tale is known almost by heart. Adults, who have grown a little weary of reading the same story so many times and have tried to take a short cut through the text, know the feeling of being brought suddenly to a halt by the anguished cry 'You've left something out!' Obviously a story so well loved must have a great deal of meaning for the child.

Stories and picture-story books help a young child to create an imaginary world, rich in fantasy, and within it, secret places that can be explored in wonderful flights of fancy. The child fills this 'pretending world' with all kinds of make-believe characters with whom to interact either solely in imagination or else in games of 'let's pretend'. Children need an imaginary world they can enter at will because it is in fantasy that they are able to rationalise their fears and doubts and form acceptable interpretations of the real world in which they are daily meeting with new, and sometimes puzzling or frightening, experiences.

13

Court Oldmeadow in one room of the cramped quarters at Maltravers Road, where Oldmeadow Booksellers operated in 1959.

Double-page spread from Squik the Squirrel Possum *by Eve Pownall, illustrated by Raymond Johnson and published in 1949 for the pre-school market.*

In relation to somewhat older children, many adults will recall being told as a child or teenager that it was time to switch off the bedroom light just when they were so completely engrossed in a story that to have put down the book at that stage would have been unthinkable. How many smuggled a torch into bed and continued to read the book under the bedclothes? How meaningful that story must have been!

It was while she was a student at the Kindergarten Teacher's Training College that Joyce Oldmeadow became aware of the many aspects of child development, including a young child's need for stories, all of which were to be of benefit to her in later years in her capacity as a retailer of children's books. After graduating, she accepted a position as a kindergarten teacher, and it was during the early years of the war, while she was teaching, that she met Court Oldmeadow. They were married in 1942 and throughout their married life they shared an intense love of literature and music.

Court Oldmeadow

Court Oldmeadow's passion for books and love of literature developed during his school days. On the completion of his matriculation year, he was awarded a university scholarship, but as those were the years of the Great Depression, he was unable to take advantage of his award and he decided on banking as a career. His first position was at the Dandenong branch of the Bank of Australasia.

Shortly after the outbreak of the Second World War, Court Oldmeadow joined the Royal Australian Air Force, and as a

Flight Lieutenant he flew missions in the Pacific area. When the war ended, he no longer felt he could settle into the world of banking and he began to look around for a suitable opening in private enterprise. His first venture in this field was the purchase of a small business in the Melbourne suburb of East Ivanhoe. Joyce Oldmeadow recalls that period in their lives:

It was a type of mixed business with a sub-post office and a small newsagency. We also stocked sweets, cigarettes, tobacco — things like that. Shortly afterwards, we sold the newsagency section because Court wanted to concentrate on building up a library of adult novels, for literature was the love of his life. We kept the other side of the business, however — the post office, sweets and so forth — because without these we couldn't have survived. Then Court started to expand the library by adding a section for children, but he did this gradually, as he could afford it. Then he decided to retail children's books as well. We sold books for very young children through to teenage novels — hard-back books because there were no paperbacks in Australia at that time.

Bookselling Days

The business in East Ivanhoe prospered and, in 1958, Court Oldmeadow took a major step in his career. Booksellers, Ormond Yeo and his wife, travelled from school to school selling educational materials from a small van. The Oldmeadows became interested in this type of operation, and in 1958 they sold their mixed business in East Ivanhoe and worked with the Yeos for twelve months. In 1959 they bought the primary-

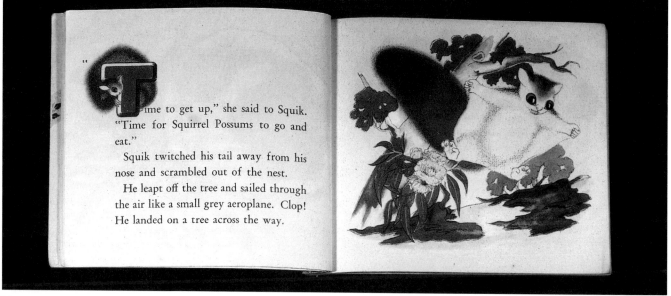

"T ime to get up," she said to Squik. "Time for Squirrel Possums to go and eat."

Squik twitched his tail away from his nose and scrambled out of the nest.

He leapt off the tree and sailed through the air like a small grey aeroplane. Clop! He landed on a tree across the way.

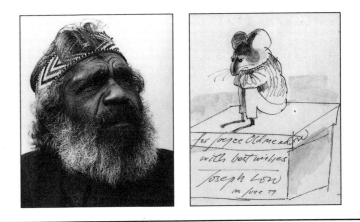

Dick Roughsey, the Aboriginal artist who illustrated The Giant Devil-Dingo *and* Rainbow Serpent.

Original illustration by Joseph Low for The Christmas Grump, *sent to Joyce Oldmeadow from America.*

Michael Dugan and Joyce Oldmeadow sharing a picture story book with a young reader.

school side of the business; the secondary side was bought by L. & S. School Library Service.

The Oldmeadows conducted their educational bookselling business from the large garage behind their home in Maltravers Road, East Ivanhoe, and serviced schools from the van. Those days were filled with long hours of strenuous work, but they were encouraging and rewarding times because Court had achieved an important goal in his life: he was now involved in a business that concentrated solely on the retailing of books.

Teachers and librarians flocked to buy their supplies from 'the bookshop in the garage', as the business was often called. The Oldmeadows stocked almost everything in the way of books and materials that primary schools required and teachers came to respect the advice, always available on request, concerning the relevance of various books and materials to their particular teaching needs. The atmosphere at the Oldmeadows' bookshop was one of informality, friendliness and hospitality. Customers of those days remember well being served tea in a silver teapot on a silver tray, and feeling free to wander around the garden.

The reputation the bookshop earned as a source of expert advice was well deserved. Both Joyce and Court seemed to sense the type of books and educational materials their customers needed, and with almost unerring judgement, to recommend those best suited to their requirements. Court was a good listener, and this, in turn, helped him to keep well informed of the needs created by changing attitudes in education. One librarian who frequented the bookshop in Maltravers Road remarked: 'If you were talking to Court Oldmeadow, you knew for certain that you had his complete attention and that he respected your requests and opinions.'

Court found that trying to combine his love of books with his business activities was often frustrating because he never had sufficient time to read all the books he wished. He read all he could, and the extent of his reading was reflected in discussions with customers as to the merits, or otherwise, of a particular publication, and he was constantly recommending, lending, and even giving away books he had found stimulating or useful. Customers often noticed, with surprise, that they seemed to be regarded more as personal friends than the purchasing public.

The business at Maltravers Road continued to grow. Joyce Oldmeadow remembers those days very well:

Initially, the business occupied two rooms built into the garage, plus a bungalow. However, the family soon came to realise that books have a life and impetus of their own. Books invaded our home, even the children's bedrooms. Court considered himself something of a handy-man and he put up

shelves everywhere. Eventually we had to build an upstairs section on the house, so that the books could take over the downstairs rooms, and the three children, teenagers by then, could move upstairs.

In 1967, Beverley Burt, a high-school teacher, joined the business on a part-time basis, and Michael Dugan, a family connection of Court Oldmeadow, and now a children's author in his own right, became the Oldmeadows' first full-time employee, working mainly in the development of the section devoted to books for school libraries.

Books continued to encroach on the domestic quarters of the Oldmeadows' home, spreading through the passages until, in 1968, the business was moved to a large, brick building in Beatrice Avenue, West Heidelberg.

If space had been a limiting factor at Maltravers Road, it was the most impressive feature of the new store, which was a cavernous warehouse with a huge expanse of concrete floor. The move took place in February, 1968. Carpets were laid, shelves were installed and quickly packed with books, customers arrived and continued to arrive, and the business flourished.

At that time, teachers were taking an increasing interest in the processes of reading: how a child learns to read, and also how to promote a child's desire to continue to read. Wide reading schemes were being introduced into schools, and there was a growth of interest in picture-story books suitable for children in

Interior of Oldmeadow Booksellers, Beatrice Avenue; Court Oldmeadow and Beverly Burt checking stock.

Humorous illustration sent to Joyce Oldmeadow from England by the creator of the Mr Men series, Roger Hargreaves.

pre-school and early primary-school grades. Libraries, particularly in primary schools, were being built or extended.

Now specialising in educational material for both primary and junior-secondary schools, the Oldmeadows' bookshop became renowned throughout Victoria for its range and scope of children's literature. Texts, picture-story books by the hundreds, factual books and children's novels, many by that time in paperback format, crammed the shelves.

Joyce Oldmeadow was involved in all aspects of the bookshop — administration, ordering and sales. Her particular love was picture-story books. She often spoke at meetings of parent groups throughout the Melbourne metropolitan and outer suburban areas, and almost without exception she centred her address on children and their books. She recalls that children who came into the bookshop were never slow to ask questions about books, and most of their queries indicated their lack of understanding of how a book is created.

'Where did this book come from? Did you have to make it?'
'Do you know the person who wrote this story?'
'Did a real person draw these pictures?'
'How does a book get printed?'

No matter how carefully the questions were answered, it became obvious that children could have no true grasp of the stages in the production of a book unless they could in some way experience the creative processes that lie behind its making. What seemed to be needed was a permanent exhibition of materials and illustrative work which showed the various stages in a book's production.

Over the years, 'Meet-the-Author' nights and book launchings had become features of the Oldmeadows' bookshop in West Heidelberg. These occasions involved adults, not children, and were held in the evenings when the bookshop was not crowded with customers. A permanent exhibition for children would mean having space in the bookshop for day-time viewing — and there was no space. There seemed to be no solution to the problem.

The children's literature section of the bookshop was Court Oldmeadow's special interest and this eventually prompted business trips to overseas publishers, as well as to those in Australia, in search of new titles. Direct contact with overseas publishing houses resulted in the Oldmeadows being constantly aware of new trends in children's books in other countries. During these trips, Joyce and Court Oldmeadow's sincerity of approach to children's literature and their ease of manner made them many friends among authors, illustrators and publishers of children's books.

On a book-buying excursion overseas in 1971, Joyce and Court found time to visit three important collections of children's literature: the Osborne Collection at the Toronto Public Library in Canada; Selma Lagerlöf's collection at her home in Sweden; and the collection of the works of Beatrix Potter at her cottage in the Lake District in England. Joyce and Court were entranced with Beatrix Potter's old world cottage. Everything she had used when she lived and worked there was still in place, and many preliminary sketches and pieces of completed artwork for her books were on display.

The cottage where Beatrix Potter had created so many of the well-loved characters for her children's books seemed to Joyce and Court to be the perfect home for such a valuable and nostalgic collection. Their visit to the cottage generated an idea that was to take their dream of gathering a collection of their own a stage further. A home, not a bookshop, was exactly what was needed in Australia for displaying examples of artwork for children's books on a permanent basis. However, it would have to be just the right kind of home, a place with an aura of history about it. The idea was destined to lie dormant for some years.

When purchasing stock in Sydney early in 1973, Joyce and Court Oldmeadow visited the premises of the publishing company William Collins, where they met the children's editor, Anne Ingram. The artwork for the book *Barnaby and the Rocket*, written by Lydia Pender and illustrated by Judy Cowell, was displayed in Anne Ingram's office. This was the first time

Lydia Pender, Australian children's author.

Illustrator of Barnaby and the Rocket, *Judy Cowell, with her young son.*

A piece of artwork for Barnaby and the Rocket *by Lydia Pender, illustrated by Judy Cowell.* (Original artwork)

that Joyce and Court had seen artwork for a contemporary Australian children's book and the impact that the freshness and vitality of the paintings made came as a surprise. To quote Joyce Oldmeadow:

> I remember thinking at the time, wouldn't it be marvellous if we could have a piece of that artwork and display it for children to see. It would make books far more real for them. You see, the artwork was so much more vibrant than the reproductions in the printed book.

Hopes of some day commencing a small collection of Australian artwork for children's books and displaying it where children could enjoy it were rekindled. But although the Oldmeadows often discussed the idea, they were unable to see any means of putting it into practice.

During this period, the bookshop in Beatrice Avenue was presenting some pressing problems. The business had once again expanded beyond the limits of the premises to accommodate both the requirements of the shop and the space needed to warehouse the stock, even though a mezzanine floor had been constructed to allow space for the office and the ever-increasing range of children's paperbacks. A certain measure of relief regarding space for storing stock was gained when another building in Beatrice Avenue was leased as a bulk-handling store. But still the business grew, and the Oldmeadows began seriously to consider finding a place outside Melbourne that could be used both as a bulk store and a freight centre for imported books.

Dromkeen Homestead

One spring day in 1973, Joyce Oldmeadow decided to drive to Riddells Creek to visit Marjorie Amess, a friend she had made when she was studying china painting, an art she still pursues as a hobby. During the course of their conversation, Marjorie Amess suggested that the Oldmeadows consider the homestead

on the hill at the back of her house as a place in which to store books. The property was called Dromkeen. The old homestead had been empty for two years and previously had been the residence of Jack Manton, a well-known art entrepreneur. He had built a large wing on the house in which to display his valuable collection of Australian impressionist paintings, known as the Heidelberg Collection.

Marjorie Amess and Joyce walked up the hill to look at the homestead. Not only did it appear a suitable place for storing large numbers of books, but also an ideal place in which to live. After her visit, Joyce discussed with Court the possibility of purchasing Dromkeen and eventually they drove back to Riddells Creek, where the agent showed them through the homestead and around the ten-hectare property. In Joyce Oldmeadow's words:

> And then, as always, I became wildly enthusiastic. I already had the homestead as a home for children's literature and all sorts of things. Court made me take things slowly and be practical. I was the one who had wild ideas; he was the one who made ideas and dreams a reality.

The Oldmeadows purchased the property and moved in on Boxing Day, 1973, and Court commuted to West Heidelberg each day. The large wing of the homestead in which Jack Manton had housed his collection of paintings became the bulk store and freight centre for the bookshop in West Heidelberg.

Shortly after the move to Dromkeen, Ross and Lucy Lindholm were engaged as members of staff for the new venture. Lucy was a nursing sister accustomed to working in the hectic conditions of a hospital casualty ward and she was soon managing the bulk book-store and freight centre with calmness and efficiency. Ross had accrued a great deal of experience with livestock and machinery on large Australian grazing properties, and his energy and ingenuity were often put to good effect at Dromkeen, where he was called upon to solve a multitude of practical problems, varying from suitable methods of tearing out ancient and stubborn clumps of agapanthus to handling the transportation of tonnes of books from Riddells Creek railway-station to the bulk store at the homestead.

While all these changes to their lifestyle and business were taking place, Joyce and Court Oldmeadow's days had been too occupied for dreams. It had become clear that there was a definite requirement for a retail bookshop at Dromkeen. Geographically, the homestead offered easy access to country areas and schools north of Melbourne. Plans for a bookshop went ahead and the bulk stock was again located at a building in Melbourne. The Dromkeen bookshop was established in the

wing that had once been the bulk store, and Lucy Lindholm was placed in charge.

The Dream Becomes Reality

On reviewing their domestic and business arrangements, Joyce and Court Oldmeadow became aware that they now had sufficient space in which to set up a permanent display of artwork by illustrators of Australian children's books and to make it accessible to children. It was with joy and enthusiasm that they embarked on the purchase of the first pieces of artwork for their collection.

Anne Ingram made arrangements for the Oldmeadows to buy one of the pieces of artwork by Judy Cowell for *Barnaby and the Rocket*, which had impressed them so much when they had seen it in Sydney the previous year. Michael Dugan suggested that Joyce go with him to meet the illustrator and author Peg Maltby at her cottage at Olinda in the Dandenong Ranges. The cover design and two original illustrations for one of Peg Maltby's fairy-tale books published during the 1940s, *Ben and Bella and the Apple Tree*, were purchased, and the artist donated one of her last remaining copies of the first edition to the new collection. A major acquisition, a short time later, was a large watercolour by Ida Rentoul Outhwaite, whose illustrations of fairyland fantasies were so admired earlier this century. These few pieces formed the nucleus of the Collection and were displayed in what was then the dining-room of the homestead, adjacent to the new bookshop.

Although Joyce and Court Oldmeadow's dream had quickened and emerged, it was some time before it was to come to complete fruition. After the opening of the Dromkeen Collection in October 1974, interest in the Collection, and curiosity about the Oldmeadows' philosophy concerning its uses, prompted an increasing number of groups of children and adults to visit Dromkeen. Concurrently, the arrival of new material for the Collection increased from a trickle to a steady flow, until eventually it took over the whole of the dining-room area and showed every sign of spreading into the adjoining rooms.

Joyce and Court realised that if artwork and other materials were to be displayed on a permanent basis and made accessible to children, constant adult supervision was essential. If this was not arranged, items might be damaged, even though unintentionally, and the preservation of such valuable and irreplaceable material was of immense importance to them. However, Joyce was adamant that the accessibility of the Collection to children must remain of paramount concern, and she was determined that nothing should sway her from this resolve, no matter how difficult such matters as supervision may become.

Shared enthusiasm is an incredible stimulant for ideas, and plans for activities related to children's literature to take place at Dromkeen followed one upon the other — a puppet theatre, more book launchings, a wider range of story-telling sessions, special exhibitions of all the artwork for a new children's book and further workshops in which children, authors and artists could work together.

By 1977, Joyce and Court Oldmeadow's dream of Dromkeen as a home for children's literature where children could be actively engaged in on-going programmes associated with children's books had become a magnificent reality.

Providentially, at this busy time, Libby Dalrymple called at Dromkeen in search of a part-time situation. She was engaged immediately, her duties being to help with the running of the homestead, with hospitality and catering, and also with various types of work concerned with the Collection.

Picturesque view of Dromkeen showing the patio with swimming-pool, where book launchings often take place.

Joyce Oldmeadow discussing children's books with an Indonesian publisher visiting Dromkeen.

Original illustration by the Japanese artist Mitsumasa Anno, who visited Dromkeen in 1983.

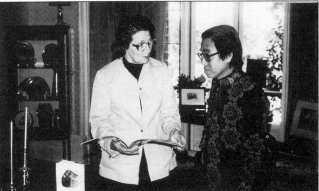

As the Collection grew steadily larger, the problem of constant supervision was solved. Story-telling sessions had been introduced early in the life of the Collection, and now educational programmes, each designed to suit a different age group of visiting children, were initiated. Other programmes were formulated to cater for adults. To begin with, the programmes were conducted by Joyce Oldmeadow, but when demands on her time became too great, the programmes were taken over by members of the Dromkeen staff.

International interest in the Dromkeen Collection, aroused when Joyce and Court Oldmeadow were awarded the Eleanor Farjeon Award in 1976, resulted in offers of artwork and other materials related to children's books, from Britain, the United States, Japan, Malaysia and Singapore.

The Courtney Oldmeadow Children's Literature Foundation

While the Dromkeen Collection had been expanding, so had the Oldmeadows' bookselling business in Melbourne. Once again, it was time to seek new premises, but now the building would have to be large enough to accommodate the main bookshop, the bulk store and the freight centre under one roof. Finally, the ex-Telecom building in McEwan Road, Heidelberg, was purchased and business commenced there in June 1977.

Tragically, during the past year, Court Oldmeadow had become extremely ill. After his death in July 1977, Joyce continued to develop the Collection at Dromkeen homestead. On 26 February 1982, the Dromkeen Collection was renamed the Courtney Oldmeadow Children's Literature Foundation in recognition of the vital part Court Oldmeadow had played in the founding and development of the Collection and his valuable contribution to children's literature.

Since 1977, many changes have taken place at Dromkeen and within the firm of Oldmeadow Booksellers. At the homestead, the Collection has spread through all the main rooms, with the exception of the bedrooms reserved for guests. Finding sufficient time to devote to both the Dromkeen Collection and the administration of the bookselling business proved too time-consuming and Joyce Oldmeadow eventually decided to concentrate on the Collection, and to accept a merger of Oldmeadow Booksellers with Ashton Scholastic Books.

Today, Dromkeen continues to cast its spell over all who visit the homestead. More than 8000 visitors, including tertiary students and research scholars, but mostly school children accompanied by teachers and librarians, now visit Dromkeen homestead each year. To spend a few hours enjoying the variety of artwork on display, exploring manuscripts, browsing through rare or contemporary children's books, or taking part in some of the creative activities, is a memorable experience for children and adults alike. As one might expect of a reality that has materialised from a dream, Dromkeen — the home of the Dromkeen Collection of children's literature — has developed a lingering mystique, completely its own.

A view of distant Mount Macedon from the Sunbury Road.

A link with the past: the old bluestone railway bridge straddling the road to Riddells Creek.

The railway-station at Riddells Creek.

Chapter 2
The Fascination of Dromkeen —
A Home for Children's Literature

In this chapter, the early history of Dromkeen homestead is outlined before a 'tour' is taken through the main display rooms.

As the Dromkeen Collection is continually growing and changing, artwork on loan may be exhibited for only a few months, or even weeks. Therefore, some of the artwork discussed in this chapter may have been in the homestead only during the period in which this book was being written.

Links with the Past

Dromkeen homestead is some sixty kilometres from Melbourne and one has a choice of route — along the Calder Highway through Gisborne to Riddells Creek, or via the Sunbury Road. The latter offers a pleasant drive with views across undulating grazing land to the ranges. The brooding hump of Mount Macedon, rising indigo-blue above its surrounding hills, dominates the skyline for most of the journey, but a short distance from Riddells Creek the land dips suddenly and Mount Macedon sinks from view as the road twists and turns on its way to lower ground. On rounding a bend, an imposing bluestone railway bridge appears silhouetted against the sky; its single arch straddles the road.

The wide, curved archway makes an impressive entrance to the Riddells Creek area where Dromkeen is situated. That the arched, stone bridge should mark the approach to Dromkeen is appropriate because the bridge and the railway-line that crosses it provide tangible links that connect the homestead's historic past with its present role as a home for the Dromkeen Collection.

The railway is the main line linking Melbourne and Bendigo and it passes through the township of Riddells Creek. The line was constructed during the gold rush days of the last century,

Judge Arthur Chomley.

Chomley family group on the front steps of Dromkeen homestead early this century.

An eastern view of Dromkeen homestead, showing the school-house where the young Chomley children were taught by their governess. The school-house has been demolished.

and both the bluestone railway bridge that spans the road and its companion arching across the creek were completed early in 1860. The man in charge of the building of these bridges was Samuel Amess, an experienced stonemason. It was Samuel Amess' grand-daughter, Marjorie Amess, who drew Joyce and Court Oldmeadow's attention to Dromkeen homestead as a suitable place for both a bulk book store and a residence — a suggestion which resulted in the Oldmeadows' purchasing the property late in 1973 and, in due course, to the founding of the Dromkeen Collection.

Riddells Creek railway-station became operational in the latter half of 1860. At that time, the train journey to Melbourne from Riddells Creek took about one and a half hours. Almost thirty years later, Riddells Creek and its convenient daily train service to and from Melbourne came to the notice of Judge Arthur Chomley, a kindly and respected gentleman, whose wife suffered from distressing attacks of asthma and had been advised to move from Melbourne to a country area as soon as possible. This posed a problem because Judge Chomley's professional life was centred in the city. In addition, he had his children's education to consider. There were eight children; the youngest, a daughter, Aubrey, was only six years of age.

It was the ease of access to Melbourne from Riddells Creek by

Horse and carriage days at Dromkeen.

train that prompted Judge Chomley's decision to purchase a property adjacent to the township and to build a homestead there. The youngest children could be taught by a governess, while arrangements could be made for the older ones to attend schools, or university, in Melbourne.

Arthur Chomley was Irish-born, the fifth of seven sons. Not long after being widowed, his mother brought all her sons to Australia, embarking on the sailing vessel *Stag* and arriving in Melbourne in 1849. On the completion of his secondary education, Arthur Chomley studied law, subsequently rising through the ranks of the legal profession until, in 1885, he was appointed a County Court Judge.

The Chomley family moved into their new home in 1889, and the judge named his estate 'Dromkeen', after the property belonging to his mother's family in County Tipperary in Ireland. On week-days, Judge Chomley travelled the short distance from Dromkeen to Riddells Creek railway-station by horse-drawn carriage, caught the early morning steam train to the city, and

returned by train that evening. It was an admirable solution to his problems.

Today, many groups of school children on an excursion to Dromkeen to view the Collection make the journey from Melbourne to Riddells Creek, and back again, by train. It is a diesel-engined train now, not the smoke-belching steam engine of Judge Chomley's day. However, it travels along exactly the same stretch of line that carried the judge to and from Melbourne almost one hundred years ago.

Visitors to Dromkeen, who travel along the Sunbury Road by car or bus, pass under the arched, bluestone railway bridge. A sharp turn to the right and a neat, white church, its surprisingly bright-red spire pointing above the trees on a hillside, indicates Riddells Creek township. Dromkeen lies a few kilometres further on along the Monegeetta Road, and a sign beside the gate directs visitors to the gravelled drive that leads into a grove of gnarled pine trees. The pines were planted when the Chomley family lived at Dromkeen and were allowed to grow undisturbed

by subsequent owners of the property. They are now so huge that they conceal the homestead from the road.

In 1974, after Joyce and Court Oldmeadow had settled into Dromkeen, they discovered that Miss Aubrey Chomley, the Judge's youngest daughter, was still alive and living in Melbourne. Excited at the thought of meeting a member of the Chomley family who had actually lived at Dromkeen as a child, the Oldmeadows invited her to visit them. Aubrey Chomley was by that time ninety-one years of age and still very alert. She was delighted to be once again in the homestead where she had spent her childhood and surprised at how few basic changes had been made to the building over the years. She eagerly pointed out the small room lined with deep bookshelves at the front of the house that had been her father's study.

Judge Chomley's study is known now as the 'Judge's Room' and it houses a valuable collection of children's books, many of which date back to the middle of the last century.

The Red Room

That Dromkeen is today a 'home for children's literature' becomes apparent immediately one steps inside the glassed-in entrance to the homestead, because several large illustrations for children's books are displayed on the walls. One is a contemporary drawing by Donna Rawlins, for the book *Time for a Number Rhyme*, illustrating the nursery rhyme 'Rub-a-dub-dub, Three Men in a Tub'. The three well-known characters are there: 'the butcher, the baker and the candlestick maker' and they are all in a tub, but not a wooden wash-tub as shown in more traditional illustrations of this rhyme. This tub is a large, white, claw-footed Victorian bath!

A few paces inside the first room of the homestead and one has the impression of having been suddenly transported into another world, yet one that is hauntingly familiar — the magical world of childhood. Paintings of fairies, gnomes, kings and castles cover the walls, while others can be seen on the covers of books inside glass-fronted bookcases. The pictures on display

Painting by Ida Rentoul Outhwaite, previously unpublished.
(Original artwork)

glow with colour; an antique iron printing press stands in front of a window; fresh flowers decorate small tables; soft carpets are underfoot.

This room is known as the 'Red Room' because the carpet is deep crimson. It is here that the earliest examples in the Collection of artwork by illustrators of Australian children's books are exhibited. Other rooms can be seen opening one into the other for the length of the building.

The Fairyland of Ida Rentoul Outhwaite

On one wall of the Red Room is a large water colour of a fairy poised between the outstretched wings of a bat as it flies through a moonlit night. The painting is by Ida Rentoul Outhwaite; the style is unmistakable.

Ida Rentoul Outhwaite's fanciful drawings and paintings of fairyland themes captured the imagination of both children and adults in the early decades of this century. Under her pen and brush, fairyland achieved a special character that was always recognisably hers. It was an idealised world into which nothing harsh or ugly was allowed to enter.

Although Ida Rentoul Outhwaite included many Australian native plants in her fairyland scenes, her concept of fairy folk was essentially English and remained so throughout her career. Books were important in the Rentoul home, and it seems that Ida was influenced early in her life by English illustrators of fairyland themes. Yet, the fairy creatures of her imagination appeared to blend with their Australian settings rather than to be out of place, a situation made possible by the artist's naturally decorative style which lent a distinctive dream-like quality to many of her drawings and paintings.

Although Ida Rentoul Outhwaite is represented at Dromkeen by several pieces of work, as yet there are no originals of her water colour illustrations for published books. However, most first, or early, editions of the children's books she illustrated are in the Collection, some produced when she was in her mid-teenage years.

Ida Rentoul Outhwaite's maiden name was Ida Sherbourn Rentoul. She was born in Melbourne in 1888 and educated at the Presbyterian Ladies College. The extraordinary talent for drawing that she showed from her earliest years was encouraged by her father, Laurence Rentoul, a scholarly Irishman and a poet. He became Professor of New Testament Greek Literature and Christian Philosophy at Ormond College, Melbourne University, and later, Moderator-General of the Presbyterian Church.

Ida Rentoul did not attend any formal art classes, but was aided in her work by her versatile father, her mother and other members of her gifted family. Spurred on by their encourage-

ment, criticism or praise, she worked with unflagging determination to improve her graphic skills and to develop her natural sense of design and composition. And improve she did! By the time Ida Rentoul had turned twenty, the public was becoming aware of the young artist who drew such imaginative and enchanting pictures of fairyland.

But fairy creatures were not the only subjects Ida Rentoul drew. In the Red Room at Dromkeen there is a pen-and-ink drawing signed by Ida S. Rentoul. The two figures in the drawing are obviously characters from a pantomime; one is Humpty Dumpty, the other is a middle-aged Edwardian lady. The caption reads: 'My Boy Humpty'. The signature dates the work as having been drawn prior to 1909 when Ida Rentoul married Arthur Grenbry Outhwaite, a prominent Melbourne solicitor, because after her marriage she signed herself either I.R.O. or Ida Rentoul Outhwaite.

When the drawing 'My Boy Humpty' was donated to Dromkeen, its history was unknown. A researcher, Sue Lowe, became curious about its origin and contacted the Mitchell

'Grasshoppers', a previously unpublished watercolour by Ida Rentoul Outhwaite. (Original artwork)

Illustration by Ida S. Rentoul for the booklet telling the story of the pantomime 'My Boy Humpty'. (Original artwork)

Library in Sydney, hoping that the library would have some reference concerning its background. She received the following reply:

Dear Mrs Lowe,
Further to your telephone call of 2nd August 1979, please find enclosed a photocopy of the picture 'My Boy Humpty', by Ida S. Rentoul, which was published in The Story of the Pantomime of Humpty Dumpty, *specially written for little ones by Annie R. Rentoul, Sydney, J. C. Williamson, n.d. (ML Ref: Q792. 4/R) The colours are indicated on the photocopy.*

So the mystery was solved. The drawing 'My Boy Humpty' was the original drawing for page 11 of the story of the pantomime produced by the theatrical company J. C. Williamson in the Christmas season of 1907.

It was not until after her marriage that Ida Rentoul Outhwaite concentrated on developing her skill in watercolour. She

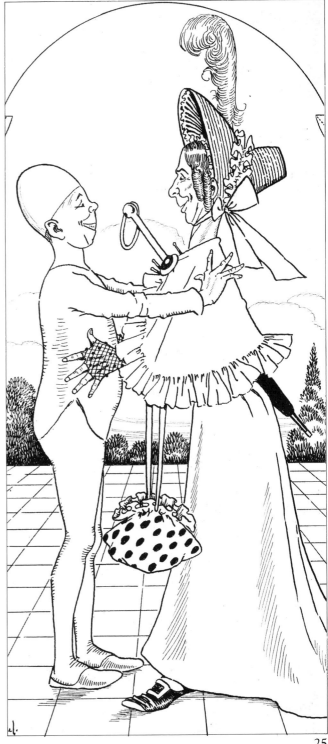

became proficient in this medium and worked hard to gather a collection of paintings which she planned to exhibit in London, but the First World War interrupted those plans.

As the voyage to England had become impossible, Ida directed her efforts towards illustrating a book of poems written for children by her sister, Annie Rentoul, and also to producing sufficient paintings and drawings for her first exhibition. This took place in Melbourne in October 1916 and coincided with the publication of the book of poems, titled *Elves and Fairies*. The exhibition was an outstanding success, as also was the one she held in Sydney the following year.

Critics have suggested that certain weaknesses can be detected in Ida Rentoul Outhwaite's work and that these are probably due to her lack of formal training in art and also, perhaps, to her decorative style. However, at the height of her popularity, an adoring public could find little fault with her illustrations or the work she exhibited. She continued to people her pictures with imaginative fairyland characters, such as the grasshoppers featured in a small watercolour on display at Dromkeen.

In 1920, Ida Rentoul Outhwaite eventually sailed for England with her husband and children and held successful exhibitions of her work in both London and Paris. An article in the *Melbourne Punch* of 10 February 1921 records her return to Australia. Titled 'A Creator of Fairies — Ida Rentoul Outhwaite is Back in Melbourne after a Tour Abroad', it reports:

" MY BOY HUMPTY."

Melbourne has not produced many women artists who have succeeded in getting a safe niche on the slippery heights of international fame . . . Ida Rentoul Outhwaite had made a reputation for herself in Australia before she went abroad thirteen months ago. She returns hall-marked with the appreciation of the art worlds of London and the Continent . . . Queen Mary set the seal of practical approval on Mrs Outhwaite's work. H.M. bought one picture, 'The Bud' . . . an infant cradled in a flower . . .

It is perhaps the Celtic strain cropping up that makes Mrs Outhwaite confess to loving a risk. She adores flying, and puts a red mark against her journey from London to Paris by 'plane . . . anything that involves taking a chance intrigues her . . .

(Punch, p. 14)

Perhaps it is but a step from having sufficient imagination to create a painting of a fairy balanced on the shoulders of a bat in flight, such as the one displayed at Dromkeen, to having sufficient spirit of adventure to make a flight in an aeroplane of 1920 vintage!

Front cover of the first edition of Tales of Snugglepot and Cuddlepie *showing the gumnut babies, created by May Gibbs.*

May Gibbs' Bushland Babies

In a glass-fronted bookcase in the Red Room is a complete set of children's books by May Gibbs, the author and artist who contributed unique and enduring fantasies to Australian children's literature.

There are no fairies floating on gossamer wings through the night sky in May Gibbs' fantasies, nor elves perched on toadstools in ferny gullies. As settings for her stories, May Gibbs chose the harsh bushland where stones, twigs and fallen gumnuts clutter the ground, tough grasses grow, and all manner of Australian animals, birds, insects and reptiles make their homes. At other times, she favoured the ocean depths where mysterious creatures live among the rocks and seaweeds on the sandy bed.

Into these settings, the author introduced the tiny beings of her imagination: her chubby, naked gumnut babies, Snugglepot and Cuddlepie, Little Ragged Blossom, and many others. When *Tales of Snugglepot and Cuddlepie* was published in 1918, May Gibbs' bushland babies quickly found their way into the hearts of Australian children, and have been doing so ever since.

As there is no original artwork by May Gibbs in the Dromkeen Collection, the cover of the first edition of *Tales of Snugglepot and Cuddlepie*, and several illustrations from other books in the series, have been reproduced here. An account of some aspects of May Gibbs' life and her work, and references to her children's books, are given in Chapter 3.

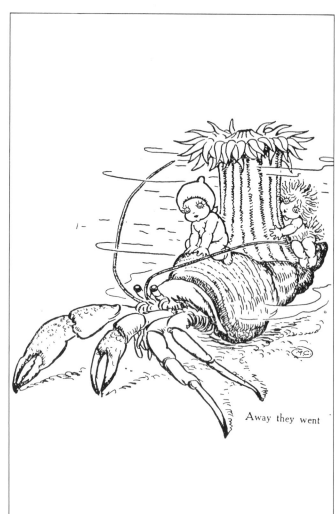

Away they went

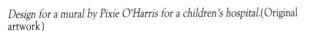

Pixie O'Harris and Pixies and Fairies

There are several sketches signed by Pixie O'Harris on a wall in the Red Room. Some sketches are in pencil, others are in pencil and wash. All are preliminary drawings for murals intended for children's wards in hospitals in New South Wales.

Pixie O'Harris! An apt name for a writer of fairy stories and creator of fairy folk in over forty children's books and in at least fifty murals in children's wards in hospitals and other institutions. However, it surprises many who have loved this artist's work since childhood to learn that her real name is neither Pixie, nor O'Harris. She was born in Wales in 1904 and christened Rhona Olive Harris. Her father was a portrait painter, and when Rhona was still a young child he encouraged her to draw and paint, and later to write verse and stories.

She was sixteen when she boarded a liner for Perth with her family in 1920, and it was during the voyage to Australia that she was given the name 'Pixie'. On the ship, she was always leading groups of children into mischief, laughing and playing with them, until one officer, complaining of the noise and looking for the ring-leader, exclaimed: 'It's that Welsh pixie, playing hide and seek!'

In her new country, Pixie no longer signed her drawings or stories Rhona Harris, but Pixie O. Harris. It was not until the family moved to Sydney and she sold a collection of her work to the editor of the magazine the *Sydney Mail* that she changed the spelling of her surname. An elderly printer persuaded her that

her signature would look better with an apostrophe. She took his advice and from then on, professionally, she became Pixie O'Harris.

Pixie was seventeen when the Harris family moved to Sydney, and she fell in love with the bright, bustling city. After a year in the art department of the printing firm John Sands, she joined her father in his studio where she illustrated theatre programmes, drew cartoons for joke blocks and did illustrations for magazines. She also illustrated children's books.

Cinderella's Party by Maud Liston, illustrated by Pixie O'Harris, was published in 1923. The book was successful and two years later, the *Pixie O'Harris Fairy Book*, containing a collection of stories by other authors besides Pixie, was published. Pixie was delighted, for she had set her heart on writing and illustrating books for children. A signed copy of the *Pixie O'Harris Fairy Book* is in the Red Room at Dromkeen.

Pixie O'Harris was married in June 1928, and it was when she was in hospital after the birth of her third daughter that the idea of painting murals for children's wards came to her. She firmly believes that it is in the world of imagination, removed from the realities of everyday life, that children gain inner strength and are revitalised. Often when Pixie was painting a mural, children in the ward decided what should be drawn and watched with delight as she included their ideas in her design.

Other examples of this artist's work are also in the Red Room. Four items together show various stages in the production of a

book of poems by Lydia Pender: the dummy (a publisher's production sample, containing drafts of the text and sample illustrations), a piece of black-and-white artwork and the metal letterpress block that was made from it and then used in the printing of the illustration. There is also a first-edition copy of the book signed by both the author and Pixie. The cover of the dummy bears the title 'Verses for Judy', but the book was retitled *Marbles in My Pocket* before going to press. The small book has a fawn jacket, but the hard cover is deep green with both the lettering and a drawing of a lively pixie printed in gold. The three toadstools on the title page and the line drawing of the child opposite have the characteristic Pixie O'Harris lightness of touch. The book was published in about 1958.

Today, Pixie O'Harris lives in a cottage tucked away among the trees of her rambling garden at Vaucluse, Sydney. Her studio is crammed with paintings and drawings, some completed many years ago, others not yet finished. Her brushes stand ready in a large jug and a drawing is pinned to the drawing-board on her work table, because she is still illustrating and writing — still creating the fairyland folk and other creatures of fantasy that have delighted generations of children.

For her contribution to children, Pixie O'Harris has been awarded the Coronation Medal, the Jubilee Medal and, in 1976, she became a Member of the British Empire. In 1977, she was made a Patron of the Royal Alexandra Hospital for Children.

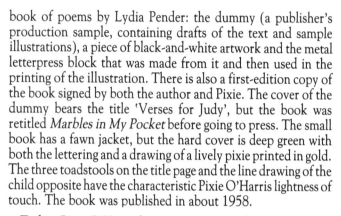

Display of publication material for Marbles in My Pocket *by Lydia Pender and Pixie O'Harris.*

Double-page spread from Peg's Fairy Book.

Peg Maltby

Several paintings by Peg Maltby, another writer and illustrator of fairyland themes, are displayed in the Red Room. As mentioned previously, two of these, the artwork for the cover of *Ben and Bella and the Apple Tree* and the original of one of the illustrations for the story, were purchased from the artist by Joyce Oldmeadow in 1974.

Peg Maltby was born in England. In 1924, she migrated to Australia with her husband and eventually settled in the Dandenong Ranges in Victoria. Painting was Peg Maltby's hobby, but it was purely by chance that she became involved in writing and illustrating books for children.

The bushland surrounding her Australian home, the treeferns, the unfamiliar wildflowers, native animals and birds, were a constant source of delight to her. She joined the Victorian Artists' Society and held several exhibitions of her work. In 1943, Edward D. Barry, a partner in the ownership of a recently formed publishing company, Murfett Proprietary Limited, attended one of her exhibitions and decided there was an outlet for her talent in the illustration of children's books.

At that time, the Second World War was in progress, and due to war-time restrictions few children's books were arriving in Australia from overseas. This factor, coupled with a lack of children's books with Australian content on the market, resulted in a strong local demand for books for children, especially picture-story books. It was in this social and economic climate that Edward Barry, a man of charm and infectious enthusiasm, set out to persuade Peg Maltby to try her hand at writing and illustrating a book of fairy stories for children.

Author and illustrator, Peg Maltby.

Delicate watercolour by Peg Maltby. (Original artwork)

Bookmark painted by Peg Maltby. (Original artwork)

At first, Peg Maltby was convinced that she would never be able to write the stories; however, she was extremely interested in doing the illustrations. Barry commissioned her to paint fifteen pictures of fairyland scenes incorporating Australian flora and fauna. When the work was completed, he encouraged her to review the descriptive notes he had asked her to write for each painting and to expand these into story form.

From this surprising beginning, *Peg's Fairy Book* came into being. Published in 1944, the book was a remarkable success, and thousands of copies were sold within a few weeks. A first edition copy of *Peg's Fairy Book* is in the Collection at Dromkeen, as also are copies of many other children's books by Peg Maltby that were popular thirty or forty years ago.

Not all examples of Peg Maltby's artwork at Dromkeen are originals of illustrations for her children's books. One picture,

showing a quaint, elfin figure and a fairy tinting apple blossoms pink, was painted for a little girl to hang in her bedroom. This picture, and two others painted for the same reason, are on loan to the Collection.

A skinny pixie in a red jacket and blue hose stares down from a wall in the Red Room. This tiny work measures only 7 cm by 13 cm and was originally intended as a bookmark. It arrived at Dromkeen by mail with a letter from a Miss Ethel Sims, a retired schoolteacher. The bookmark had been given to her as a Christmas present by one of Peg Maltby's sons, a pupil of Miss Sims. She had protected the small painting over the years, had never used it as a bookmark, and had eventually decided that Dromkeen was the ideal home for it.

Peg Maltby visited Dromkeen several times before her death in 1984.

Dorothy Wall and Her Stories About Blinky Bill

Two well-known characters in Australian children's literature appear in a large painting on a wall in the Red Room. One is the mischievous young koala, Blinky Bill; the other is his mother. Their creator was Dorothy Wall. Her first book about Blinky Bill's escapades, *Blinky Bill: The Quaint Little Australian*, published in 1933, was a success.

Dorothy Wall was born in New Zealand in 1894. She studied at the Christchurch School of Arts and, at the age of twenty, came to Australia and settled in Sydney. She was extremely creative and talented, and had no trouble finding employment as a commercial artist. Her first work published in Australia seems to have been an illustration that appeared in the magazine *The Lone Hand* in October 1914. This magazine reported European literary and art movements, and published fiction, poetry and illustrations by the best writers and illustrators of the day.

In 1921, Dorothy Wall married Andrew Delfosse Badgery, one of Australia's pioneer aviators, and a son was born in 1925. The marriage did not last, and over the ensuing years Dorothy Wall and her son moved often, living at various times either in Sydney or in the Blue Mountains. When in the mountains, they would wander through the bushland observing the local animals and plants. At night, the artist drew and painted by the light of an oil-lamp, for there was no electricity in the house. It was while she was living at Warrimoo, in the eastern foothills of the Blue Mountains, that Dorothy Wall created her koala character,

"Did you pull my tail?"
Madam Hare demanded.

"Little bear," he cried softly,
"it is too light for me to see farther."

34

Blinky Bill.

Young children loved Blinky Bill, perhaps because they could readily identify with many of his pranks. Although Dorothy Wall's koala characters lived in gum trees, they wore clothes and behaved in a similar fashion to the people of Sydney's suburbia; her naughty koalas behaved much like naughty children. These anthropomorphic ideas later were to be frowned on by critics, but when the first of the Blinky Bill books arrived in the bookshops, the small koala and his family and friends were greeted with delight and affection.

The painting of Blinky Bill and his mother, which is displayed in the Red Room, is typical of Dorothy Wall's style in her coloured illustrations for the Blinky Bill series. The colours are fresh and bright, and the two koalas are behaving true to character. Blinky Bill has a shanghai clutched in his right hand, while his mother has a firm grip on his other hand — a positive way of ensuring that the shanghai will not be used. This painting is not an original of an illustration for one of the Blinky Bill books: it was commissioned by the publishers as a poster, part of a publicity campaign to advertise a new book in the series.

Hanging beside the painting of Blinky Bill and his mother are two black-and-white drawings which *are* originals of illustrations for Blinky Bill books. One, showing Madam Hare in a fury after her tail has been pulled by Blinky Bill, was drawn for *Blinky Bill: The Quaint Little Australian*; the other was drawn for *Blinky Bill Grows Up* and illustrates Blinky Bill talking to a wise owl in a gum tree.

Dorothy Wall was extremely skilful in capturing emotion, mood and action in her drawings. Expressions on the faces of her animal characters were readily interpreted by children, and they delighted in the situations presented — perhaps mother koala reaching out to grab Blinky Bill and give him a sound whack on the pants, or Blinky Bill racing away from an explosive situation caused by his mischief.

Today, many of the situations Dorothy Wall created around her animal characters have dated, but children still delight in Blinky Bill as a character, and enjoy the numerous small illustrations that enliven the margins of the pages in the Blinky Bill books.

In 1939, the first three Blinky Bill titles, *Blinky Bill: The Quaint Little Australian*, *Blinky Bill Grows Up* and *Blinky Bill and Nutsy*, were combined in one volume, *The Complete Adventures of Blinky Bill*. It has been in print ever since.

Nine years after the publication of her first Blinky Bill book, Dorothy Wall died of pneumonia in the Sydney suburb of Cremorne. Through her stories about Blinky Bill, Dorothy Wall made her own particular contribution to the Australian genre in children's literature.

Elizabeth Durack

A large picture of an Aboriginal child holding a white angora goat in her arms hangs in the Red Room. Titled *The Kid*, it is the work of the West Australian artist Elizabeth Durack and was donated by her to the Dromkeen Collection. The picture is a hand-print of a painting by Elizabeth Durack, and it arrived at Dromkeen accompanied by a letter from the artist that explained the circumstances in which the original was painted and how the facsimile she had donated was produced. Her letter has been reproduced here.

Elizabeth Durack and her sister, Mary, spent many years on their father's properties in the Kimberley area of north-west Australia. The sympathy, affection and understanding which the sisters developed for the Aboriginal people, their customs, and the wild, often harsh, land they inhabited is apparent in much of their work. A first edition copy of their best known

children's book, *The Way of the Whirlwind*, is in the Dromkeen Collection.

An Antique Printing-Press

Also in the Red Room, and on loan to Dromkeen, is an Albion printing-press. With its cast-iron Grecian columns, claw feet and brass decorations, this antique printing-press is an interesting example of industrial design of the last century. Made by Hopkinson and Cope of London in the early 1860s, the hand-press was used in the offices of the *Bendigo Advertiser* during the latter half of the nineteenth century. It has been restored to perfect working order.

Accompanying the press is a type-case, together with a tray of hand-cut wooden letters and printer's blocks. The wooden blocks were used to separate the composed words and lines of

type, and also to keep the set type jammed tightly inside the 'chase' (frame) when printing. The type-case displayed at Dromkeen, however, was designed to hold metal, not wooden, type.

Until well into the last century, large carved wooden letters were used in printing-presses in conjunction with cast-metal type. Wood was cheap, and wood-carving as a craft was prevalent. Metal was expensive, and even though metal type could be continually melted down and re-cast, it would have been extravagant to have tied up the amount of metal needed for large letters. All letters were made as mirror images and were raised above the block of metal or wood of which they were a part. When inked, only the raised surface printed. This kind of printing is known as 'letter-press' and is still used occasionally today.

Beside the antique printing-press in the Red Room is a lithographic stone. This stone is a variety of limestone. Lithographic stones were used during the nineteenth century and into the early years of the present century for printing illustrations and other artwork, particularly in colour. The stone was ground to a perfectly flat, polished surface on which the illustration to be printed was drawn. All drawings were mirror images, but no raised printing surface was required in lithographic stone printing because the process was a chemical one based on the principle that oil and water do not mix. The stone was treated chemically in such a way that the oil-based printer's ink adhered to the greasy areas (the drawing) and not to the remainder of the surface of the stone. A variety of effects could be achieved by drawing lightly, or heavily, or by stippling, or by using lines for shading. The lithographic stone was locked into a manually controlled letter-press machine for printing.

Beautifully coloured children's books were produced in England in the latter half of the nineteenth century by means of lithographic printing. Several of these books are in the Collection; *The Baby's Opera* by Walter Crane is one example.

Technological discoveries in the printing industry which took place at the beginning of this century resulted in a change from the use of lithographic stones to that of metal plates. These discoveries revolutionised printing methods and had a direct effect on the production of books for children. Advances in methods of printing are still continuing.

Original artwork of Bunyip and Crocodile from pages of Kangapossum & Crocoroo.

Top half of Bunyip and bottom half of Crocodile from pages of Kangapossum & Crocoroo.

The Green Room

The other main display-rooms at Dromkeen are the Green Room, also named for the colour of its carpet, the English Room and the American Room.

When walking through the display-rooms examining the examples of artwork on the walls, one becomes very much aware of the changes in taste and style in children's book illustration that have taken place since the early decades of this century. The most obvious are the wider range of subject-matter and the tremendous variety in both style and use of medium.

The children's books and artwork featured in this section of Chapter 2 are by contemporary Australian authors and illustrators. The illustrations and other pre-publication material mentioned were among those on display during 1984.

Fun and Fantasy

In 1969 an unusual full colour picture book titled *Kangapossum & Crocoroo* was published in Melbourne, and some of the illustrations prepared for the book are in the Dromkeen Collection. *Kangapossum & Crocoroo* is a fun-book; the illustrations are mainly of Australian native animals, including the fabled bunyip. Each page of the book is split horizontally so that the

top half of one animal can be fitted exactly to the bottom half of another.

The humorous verses for *Kangapossum & Crocoroo* were written by David Rankine who was at that time senior sub-editor and feature writer with the *Sun News Pictorial* in Melbourne. The book was illustrated by Geoff Hook, staff cartoonist at the *Sun*.

As a professional newspaper cartoonist, Geoff Hook signs his work 'Jeff', and somewhere in each of his black and white cartoons he always includes a tiny fish hook for which his readers invariably search.

Among other books, Geoff Hook has also illustrated three children's books by Osmar White which feature 'the greatest explorer of all time', Dr Alastair Angus Archibald McGurk and his remarkable double-humped riding camel, Cathie Can. The stories are fantasies filled with absurdities to which young readers respond with enthusiasm, but underneath all the fun lie positive messages about the need for conservation of the environment and its animals and plant life.

The black and white artwork for the second book in the series, *The Further Adventures of Dr A. A. A. McGurk*, is in the Green Room at Dromkeen and Geoff Hook has incorporated that small, elusive fish hook in each drawing.

Amanda Walsh, children's book illustrator and a distant relative of the famous English illustrator of children's books in the nineteenth century, Randolph Caldecott.

Egrin, the kindly wizard. (Original artwork)

The evil, painted wizard. (Original artwork)

Fantasy and Magic

Several pieces of artwork for *Egrin and the Painted Wizard* are in the Green Room. All children love magic and weird or wonderful wizards and witches with magic wands and magic powders, who can perform all manner of tricks and spells, good and evil. So it is not surprising that the whimsical fantasy about the kindly wizard, Egrin, and the evil, 'painted' wizard, has proved so popular since it was published in 1972. The blurb in the book presents the idea of the story:

> *Like most wizards, Egrin wore a tall hat and had lots of magic powders and a magic wand, but he only ever used it to help his friends. One day, the picture he was painting suddenly came alive, and Egrin found himself facing the meanest looking wizard he had ever seen.*

The mean wizard 'turned Egrin into a toad, and shut him in a cage', but when the painted wizard is reduced to a puddle of paint by a providential shower of rain, his evil spells are negated.

Egrin and the Painted Wizard was created by Amanda Walsh. In an interview, she explained that the idea for her book evolved from a dream, and that she wrote the story and completed the pen and ink and water colour illustrations in six weeks.

Egrin and the Painted Wizard was translated and published as a French edition in 1976. Amanda Walsh's second children's book, *Egrin and the Wicked Witch*, was published in 1978.

A Very Long Fantasy

The artwork for an extraordinary children's book, *The Train*, is displayed in the Green Room. Consisting entirely of illustrations (there are no words except in labels), this is indeed a different kind of fantasy.

The body of the book is folded concertina-fashion between the hardback covers and attached to the cover at the last page. Purported to be 'one of the longest books in the world', *The Train* unfolds to over five metres in length, and in one picture after another, the continuous 'story' of two robbers who jump on the train to escape pursuit by two policemen 'unfolds'. However, the police are close behind the robbers and they too jump on the train. The exuberant illustrations present a series of ridiculous situations as the robbers flee from one railway flat-top with its strange cargo to the next. There is a monster Krollsnork breaking out of its cage; a travelling circus, and all the disruptive effects the escaped circus animals have on other cargo are shown; there is even a functioning, mechanised milking-shed. The situations provide plenty of scope for imaginative story interpretation.

39

Witold Generowicz's book *The Train* is a direct result of his own fascination for trains: both his home and his place of work are situated close to railway-lines.

Adventure Fantasy

The moon is full, the night is warm, and young Jack can't sleep. Off go the bedclothes, off go Jack's pyjamas, on go his boots — and Jack is out and away through the scrub 'on the track of the moon'.

Illustrated with pencil drawings by Betty Greenhatch, the adventure fantasy *Jack in the Bush* is set in moonlit bushland inhabited by all kinds of Australian animals, birds and small creatures. The author is the poet Barbara Giles. She wrote the book in 1979, but it was not published until 1983, and therein lies a story.

Freelance artist and fashion designer, Betty Greenhatch; she designed the outfits worn by the Australian team at the opening ceremony of the Olympic Games in Los Angeles in 1984.

El Nino, the Sea God, from The Voyage of the Poppykettle *by Robert Ingpen.*

Barbara Giles and Betty Greenhatch exhibited the manuscript for *Jack in the Bush* with several sample illustrations in an exhibition held by Webber's Bookshop in 1979. The illustrations which Betty Greenhatch prepared were in full colour. Representatives from the publishers, Penguin Books, attended the exhibition, noticed the manuscript and illustrations for *Jack in the Bush*, and wanted to publish the work, but felt that the story, set in a moonlit scene, lent itself admirably to black and white illustrations. They pointed out that the cost of printing full colour illustrations would be prohibitive. Black and white illustrations were eventually agreed on and it took Betty Greenhatch two years working part time to complete her superb pencil illustrations.

Jack in the Bush was launched at Dromkeen by Joyce Oldmeadow in November 1983, and all the original artwork was exhibited there. A piece now belongs to the Dromkeen Collection.

In 1984, *Jack in the Bush* shared the position of runner-up in the Noma Concours Award with another Australian picture-story book, *Tiddalick: The Frog Who Caused a Flood*, by Robert Roennfeldt.

Noma Concours Award

The Noma Concours Award for Children's Picture Book Illustrators, sponsored by the Asian Cultural Centre for UNESCO, Tokyo, Japan, is a biennial competition for which countries in the Asia-Pacific, Arab-Africa and Latin America-Caribbean regions are eligible.

The Award was established to encourage illustrators of children's books who are talented but who do not necessarily have the opportunity to have their work promoted world-wide.

Robert Ingpen

A black-and-white drawing by Robert Ingpen of the sea-god of the ancient Incas of South America, El Nino, is in the Green Room at Dromkeen. It is the original of an illustration for the book Robert Ingpen wrote and illustrated, *The Voyage of the Poppykettle*.

Robert Ingpen was born at Geelong in Victoria. After completing his secondary education at Geelong College, he enrolled at the Royal Melbourne Institute of Technology where he studied art. In 1958, he was employed by the Commonwealth Scientific and Industrial Research Organisation (CSIRO) as a designer and illustrator of graphic periodicals.

While working closely with scientists, Robert developed a respect for scientific disciplines. This, in turn, influenced his attitude towards his own work and set him pondering about the inter-relationship of man and the environment, one of the con-

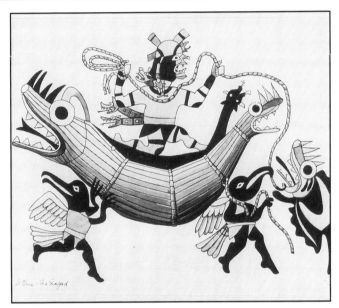

cerns of the CSIRO. He developed a deep sense of history; all aspects of the past intrigued him.

Eventually, Robert Ingpen left the CSIRO and worked as a private consultant for federal and state governments, while also pursuing other interests connected with illustrating. Some years ago, as a result of his previous involvement with the CSIRO, he spent some time working in Peru for the United Nations on a scientific project. Stories of the ancient Incas, which he heard in Peru, fascinated him. From this impetus came his book *The Voyage of the Poppykettle*.

The imaginative tale of the diminutive Hairy Peruvians who ventured across the Pacific Ocean in the 'Poppykettle' to escape from the Shining Spaniards and landed at what is now called Limeburner's Point, not far from Geelong, has intrigued many children. Apart from the appeal of the characters in the story, there is the question of the metal keys which the Hairy Peruvians used as ballast in their poppykettle boat. Is it possible that the keys dug up at Limeburner's Point by early settlers in 1847 were from the Poppykettle?

If one considers Robert Ingpen's love of old homes and buildings, and his interest in books and illustrating, it is of no surprise to learn that he has been actively involved with Dromkeen for some time. He is an Honorary Governor of the Courtney Oldmeadow Children's Literature Foundation. He designed the Dromkeen Medal, which is awarded annually to a person who has made a significant contribution to the appreciation and development of children's literature in Australia, and has been a member of the panel of judges who select the recipient of the Medal.

Author and illustrator, Peter Pavey.

Page of original artwork for Peter Pavey's innovative children's picture-story-book-and-counting-book-combined, One Dragon's Dream.

Peter Pavey's Counting Book Fantasy

In 1979, a most unusual, innovative and imaginative children's book was published. It was a picture-story book and counting-book combined. Titled *One Dragon's Dream*, it was the brainchild of Peter Pavey — the first children's book he had both written and illustrated.

Peter Pavey had been drawing pictures of dragons and selling them to friends for some time before the concept of *One Dragon's Dream* came to him. He completed his number rhymes and several drawings, and showed his work to the Melbourne-based publishing company Thomas Nelson. At first, the publisher had reservations about a counting-book and picture-story book 'all in one', but Pavey eventually won the day.

The piece of artwork '. . . four frogs seized him' for *One Dragon's Dream* is in the Dromkeen Collection. As well as four frogs, there are four horses, four penguins, four chimneys, four pools of water — and so on. All the pictures in the book are filled with the exotic paraphernalia of dreams and provide exciting puzzles for children as they recognise and count the various objects, often having to search diligently to find an elusive one to complete the number. But quite apart from the counting aspect of the book, the pictures tell a sequential story.

Peter Pavey was born in Melbourne and trained in advertising and design at Swinburne Institute of Technology. During the last year of his four-year course, he became convinced that he did not have the natural aggressiveness necessary to be successful in advertising, no matter how good an artist he was. In a talk he gave at Hall Primary School, ACT, in 1980, Peter Pavey spoke about his growing disenchantment with advertising and explained how his interest in children's books was aroused:

> . . . I discovered The Little Bookroom in Melbourne, run by Albert Ullin. I used to spend hours in his little shop devoted to children's books. New books have a magnificent smell about them. I'd sit in a corner and go through the new books and buy the ones that I liked. I saw them as an alternative to advertising for my inventiveness. Rather than just emulate reality I like to create my own, and I saw children's books as an avenue for that. (Writing and Illustrating For Children, p. 222)

Pavey has a feeling of responsibility for the age group for whom he writes:

> I'm interested in picture books, and particularly in ones that kids can read on their own. I think that if kids can read and look at books on their own that's a start in getting them interested in books. If parents read to them that's great, but I think they've got to have the personal contact of playing with books and understanding a certain amount themselves. And

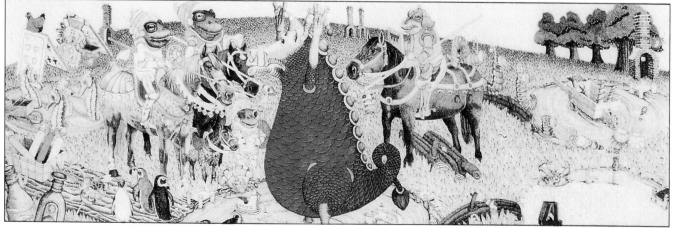

Original artwork by Walter Stackpool for the book Banjo Paterson's Horses, *in Angus & Robertson's Young Australia Series.*

Original artwork for A. B. (Banjo) Paterson's ballad, 'Mulga Bill's Bicycle' by the sisters Kilmeny and Deborah Niland.

that's the area I'm most interested in. (Writing and Illustrating For Children, *p. 223*)

One Dragon's Dream took about three years to complete, and in 1980 it won the Children's Book Council of Australia Picture Book of the Year Award. It has been a great success with children, as also has another of Pavey's picture-story books, *I'm Taggerty Toad.*

Deborah Niland and Kilmeny Niland

The republication, as profusely illustrated children's picture-story books, of many well-known Australian bush ballads, some by 'Banjo' Paterson and others by Henry Lawson, became a popular publishing practice in the early 1970s. The sisters Kilmeny and Deborah Niland captured the mood and humour of Paterson's story 'Mulga Bill's Bicycle' in their illustrations for the edition published by William Collins in 1973, and a piece of artwork prepared for this edition is on display in the Green Room.

Mulga Bill's Bicycle won the Commonwealth Visual Arts Board, Best Illustrated Children's Book of the Year Award in 1974, and in the same year, the Australian Book Publishers Association, Children's Category, Book Design Award.

Author and illustrator, Robert Roennfeldt.

Cover of Roennfeldt's book Tiddalick.

Original artwork for Tiddalick, *held in the Dromkeen Collection.*

Robert Roennfeldt's directions, written for children, concerning the technique he used when illustrating Tiddalick. *(Original artwork)*

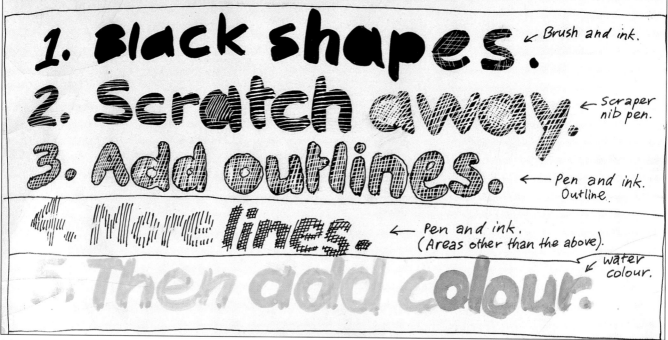

How Tiddalick was drawn on Scraper Board.

1. **Black shapes.** ← Brush and ink.

2. **Scratch away.** ← Scraper nib pen.

3. **Add outlines.** ← Pen and ink. Outline.

4. **More lines.** ← Pen and ink. (Areas other than the above).

5. **Then add colour.** ← water colour.

Astra Lacis, children's book illustrator, with Christobel Mattingley, author of children's books.

Original artwork for Moon-Eyes, *written by Jean Chapman and illustrated by Astra Lacis.*

Patricia Mullins in her studio.

A Legend

The artwork for Robert Roennfeldt's first children's book, *Tiddalick: The Frog Who Caused a Flood*, is displayed at Dromkeen.

Published in 1980, Roennfeldt's adaptation of an Aboriginal legend has proved extremely popular. *Tiddalick* is the story of a huge frog with an enormous thirst, who selfishly drank all the water in the billabongs, rivers and lakes until there was not a drop left in the land. As there was now no water to drink, the other animals were in dire distress. They held a meeting and decided that the only way to force the enormously bloated Tiddalick to give back the water he had consumed was to make him laugh, and in this they were eventually successful.

Robert Roennfeldt's art style is individualistic and expressive. The antics of the animals in *Tiddalick*, and the expressions on their faces, delight both children and adults. Roennfeldt has provided Dromkeen with step-by-step instructions that show how he achieved the effects he wanted by using scraper-board, ink and paint. These instructions are used when the original artwork for *Tiddalick* is being discussed with groups of children who visit Dromkeen.

Astra Lacis — Creator of Mood and Atmosphere

An experienced, versatile illustrator with an extremely individual decorative flair, Astra Lacis varies her style in order to capture the mood of a story or poem, as she has in her illustrations for the picture-story book *Moon-Eyes*, written by Jean Chapman. *Moon-Eyes* is the story of a half-starved alley cat living in an underprivileged area of Rome. It is Christmas, and the weather is cold and bleak — an atmosphere that Astra Lacis has captured most effectively in her illustration of the cat, Moon-Eyes, displayed in the Green Room.

Astra Lacis was born in Latvia and migrated to Australia with her family in 1949. She has illustrated many articles, stories and children's books in her career, one of the latest being *The Angel With a Mouth-Organ*, written by Christobel Mattingley. This book resulted from a conversation one day between the author and the illustrator in which Astra Lacis mentioned some of her experiences as a child in Europe during the last war. Christobel had the idea of incorporating some of these experiences in a children's book which Astra would illustrate. The result was *The Angel With a Mouth-Organ*, published in 1984.

Realism

The design layout for the jacket of the hardcover edition of the children's picture-story book *Rummage* is displayed on a wall in the Green Room. The designer's directions to the printer can be

Layout of the jacket of the hardcover edition of Rummage *showing instructions to the Asian printer.* (Original artwork)

seen above and below the pictorial layout and have been translated into Chinese by the Asian printing firm involved. Strips of type laid on the artwork indicate to the printer where the equivalent areas will appear on the final printed jacket.

Rummage was written by Christobel Mattingley and illustrated by Patricia Mullins. Christobel Mattingley was born in Brighton, South Australia, and is the author of many children's books. On an overseas trip in 1977, she paid a visit to Covent Garden in London. She had been looking forward to experiencing the atmosphere of this famous market and was unprepared for the changes that had taken place there. The old-world atmosphere had almost disappeared — the market stalls now reflected a new slickness designed to attract the tourist trade. Disappointed, and feeling sad that so many historic places seemed to be changing, she turned away. An old, gold-lettered sign on an equally old corner-shop window caught her eye: PORTWINE & SONS — PORK BUTCHERS. From this sign, and her feelings about the changed atmosphere of Covent Garden, as well as her impressions of stall-holders and customers, the idea for her story, *Rummage*, was born.

The main character in the story is Mr Septimus Portwine who runs a rummage stall in the market. Mr Portwine has a big, bushy beard and many friends. He likes to sit on a box beside his stall, 'reading the old newspapers he used for wrapping purchases,

while people poked and delved and hunted through boxes of clocks and candlesticks, kettles and keys, wheels and tools . . .'

When the publisher Angus and Robertson accepted the manuscript of *Rummage*, they engaged the artist Patricia Mullins to illustrate the book. Fortunately, Patricia Mullins had planned a trip to London and so was able to visit Covent Garden. There she made sketches of the stalls, the people and the buildings in the area and so obtained sufficient material to enable her to capture the atmosphere of the market once she began to do the illustrations. When that time came, she decided on collage, and her mixture of materials — synthetic fur, wool, lace and other fabrics, newspaper, and so forth, in combination with paint, crayon and ink, gives both a feeling of reality and texture to her illustrations.

Patricia Mullins lives in the inner Melbourne suburb of Fitzroy, in a house built in the Victorian era. A short distance from the rear of the house is her studio, a more recent building with a mezzanine floor where the artist works. The ground floor is filled with all manner of models of horses — rocking-horses, horses that have spent their working life on a carousel, hobbyhorses, stuffed toy horses — small models, large models!

Considering Patricia Mullins' love of models of horses, it is probably not surprising to discover quite a few renderings of horses in her illustrations for *Rummage* — a painting of a horse,

Noela Young, illustrator and author of children's books.

Original artwork by Noela Young for her book Torty Longneck.

a toy horse on wheels, a model of a draught-horse, cavalry, and a glazed china statuette of a horse and rider. There is even a picture of a dappled grey horse on the wall of Mr Septimus Portwine's bedroom. But the horses in her illustrations are not at all obvious: one has to search for them.

Rummage was commended by the Children's Book Council of Australia in the awards given in 1982.

Noela Young

A piece of artwork showing two tortoises swimming together is displayed in the Green Room. This painting is an illustration for Noela Young's delightful picture-story book *Torty Longneck*, which was published in 1977.

Torty Longneck is a story about the adventures of a small tortoise which continually wanders away from its owner, Nick. The mystery of why Torty is continually disappearing is solved when it is discovered that he has been searching for a mate, and a suitable mate is found.

A freelance illustrator since 1952, Noela Young's work in book illustration has been commended and highly commended in awards over the years. Besides *Torty Longneck*, Noela Young has both written and illustrated three other picture-story books, *Keep Out, Flip the Flying Possum* and *Mrs Pademelon's Joey*. Her illustrations for the 'Muddle-headed Wombat' series of children's books written by Ruth Park are well known and well loved.

Of Noela Young's illustrations for Hesba Brinsmead's children's book *Once There Was a Swagman*, Marcie Muir, a researcher of Australian children's literature, comments: 'Noela Young in this book created illustrations of sensitivity and beauty which are the most imaginative she has ever drawn.' The manuscript for *Once There Was a Swagman* is in the Dromkeen Collection, together with one of the artist's original black-and-white illustrations and some other pre-publication material.

The English Room

A large room, known as the English Room, is located at the end of one wing of the homestead and is the lounge room used by resident guests. Displayed on its walls are illustrations for children's books by illustrators from the United Kingdom, some of whom have visited the homestead.

A Tiger Comes to Tea

In the English Room is a piece of artwork for the children's book *The Tiger Who Came to Tea*, written and illustrated by Judith Kerr and published in 1968.

This book is a fun-fantasy for the under-fives and tells the story of an amiable tiger who knocked on the door one afternoon when Sophie and her mother were having their tea. The tiger said he was hungry and so was invited to join them, which he did, happily eating his way through all the food in the house, and consuming everything there was to drink — even all the water in the tap! After that, he departed in the friendliest

The Tiger Who Came to Tea; *original artwork by the English illustrator Judith Kerr.*

Illustration for Grasshopper and Butterfly *by the English illustrator Pauline Baynes. This book was runner-up for the Kate Greenaway Medal in 1972.*

fashion. With nothing left in the house to eat or drink, Daddy takes the family to a cafe for dinner, when 'all the street lamps were lit, and all the cars had their lights on'.

At first, Judith Kerr wrote stories for her own children, but later she illustrated her stories and submitted them to the London publisher William Collins as possible picture-story books. *The Tiger Who Came to Tea* was the first to be published. Still in print, it has enjoyed tremendous popularity.

Of Insects

Another piece of artwork in the English Room was prepared for the book *Grasshopper and Butterfly*, written by Helen Piers and illustrated by Pauline Baynes. *Grasshopper and Butterfly* is a factual book that relates, in an interesting and enchanting way, the life-cycles of some of the insects that abound in the English countryside. To quote from the blurb on the jacket of the copy at Dromkeen:

> Helen Piers' keen insight into natural lore and her close attention to detail is matched by Pauline Baynes' splendid colour pictures of the [English] countryside and its small creatures.

The close-up paintings of flora and insects in *Grasshopper and Butterfly* show the subjects in graphic detail, at no time do the small creatures lose their 'insectness'.

Pauline Baynes was born in Brighton, England, in 1922. The first five years of her childhood were spent in India, after which she lived in southern England and later attended The Farnham School of Art and the Slade School of Fine Art, London. In

1968, she won the Kate Greenaway Medal for her illustrations for Grant Uden's *A Dictionary of Chivalry*. The medal is awarded to the artist who, in the opinion of the Library Association of Great Britain, has produced the most distinguished illustrative work for a children's book published in the United Kingdom during the previous year.

A Touch of Surrealism

Justin Todd's illustrations for *Moonshadow*, written by Angela Carter, provide a game for the reader, one filled with visual tricks in which shapes are defined within shapes, yet all knit together in the main image, and all complement the imaginative text. Justin Todd's style adds something new to children's book illustration — a touch of surrealism, which captures a child's interest and delight, and lends a 'real-yet-not-real' quality to the pictures. Four pieces of artwork for *Moonshadow* were on loan to Dromkeen during 1984.

The American Room

Artwork by American illustrators of children's books occupies one room at Dromkeen. Contact between Joyce Oldmeadow and a number of American artist/illustrators was the result of a visit to Dromkeen by Bill Martin Junior of the American publishing firm Holt Rinehart and Winston, when he was in Australia attending a reading conference. Surprised and intrigued by the Dromkeen Collection and its setting, Bill Martin persuaded Joyce to extend the itinerary of an overseas trip she had already planned and include New York so that she could meet some American children's book authors and illustrators and talk to them about Dromkeen and its objectives, and perhaps show some slides of items in the Collection. At a subsequent function held at Long Island, New York, and arranged by Bill Martin, Joyce Oldmeadow met a far larger gathering of illustrators and authors of children's books than she had anticipated, and their obvious interest in Dromkeen delighted her.

Symeon Shimin

It was at the gathering in New York that Joyce Oldmeadow met the artist and illustrator Symeon Shimin, whose sensitive illustrations for children's books are well known in America. Some beautiful examples of his work can be seen in the American Room, including one from the children's book *The Wentletrap Trap* which was written by Jean Craighead George. The dummy of this book, with an inscription by Symeon Shimin to Joyce Oldmeadow, is in the Collection.

Nancy Patz

The association between Dromkeen and the American author-artist of children's books Nancy Patz commenced shortly after the publication, in 1978, of her book *Pumpernickel Tickle and Mean Green Cheese*. At that time, Darren Ryan was manager of the bookshop at Dromkeen and he shared certain of the responsibilities to do with the Collection with Joyce Oldmeadow. In 1979, Darren Ryan visited the United States with a group of

Nancy Patz, American children's book author and illustrator.

Fun and action; original artwork by Nancy Patz for her book Nobody Knows I Have Delicate Toes.

Australian publishers, and while there made contact with several American publishing companies. On his return to Australia, he corresponded with some American authors and illustrators through their publishers — one author/illustrator was Nancy Patz.

At that time, *Pumpernickel Tickle and Mean Green Cheese* was enjoying outstanding success in America, Canada, Britain and Australia. In response to a suggestion that she might like to display some pieces of original artwork for the book at Dromkeen, Nancy Patz placed all the artwork, working sketches, the dummy of the book, and photographs of the city of Baltimore, which she had used as reference for some of the backgrounds for her illustrations, on loan to Dromkeen for some months. It made an impressive display.

In *Pumpernickel Tickle and Mean Green Cheese*, Elephant and little Benjamin walk through the streets of Baltimore 'to buy a loaf of dark brown pumpernickel, a piece of yellow cheese and a great big, very green, nice dill pickle'. The personality of Elephant (the elephant character's name) began to emerge as

Nancy Patz wrote, and re-wrote, the manuscript; so did the relationship between little Benjamin and his big, warm-hearted, fun-loving, goofy friend.

The originals of two illustrations from Nancy Patz' sequel to her first story about Benjamin and Elephant, *Nobody Knows I Have Delicate Toes*, are in the American Room at Dromkeen. In this story, Elephant gets stuck in the bath when he is 'helping' Benjamin to get ready for bed. *Nobody Knows I Have Delicate Toes* was published simultaneously in England, Canada, Australia and the United States in 1980.

Conclusion

It has not been possible in this 'tour' through Dromkeen homestead to discuss each piece of artwork on display during 1984, but many others have been included in the following chapters of this book. The names of all illustrators and authors whose work was represented at the homestead during 1984 appear in Appendix 1.

Chapter 3
A Journey into Australian Children's Literature

The earliest children's book in the Dromkeen Collection, *The Life of Captain James Cook*, is by an anonymous author. This small book was printed in London in 1835 by C. F. Cock of 21 Fleet Street and sold as a new edition. Through sampling children's books in the Collection in historical sequence, covering the period 1835 to 1984, gradual changes in format, content, and style of writing and illustration become apparent.

During colonial days, most books read by Australian children were written and illustrated by English authors and artists and printed and published in the United Kingdom. Few books for children were produced in the Australian colonies before the 1890s; it was in this decade that Australian authors, illustrators and publishers began to emerge, and children's books that were unmistakably Australian in character and content appeared. From the 1890s onwards, a recognisably Australian genre in children's literature developed. Today, the names of many Australian authors, illustrators and publishers of children's books are known and respected world wide.

This chapter is not intended as an in-depth survey of the development of Australian children's literature. Rather, it provides a glimpse into some aspects of this development, such as the influence of certain booksellers and publishers, the effects of advances in printing technology on the production of children's books, and most importantly, an appreciation of the works of many authors and illustrators who have contributed to the development of Australian children's literature and are represented at Dromkeen either by their published books, or by pre-publication production materials, or both. At times, biographical information concerning the lives or philosophies of people mentioned in this chapter has been included.

To reiterate, no children's books published prior to 1835 are currently in the Dromkeen Collection. However, in order to present a more complete overview of the development of children's literature in this country, a brief mention of some types of reading material most likely to have been available for children in the colony of New South Wales during its very early years has been included in 'Colonial Days', the first section of this chapter.

PART 1
Colonial Days

Thousands of years before European explorers discovered parts of the coast of the southern continent now known as Australia, the race of dark people who had lived there for over thirty thousand years had developed a rich heritage of legends and lore. They had no written language but their mythology and traditional beliefs had been zealously preserved, passed on by word of mouth from one generation to the next, over countless centuries.

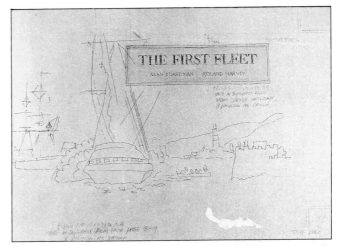

51

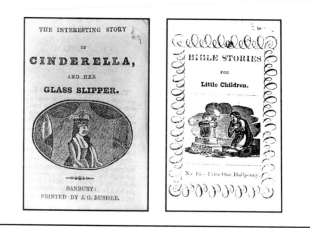

Two examples of chapbooks, from the collection in the State Library of Victoria.

A British Battledore: from a facsimile held in the collection of the State Library of Victoria.

In 1787, following the discovery of the east coast of the southern continent by Captain James Cook in 1770, a fleet of eleven ships under the command of Captain Arthur Phillip set sail from England to commence a penal settlement in the new land. On 26 January 1788, the First Fleet cast anchor in a sheltered cove on the east coast of the continent. Phillip named this place Sydney Cove.

The people who arrived aboard the vessels of the First Fleet —naval officers, marines, surgeons, a judge, a chaplain and convicts — brought to the southern continent a culture totally different from that of its Aboriginal inhabitants. This western culture included written language and its associated printed matter.

According to the records, a number of children and infants arrived with the First Fleet. Some were children of marines, who had been allowed to bring their wives and families with them to the new colony, whereas the naval officers had not; others were the children of convicts.

At first there was little time to worry about formal schooling for the children in the new settlement at Sydney Cove. A few children would have received instruction in reading and numbers from already literate parents, who were sure to have brought some children's books of the period with them, but others would have had no tuition at all. Eventually this became a matter of concern to the colonial chaplain, Richard Johnson, and he managed to have a convict woman appointed as a teacher.

In England, at that time little variety in reading matter and educational material existed for children. There were leather-bound copies of age-old favourites such as *Aesop's Fables*, *Pilgrim's Progress*, *Gulliver's Travels* and *Robinson Crusoe*. There were also other, less expensive, forms of reading matter and educational materials — for example, battledores on which the alphabet was printed, spelling-books, primers, and chapbooks of nursery rhymes, fairy-tales and biblical stories, most of which were illustrated with cheap woodcuts.

A Scarcity of Books for Young Colonials

By the year 1800, there were over nine hundred children in the colony. Some parochial schools had been established but it was not compulsory for children to attend school, and as fees had to be paid for schooling, the education of some children was neglected completely. Many well-educated parents taught their children 'the three R's' at home, while others were tutored privately by educated men and women who had immigrated from England.

In 1798, Reverend Richard Johnson formulated some 'Rules or Articles' for a parochial school in Sydney. Rule 15 stated:

> *As books of learning are at present scarce in the Colony, the children are to give up their Books to the Master every noon & evening, except on Saturday, when they may be allowed to take them home, that the Parents, on Sundays, during the Interval of Divine Service, may hear their lessons . . .*
> (Mackaness, Some letters of Rev. Richard Johnson, p.29)

Most books of learning to which the Reverend Johnson referred would have been spelling-books, primers, grammar books and catechisms. The inclusion of catechisms among instructional books for children was due mainly to the influence of some extremely active religious societies that flourished both prior to and during the first century of European settlement in Australia.

Two leading religious societies in England, The Society for Promoting Christian Knowledge, dating from 1699, and The Religious Tract Society, dating from 1799, became prolific

Back and front pages of an original religious tract, used in the Australian colonies during the 1850s.

publishers during the nineteenth century. Their books and religious tracts flowed into the Australian colonies, to which the societies also sent teachers. Examples of publications by both these societies, and others, are in the Dromkeen Collection.

The desperate need to acquire reading matter suitable for children during the early years of colonisation is recorded in correspondence and despatches sent to London by various persons interested in the education of the young.

The Reverend William Pascoe Crook, a teacher at the elementary school at Parramatta, a new settlement near Sydney Cove, wrote to the London Missionary Society in 1804:

This is an extraordinary place for children. There are vast numbers of them in the colony. Books are much wanted here — spelling books, Watt's Catechisms . . . Scott's Diction-ary, arts, grammars, Bibles, etc. . . . I shall be thankful for any and will make the best use of them . . . (Historical Records of New South Wales Vol.5, *p.314*)

In 1821, Governor Macquarie's concern about the need for suitable books for schools in the growing colony prompted a request to the government in London for slates, school books, and other materials. Among the Bibles, prayer-books and instructional books he received were also books suitable for awarding as prizes for achievement at schools and Sunday-schools.

In October 1824, Thomas Hobbes Scott was appointed Archdeacon of New South Wales and he arrived in the colony in the follow year. Before he departed in 1829, he made a final report to Governor Darling, justifying his period of residence.

---

8   HISTORY OF THOMAS BROWN.

Every week from my wages a sixpence I spare,
   A Bible to buy, for I need it;
And when time I can spare to a friend I'll repair,
   Who has promised to teach me to read it.

And you, sir, have been a most kind friend to me
   This I own, though I cannot repay;
But yet there is One, who this kindness will own
   At the last and the great judgment day.

For myself, as becomes a poor, weak, sinful man,
   I will pray for support from on high;
To walk in God's ways, my Saviour to praise,
   And to trust in his grace till I die.

And though poor and unwise in the ways of the
      world,
   I believe in the truth of God's word,
That, true riches are they, which will not pass away,
   And true wisdom, the fear of the Lord.

THE RELIGIOUS TRACT SOCIETY;
56, PATERNOSTER ROW, AND 65, ST. PAUL'S CHURCHYARD.

THE

SABBATH BREAKER RECLAIMED:

OR,

THE PLEASING HISTORY

OF

THOMAS BROWN.

LONDON:
THE RELIGIOUS TRACT SOCIETY
56, PATERNOSTER ROW, AND 65, ST. PAUL'S CHURCHYARD.

Price One Penny.

No. 1581.

His closing remarks stated in part:

> *I requested each chaplain to establish a lending library for the use of children, lending such books as are calculated for their capacities, selected from the catalogue of The Society For Promoting Christian Knowledge, and other useful publications . . .* (Historical Records of Australia Vol.15, p.214)

Scott's suggestion that each school have a library was certainly ahead of its time. It was probable, however, that much of the reading matter he advocated would not have proved very exciting since most books for children at the beginning of the nineteenth century were expected to be both instructional and informative.

Some Early Children's Books in the Dromkeen Collection

As mentioned previously, the earliest children's book in the Dromkeen Collection is *The Life of Captain James Cook* which was printed in London as a new edition in 1835. This book offers children 'instructive encouragement'. The preface states:

> *The young reader will perceive from it* (the story), *that the humble birth of this illustrious seaman was no bar to his advancement in life; his excellent character, not less than his professional skill, always recommended him to the notice of his superiors, and at last gave him those opportunities which have placed him in the first rank of naval discoverors.*

The book is illustrated with wood-engravings depicting 'life in the South Seas'.

However, early in the nineteenth century, some English and American writers of children's books were attracted by accounts of the strange, frequently hostile environment of the new colonies in Australia, and they took as themes for their stories adventures which the characters they created encountered in this new land.

As most of the authors of these books, and the artists who illustrated them, had never visited the colonies, their conceptions of the Australian landscape and way of life of both the Aborigines and the settlers were often incorrect. Artists were forced to fall back on personal visual experiences of their own environment, as well as pictures of Africa, America and various tropical islands that had been explored many years previously

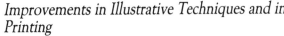

and had been well documented pictorially. Therefore, it was not surprising that in their illustrations the Australian outback sometimes resembled an English scene, that Australian trees looked very like European varieties in full leaf or the palms of equatorial islands, and that the Australian Aborigine resembled an African negro or an American Red Indian, or a combination of both.

A popular American writer of children's stories at that time was 'Peter Parley', a pseudonym for Samuel Grimswold Goodrich. His *Tales About America and Australia*, published about 1840, contains some ill-informed judgements of life in the Australian colonies, while some of the wood engravings must have resulted in his readers developing strange ideas of both the Australian Aborigines and the Australian environment. The copy of *Tales About America and Australia* at Dromkeen is an example of books presented as prizes for achievement in schools and Sunday-schools early last century.

It is inscribed:

Miss Harriet Picot, Christmas Prize for 1841. Presented by Mrs Bennet as a reward for her Perserverence and Regularity.

Improvements in Illustrative Techniques and in Printing

From the middle of the eighteenth century in England, and throughout the nineteenth century, methods of reproducing illustrations for children's books had gradually improved. Wood engravings using box wood and carving *with* the grain, which was relatively easy to do, had slowly given way to fine engravings using the end of the block of wood and carving *against* the grain. This technique took much longer to execute but allowed for a much wider range of effects, and the sharpness of each engraving lasted for many more thousands of impressions without becoming blurred as had happened with the earlier method.

Printing techniques had also improved and the beginning of the nineteenth century saw wooden hand-presses superseded by printing presses made of iron such as the Albion press in the Red Room at Dromkeen. By the 1830s, steel engraving was in common use for reproducing illustrations for children's books, and this method was used concurrently with the reproduction of fine wood engravings and lithographic work.

HUT IN VAN DIEMEN'S LAND.

Fisher's Juvenile Scrap Book, published in London in 1844, has excellent examples of steel engravings. The book comprises prose and verse, and each of the sixteen engravings is protected by a tissue guard. The initial article is a short account of the life, voyages and character of Captain James Cook. A copy of this book is in the Dromkeen Collection.

The First Australian Children's Book

In 1841, what is considered to be the first Australian children's book written and published in Australia was printed at the office of the *Gazette*, in Lower George Street, Sydney, and published by George William Evans, bookseller and explorer. The book was titled *A Mother's Offering to Her Children: By a Lady Long Resident in New South Wales*. In the preface, its author states:

> . . . *its* [the book's] *principal merit is in the truth of the subjects narrated; the accounts of the melancholy shipwrecks being drawn from printed sources; and perhaps it may claim some trifling merit also from being the first work written in the colony expressly for children.*

The exact authorship of this historic book was uncertain until patient research by Marcie Muir, a leading writer on the subject of Australian children's literature, revealed that Australia's first children's author was Charlotte Barton.

The book is written in the didactic question-and-answer style, the dialogue being between the mother (Mrs Saville) and her four children. For example, concerning a cuttle-fish that Clara had tried to catch at Bondi Bay:

> Mrs S. — *It contains a dark colored liquid, which it discharges when in danger, in order to thicken the water, so as to elude pursuit. This liquid when dried becomes a hard substance; and it is supposed to be used in the preparation of Indian ink; which you so frequently use.*
>
> *Your paint, called sepia, is also made of this liquid; it takes its name from the fish, which is called the sepia or cuttle fish.*
> Emma. — *It looks like a mass of jelly.*

Clara. — *Its skin must have been very tough; for I pressed the stick strongly on it; to hold it down.*

Mrs S. — *Yes. The skin is like leather; very coarse and strong. The kind you saw is destitute of bone, or other hard substance . . .*

A facsimile edition of *A Mother's Offering to Her Children*, published in 1979, is at Dromkeen.

Nineteenth Century Juvenile Novels

The period covering the first hundred years of the settlement of Australia through to the first decade of the twentieth century was more or less contemporaneous with the development of children's books in Britain and America. This was particularly so in the case of the development of the juvenile or junior novel. As the century advanced, many overseas writers turned their attentions to the Australian colonies because the exotic environment offered such a wealth of themes that could be used in stories. In addition to themes which incorporated the strange flora and fauna, the wild bushlands, the Aborigines and the convicts, were the dangers caused by bush fires, droughts and floods, the discovery of gold and the activities of the bushrangers.

Brenda Niall, in her book *Australia Through the Looking Glass*, suggests four main approaches to juvenile novels with Australian themes published between the early decades of the last century and the 1890s. These approaches are as follows: stories 'characterised by moral earnestness and a commitment to emigration' in which the need for an exciting story is balanced against the need to encourage emigration to the new colonies; the adventure story which 'could make the most of colonial perils'; novels 'distinguished by . . . religious impulse' wherein organisations such as The Religious Tract Society saw Australia as 'a new mission field'; and lastly, books which constituted the 'semi-documentary or diary' form of writing.

Brenda Niall points out that there is much overlapping of both content and theme in junior novels of this period, irrespective of the main intent of the author, and that this is particularly noticeable in stories which were primarily intended to excite or satisfy the reader's spirit of adventure.

Novels of pioneering days were written and published with the already large, and steadily growing, British readership market in mind, and differences between life in 'the old country' and life in the colonies were strongly emphasised. Junior novels written about Australian life and published in England, as well as those which centred on life in England, such as *Tom Brown's Schooldays*, published in 1857, were imported for colonial children by booksellers who had migrated to Australia and established businesses in the growing cities.

There are too many examples of nineteenth century junior books in the Dromkeen Collection to list here, therefore, a few which exemplify either various types of story content, style of writing and illustration, fashions in cover design, or other points of particular interest, are mentioned.

An Adventure Theme

While, in the main, *The Kangaroo Hunters* by Anne Bowman, published in London in 1859, is an adventure story, there is a strong infusion of other elements, for example, detailed information concerning Australian flora, fauna and geography, much of it incorrect.

Like many authors of her time, Anne Bowman had never visited the colonies and the information about Australia in her book makes amazing reading today. But over one hundred and twenty years ago, when she wrote *The Kangaroo Hunters*, correct information about such a little-known environment as Australia was of almost no concern to British publishers. However, publishers considered it essential that the author's ideas, expressed through the characters, complied with the strict social

Fight with the Kangaroo.— P. 336

57

Display of juvenile novels of the nineteenth century, in the Dromkeen Collection.

and moral standards that the purchasing public of the period demanded in a junior novel.

The Kangaroo Hunters describes the adventures of the Mayburn family who are forced to take to the open sea on a raft when a fire destroys their ship. Mr Mayburn is a widower and a clergyman. With him are his sixteen-year-old daughter, Margaret, two younger sons and an orphaned boy. The party also includes another boy and his sister who have been befriended by the Mayburns, a nurse-come-nanny, and a convict, named Wilkins, who has experience as a seaman.

When the party eventually reaches the coast of Western Australia, the boys construct a few implements by copying some left by Aborigines; they also make bows and arrows. Then, with an axe, several knives and a rifle salvaged from the ship, the party proceeds to live off the land. Strangely, there always seems to be an abundance of animals and birds to kill!

During their fifteen-month trek across the continent, the party is harassed by hostile Aborigines, in peril of being bitten by alligators, and constantly facing other incredible dangers. And throughout the narrative, Mr Mayburn never fails to exhude detailed information about the native plants and animals. On one occasion, hearing the boys wishing for some form of transport, he advises that 'the emu . . . is not formed for carrying burthens [burdens], not tractable enough to submit to the dominion of man . . .' This was one observation that is reasonably correct.

In the story, sixteen-year-old Margaret plays a role often allotted to women in junior novels set in early colonial days, that of the guardian of Christian principles and beliefs, and the protector of refined behaviour, even in the most stressful circumstances.

The Kangaroo Hunters is a most confusing and exceedingly long story. Most of the detailed information about the Australian environment is quite ridiculous, but as an adventure story it sold very well indeed. In fact, it was still in print, and still selling, in the early decades of the present century.

Books As Prizes

During the nineteenth century the practice of giving books as prizes for achievement at school and Sunday-school, which commenced in England, was echoed in Australia, and continued in both countries until well into the twentieth century. Many publishers of junior books last century were eager to compete in this profitable market, and also in the gift book market, and they published junior novels with attractive coloured covers on which title and decorations, or illustrations, were frequently embossed in gold leaf.

One example of this style of publication in the Dromkeen Collection is titled *The Gilpins and Their Fortunes*, published in London in about 1865 by The Society for Promoting Christian Knowledge. It is the story of a pioneer family, the Gilpins, who 'make good' in Australia; its author was a prolific writer of the period, William H. G. Kingston.

The Young Settlers

William H. G. Kingston wrote for several publishing companies. His book *Australian Adventures* was published in London

ADVENTURES IN AUSTRALIA.

AUSTRALIAN ADVENTURES

BY

WILLIAM H. G. KINGSTON

AUTHOR OF "GREAT AFRICAN TRAVELLERS," "SHIPWRECKS AND DISASTERS
AT SEA," "DIGBY HEATHCOTE," &c.

WITH THIRTY-FOUR ILLUSTRATIONS

LONDON
GEORGE ROUTLEDGE AND SONS
BROADWAY, LUDGATE HILL
GLASGOW AND NEW YORK

in about 1884 by George Routledge and Sons. On the cover of the copy in the Dromkeen Collection, 'new chum' settlers from England are shown stalking emus with bows and arrows. The theme of 'new chum' immigrants having to face and overcome the difficulties and dangers they encounter in Australia, all of which were so totally different from anything they had experienced in England, runs through many nineteenth century children's novels. In these stories it was usual for 'new chums' who overcame their problems to be accepted by established settlers, while those who failed were often dispatched home to England by their author-creators.

A Story with a Conversion Theme

Another book in the Dromkeen Collection, *The Children in the Scrub*, attributed to Sophia Tandy and published in London in 1878, is an example of a story written with the purpose of furthering the teachings of the Gospel. Subtitled 'A Story of Tasmania', this colonial tale recounts the drama of three children lost in thick scrub for five days and of their eventual rescue. The plot is used as a vehicle for the conversion theme — a bringing back 'into the fold' of the children's mother, who had turned her back on the Christian faith, and of the return to Christian ideals by the children's elder brother, Richard, after he finally finds his brothers and sisters 'under the shadow of the hollow white-gum tree'.

Factual Tales

Only an author who had grown up in the Australian colonies, or at least had been resident there for several years, could be expected to have sufficient knowledge of colonial life to write authentically about it. Some semi-documentary or diary-style books for children written by authors who had experienced life in the Australian colonies last century are in the Dromkeen Collection. A few are mentioned below.

The first, *A Mother's Offering to Her Children*, has been discussed previously. Composed in the question-and-answer style, it is an extreme example of this genre.

In contrast, *A Boy's Adventures in the Wilds of Australia* by William Howitt, published in London in 1854, is a type of informal travelogue and is written in the first person. Howitt and his wife visited Australia in 1852 and stayed for two years. Howitt's book takes the form of a diary kept by a boy, Herbert, whose travels from Melbourne to the goldfields with his father, brother and cousin are recorded and give a practical view point of colonial life.

Here they excavate the hills at that depth (50 to 100 feet), driving tunnels as far as their neighbours will let them, and clearing out all the space that they can obtain of the gold-impregnated stratum. Some of these hills here are thus excavated for miles, and one so completely so, that the other day the whole hill cracked right across, from one end to the other, with an explosion like thunder, the fissure descending from top to bottom, on which all miners emerged from their pits like rabbits from their burrows when they are invaded by the ferret. Fortunately, no one was hurt.

Another author whose writings were of a documentary nature was Louisa Anne Meredith. Born in Birmingham, England, she married Charles Meredith in 1839. Shortly after their marriage, the couple sailed for Sydney, but moved to Tasmania the following year.

In her new environment, Louisa continued to write, sketch and paint as she had in her homeland. In about 1860, a children's book she had written and illustrated while at Twamley in Tasmania was published in London. It was titled *Loved And Lost! The True Story of a Short Life Told in Gossip Verse and Illustrated*. The pages are decorated with vignettes of flowers, birds and animals, and in the text the author exhorts all people not to cage living creatures as the very thought is cruel and barbaric. The copy in the Dromkeen Collection still retains the gilt on its green cover and page-edges.

The Australian Aborigine in Nineteenth Century Children's Literature

Most children's books written during colonial days included some references to the Aboriginal people, and the stories reflected the attitude, prevalent in those days of the British Empire, that the European was superior to all other races. In general, the Aborigines were depicted sanctimoniously, as heathens whose salvation lay in their Christianisation, and it was often, quite erroneously, inferred that, as a people, they lacked worthwhile spiritual beliefs of their own. Numerous stories featured fierce clashes between Aborigines and white settlers, the Aborigines being portrayed simply as a race of savages. Most authors gave little thought to encouraging young readers to regard the Aborigines as people with feelings similar to their own. In contrast, an individual Aborigine was often shown, condescendingly, as being responsive to friendliness, and many stories included an Aborigine who becomes a faithful retainer —a 'Man Friday' as in *Robinson Crusoe*.

Although so many nineteenth century writers showed a contemptuous or patronising attitude towards the Aborigines and their customs, a number of authors did raise issues of moral consciousness and give reasons why conflict between white settlers and the Aborigines began. On these occasions, characters in stories often express the viewpoint that due to colonisa-

Page from Louisa Anne Meredith's Loved, and Lost! *printed in London by Day and Son, and published in the colonies about 1860 by George Robertson, Melbourne; W.C. Rigby, Adelaide; Walch and Sons, Hobart and Launceston.*

Posed photograph of Bett-Bett and her dog, Sue; from a first edition of The Little Black Princess, *held in the Dromkeen Collection.*

tion, Aboriginal tribes had been deprived of their hunting grounds, therefore it was no wonder that they looked upon settlers as intruders who were destroying both their livelihood and their social structure, and took retaliatory action against them.

In the Dromkeen Collection is a copy of a book titled *Blacks and Bushrangers* by E. G. Kennedy, published in London in 1889. In the preface, Kennedy sets out to authenticate many instances in his story, and speaking of a notorious outback, buckjumping horse, he states: 'one of the many I saw ridden on a northern station in 1864'. So it appears that Kennedy spent some time in Queensland and while there, it is possible that he developed a certain insight into the way of life and customs of the northern Aboriginal people, which he used later in his adventure story *Blacks and Bushrangers*.

In the story, Mat Sampson and his brother Tim are shipwrecked on the Queensland coast. The sole survivors, they manage to find food in the bushland, until they are captured by

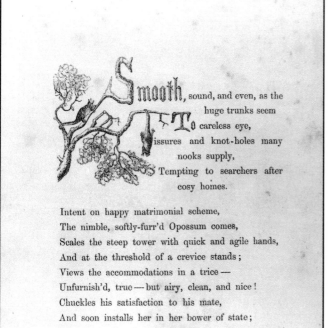

Aborigines of the Waidonga tribe. The Aborigines prove friendly, and Mat and Tim learn their ways of foraging and hunting for food and are eventually assimilated into the tribal way of life.

The emotions experienced by Mat and an elder of the Waidonga people, Drummoora, when Mat and Tim finally leave for southern parts are apparent in this quote from the novel:

> *When the white men turned their faces homewards the chief and his whole tribe accompanied them as far as the boundaries of the Waidonga country . . . when Mat turned round for a last wave of the hand he saw his old chief . . . seated on a stone, [in] the attitude of despair. The tears rose in his [Mat's] eyes as he witnessed this spectacle . . .*

Kennedy's work shows many differences in attitude towards the Aboriginal people from those of his contemporary writers.

In 1891, two years after Kennedy's book appeared, a completely new perspective on the way of life of the Australian Aborigines eventuated in the form of a collection of their legends and tales. Titled *King Bungaree's Pyalla*, it was written by Mary Anne Fitzgerald from memories of stories that were told to her during her childhood.

In 1896, Kate Langloh Parker's *Australian Legendary Tales* was published. It contained folklore of the Noongahburrahs as told to the piccaninnies, and the illustrations were by an Aboriginal artist. *More Australian Legendary Tales* followed in 1898.

In 1905, *The Little Black Princess*, written by Jeannie Gunn, was published. The little black princess was an eight-year-old Aboriginal girl named Bett-Bett who lived on Elsey cattle station in the Northern Territory where Jeannie Gunn's husband was manager. This was the first attempt to present to children of European descent an intimate picture of the way of life of an

Aboriginal child. Although, at times, the author can be criticised for condescension when she writes about adult Aborigines, the story is mostly written with humour and understanding and shows genuine affection for Aboriginal people.

Bett-Bett's group of blacks are camped on Elsey property and so are living in close proximity with the station people. There are many references to the cultural beliefs and customs of the Aborigines, and as many references to attempts by the 'Missus', as Jeannie Gunn is known, to introduce Bett-Bett to the ways of white people. For example, in the following extract the Missus has decided to introduce Bett-Bett to books, and a reading lesson ensues.

The capitals were bad enough, but when we began the little letters, things got dreadfully mixed.

'Missus! this one no more "A",' said Bett-Bett, worrying over small "a".

I told her it was a little 'a'; but she insisted that it wasn't, and to prove it showed me big 'A', and of course they were not a bit alike. To try and make her understand a little better, I said that capital 'A' was the mother, and little 'a' the baby. This pleased her very much . . . we said: 'Mumma A and piccaninny belonga mumma A; mumma B and piccaninny belonga mumma B, and so on to the very end of the alphabet . . .

Teaching roles are reversed when Bett-Bett attempts to instruct the 'Missus' in bush-craft. Jeannie Gunn proves a dull pupil for she is unable to identify even the tracks made by her own husband!

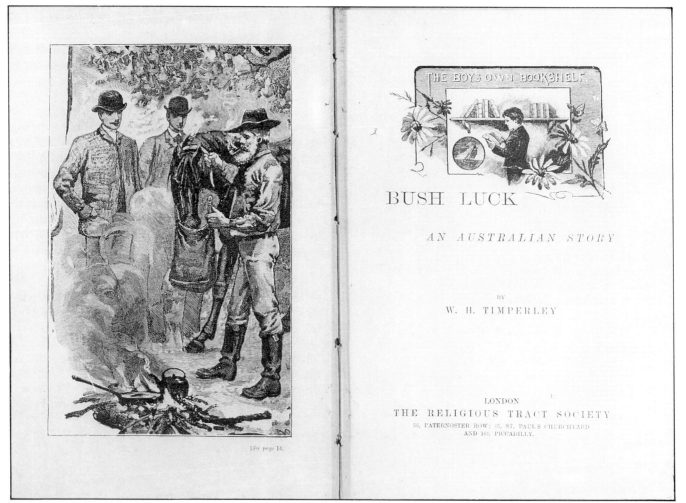

[*See page 14.*

THE BOYS OWN BOOKSHELF

BUSH LUCK

AN AUSTRALIAN STORY

BY

W. H. TIMPERLEY

LONDON
THE RELIGIOUS TRACT SOCIETY
56, PATERNOSTER ROW; 65, ST. PAUL'S CHURCHYARD
AND 164, PICCADILLY.

Three fascinating examples of juvenile reading matter published in the nineteenth century; these books are in the Dromkeen Collection.

At the time of Mrs Aeneas Gunn's death in 1961, *The Little Black Princess* had sold 280,000 copies.

Times of Change

During the greater part of the nineteenth century, there were few heroes and heroines aged less than fourteen years in junior novels set in Australia. Stories of adventure and land settlement where physical dangers and trials, as well as conflicts of 'right or wrong' attitudes and ambitions, had to be overcome, or resolved, required characters in their late teenage years, or even older. But there was more to the vogue than this. The moralistic attitudes of those times demanded characters upon whom young readers could model their own behaviour, and so all characters tended to become stereotyped.

Times were changing, however, and more realistic heroes and heroines, as well as those of a younger age-group, began to appear in children's literature around the world. These child characters retained their childlike behaviour — their sense of fun, their jibes at one another, hurtful or otherwise, their quarrelsomeness, their affections, their need for love and security, and importantly, their real interests. Hand-in-hand with this more realistic treatment of children as main characters came a feeling of realism in other aspects of stories written specifically for young readers.

In several aspects, but not all, one such book in the Dromkeen

Collection is *Tom's Nugget* by J. F. Hodgetts, published in London in 1888. Hodgetts had spent some time on the goldfields and also had experienced life in Melbourne's 'canvas town' where immigrants erected temporary homes prior to setting off to seek their fortunes in gold. His accounts of those times are both immediate and realistic.

In *Tom's Nugget*, the interests of the main character, Tom, are fairly consistent with the interests of any boy of eight years of age at that time. Speech is in the colloquial language of the day, as can be noticed in the following extract in which Tom and his friend are searching for a platypus, which Tom calls a 'Horny-floflinxus' instead of ornithorhyncus.

> There was no sign of the animal, however hard Tom pecked at the bank or Billy dug in the sand. At last our hero, tired and hungry, threw down his pick exclaiming — 'Beastly country this is! You never find what you want. In England, now, if you want frogs or anything, you know where to look and how to find them. Perhaps, after all, there are no horny-floflinxuses at all! Disappointing, isn't it?'
>
> 'You have no right to growl, considering you have the finest nugget ever found.'
>
> 'You shut up about the nugget! It was a fluke, I tell you, and has brought me nothing but bother.'

Another book in the Dromkeen Collection, *Bush Luck*, written by W. H. Timperley and published in London in 1892, was amongst the last books to be published under the imprint of The Religious Tract Society, 'The Boy's Own Bookshelf', because the Society's publications were to become submerged in *The Boy's Own Paper*. Over the previous decade, Australia had become more urbanised, and outback areas more settled, so the colonies no longer offered the attractions of an uncivilised land where misisonary intent could flourish. The mid-eighteen-nineties were to see the emergence of Australian authors whose attitudes to junior fiction were quite different from those which had dominated children's literature for the past century.

Nineteenth Century Books for Young Children

In the Dromkeen Collection are many nineteenth century books written specifically for young children. Two, *The Infant's Magazine* for 1877 and *My New Book*, one of the varied series of Toy Books and also published in 1877, are products of The Religious Tract Society.

The Infant's Magazine is profusely illustrated throughout with either fine woodcuts or steel engravings. The use of large type ensured that young children could read the print with ease. The content is varied: short stories and verse; line drawings of birds for children to copy; titbits to encourage learning; and others that emphasise the work ethic — and many a moral is taught, as can be seen in the poem 'Dirty Jack' by Jane Turner:

DIRTY JACK

There was one little Jack,
Not very long back,
And 'tis said, to his lasting disgrace,
That he never was seen
With his hands at all clean,
Nor yet ever clean was his face.

His friends were much hurt,
To see so much dirt,
And often and well did they scour;
But all was in vain —
He was dirty again
Before they had done it an hour.

When to wash he was sent,
He reluctantly went,
With water to splash himself o'er;
But he left the black streaks

Running down both his cheeks,
And made them look worse than before.

The idle and bad
May, like to this lad,
Be dirty and black, to be sure;
But good boys are seen
To be decent and clean,
Although they are ever so poor.

Another nineteenth century children's book in the Dromkeen Collection, *Jackanapes*, written by Juliana Horatia Ewing and published by The Society for Promoting Christian Knowledge in 1879, is for an older age group. The illustrations are by the famous English illustrator Randolph Caldecott, and were engraved and printed by the equally famous nineteenth century printer of children's books, Edmund Evans.

The English Engraver, Edmund Evans

By the 1860s, steel engraving and printing by means of engraved box-wood blocks and lithographic stones had become the most

R. CALDECOTT'S
PICTURE BOOK

CONTAINING

THE DIVERTING HISTORY OF JOHN GILPIN
THE THREE JOVIAL HUNTSMEN
AN ELEGY ON THE DEATH OF A MAD DOG

ALL ILLUSTRATED IN COLOUR
AND BLACK AND WHITE
BY
RANDOLPH CALDECOTT

LONDON
FREDERICK WARNE & CO.
AND NEW YORK
[*All Rights Reserved*]

commonly used techniques in the reproduction of illustrations for children's books published in England. Few artists were able to do their own engraving or litho printing and so were dependent on the skill of the engraver or litho printer for faithful reproduction of their work.

Edmund Evans, a craftsman of exceptional skill, an engraver and printer and an artist in his own right, was largely responsible for bringing tasteful colour printing to prominence in England in the latter half of the nineteenth century. Through the lithographic techniques and skills he developed, the work of English illustrators of children's books, such as Kate Greenaway, Walter Crane and Randolph Caldecott, became renowned world wide.

The Dromkeen Collection has books illustrated by two of these artists and printed by Evans — *The Baby's Opera* by Walter Crane, published in 1877, and one of Randolph Caldecott's famous picture books. The clean line drawings and fresh clear colour, indicative of illustrations by Greenaway, Crane and Caldecott, and faithfully reproduced by Evans, were quite unlike the many florid coloured illustrations for children's books produced by other illustrators and printers of the day.

The style of the illustrations by the three English artists, Kate Greenaway, Walter Crane and Randolph Caldecott, was related in essence to the Arts and Crafts Movement which was sweeping

Europe at that time — in other words to *art nouveau*. This was essentially a decorative, romantic style, sometimes embracing sweeping, curving lines, at others involving simplified or stylised figures or plant forms. Walter Crane was a leader in the Arts and Crafts Movement and his illustrations for *The Baby's Opera* show his love of the movement's decorative style.

The books by Crane and Caldecott in the Dromkeen Collection would most probably have been purchased from one of the busy bookshops in the colonies last century.

PART II
The Emergence of Australian Children's Authors and Illustrators

Australian Booksellers
The buying and selling of books in the Australian colonies during the second half of the nineteenth century followed the practices of the book trade in Britain. Between 1852 and 1882, some extremely enterprising young booksellers emigrated to the Australian colonies and were to make their mark on bookselling and publishing in the newly emerging nation.

The most prominent booksellers were: George Robertson and Samuel Mullen, who established themselves in Melbourne;

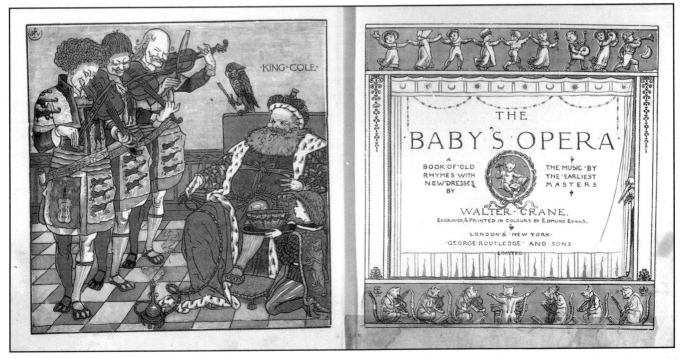

George Robertson, the Melbourne bookseller and publisher.

Samuel Mullen, the Melbourne bookseller and publisher.

William Charles Rigby, who commenced his business in Adelaide; and David Mackenzie Angus and his partner, *another* George Robertson, who built up the business of Angus and Robertson in Sydney.

George Robertson of Melbourne and Samuel Mullen

George Robertson of Melbourne was not a relative of George Robertson of Sydney, and was about thirty-five years his senior. That these two eventual giants in the Australian bookselling and publishing scene had the same names has always caused some confusion. If either man had possessed a second name this would not have happened.

George Robertson, the Melbourne bookseller and publisher, was born in Glasgow in 1825. When he was four years of age his family moved to Dublin, where George eventually became apprenticed to a leading firm of booksellers, William Curry Junior and Company. Here he met a fellow apprentice, Samuel Mullen. The two became friends and, in 1852, they decided to emigrate together to the colony of Victoria. They embarked on the *Great Britain*, the largest and fastest ship of the time, equipped with steam-driven propellers as well as sail. The *Great Britain* reached Melbourne on 12 November the same year.

It seems that on landing, Robertson found himself short of ready cash and being an enterprising young man, he opened one of the crates of books he had brought with him on the ship as stock for his proposed bookshop and commenced to sell his wares. In next to no time, he had disposed of the whole crate of books to the literature-hungry Melbournians on the wharf. Later, the bookshop he opened at 84 Russell Street became extremely successful.

Samuel Mullen had not intended to continue in the book trade in his new country, as he imagined himself well suited to a more vigorous life on the land. He took advantage of an introduction he had to Samuel Baird of Mount Bute Station in the Western District of Victoria and became a jackaroo, working with stock and assisting with the maintenance of the property.

By 1855, George Robertson's bookselling business was thriving and he had ventured into publishing. At about this time, Samuel Mullen came to the conclusion that outback life was not really to his taste and he returned to Melbourne, where he joined George Robertson's business as senior assistant.

In 1857, George Robertson opened a book-buying office in London and appointed Samuel Mullen as manager. Mullen sailed for England with his wife and infant son, but on reaching London, he received an astonishing communique from Robertson, stating that the appointment had been cancelled and that Robertson had placed his brother, William Robertson, in charge of the London office. No reason for this sudden change

Angus & Robertson, Publishers

The Melbourne booksellers George Robertson, Samuel Mullen and E. W. Cole, and the Adelaide bookseller W. C. Rigby, were contemporaries of two important Sydney booksellers, David Mackenzie Angus and the other, younger George Robertson, so often confused with George Robertson of Melbourne.

The Sydney firm Angus and Robertson, formed in 1886, had a profound effect on bookselling and publishing in Australia during the last decades of the nineteenth century. It resulted, in the twentieth century, in the publication of many outstanding Australian books for children. Some became so well loved that they have never been out of print.

David Mackenzie Angus was born in Thurso, Scotland, in 1855. Throughout his life he was troubled by periods of ill-health, and the need to live in a milder climate than that of his native Scotland eventually forced him to emigrate to Australia. He arrived in Sydney in 1882, and a short time later joined the staff of the bookshop which George Robertson of Melbourne had opened at 361 George Street.

The younger George Robertson was born at Halstead, in the county of Essex, England, in 1860, and eventually came to Australia via New Zealand. It is an amazing coincidence that he secured a position with the Sydney branch of the bookseller who had the same name as himself. There, the younger George Robertson became friends with David Angus.

David Angus left the bookshop in George Street in 1884, to start a bookselling business of his own in Market Street, but a year later he was struck again by ill-health. The young George Robertson came to the aid of his friend, an act that resulted two years later in the partnership of Angus and Robertson.

In 1888, Angus and Robertson commenced publishing works by Australian authors, success in this field eventually being achieved with *The Man From Snowy River and Other Verses* by A. B. (Banjo) Paterson, and works by Henry Lawson. Angus and Robertson published their first junior novel in 1897. Written by a young author, Louise Mack, it was titled *Teens*.

David Angus relinquished his share in Angus and Robertson and returned to England in 1900. He died in 1901. Within a few years Angus and Robertson became a public company with George Robertson as managing director.

In 1905, four years after the Australian states had joined in Federation to become a new nation — the Commonwealth of Australia — Angus and Robertson published an *Anthology of Australian Verse*. The editor was Bertram Stevens, who read manuscripts for Angus and Robertson and was formerly editor of the magazine *The Lone Hand*. In the introduction to the anthology, Stevens stated:

Australia has now come of age, and is becoming conscious of its strength and its possibilities. Its writers today are, as a rule, self-reliant and hopeful. They have faith in their own country; they write of it as they see it, and of their work and their joys and their fears, in simple, direct language . . .

These sentiments typified the literary mood of the 1890s and early 1900s in Australia.

New Styles in the Writing of Children's Books

An interest in child development was stirring in Europe and America and, as a consequence, educational philosophy and practices slowly began to change. The needs and interests of child readers became of importance and their right to be entertained by their leisure reading matter recognised. These new attitudes influenced ideas concerning the nature and content of children's literature, and children's authors of the late nineteenth century and early twentieth century responded accordingly.

Themes for children's books written by Australian authors followed trends set by English and American writers and publishers of books for children. For readers about to enter their teenage years, and those who were already in that age group, came the family story, set more often in the city than the country, and school-based stories.

The new emphasis on realism in children's books, which had already made an appearance, was developed further. It was noticeable in the portrayal of the personalities of an author's chosen characters, as well as in the interaction between the characters. Child characters became more complex and life-like: they were rebellious, naughty and mischievous, just as often as well-behaved, for it was no longer expected that they be presented as unrealistic, idealised little models of virtue. There was also realism in subject-matter, incident and environment for, by this time, Australian authors were handling the Australian setting of their stories more naturally and not labouring it, as had been the trait during the greater part of the nineteenth century.

In general, the emphasis on informative instruction and religious moralising gradually faded and junior novels began to reflect accepted middle-class values and moral codes of the times. Most Australian authors of junior novels who emerged in the 1890s and the early decades of the twentieth century came from the well-educated, middle-class of Australian society, and most of those authors were women.

Ethel Turner

Ethel Turner was the first Australian author of a junior novel featuring a family-type story centred in a city. A complete set of her junior novels is in the Judge's Room at Dromkeen homestead.

Ethel Turner's first book, *Seven Little Australians*, was written when she was twenty-one, and was published in London in 1894 by the English company Ward Lock, who had established an office in Melbourne in 1884 under the managership of William Steele. To William Steele belongs the credit, not only of

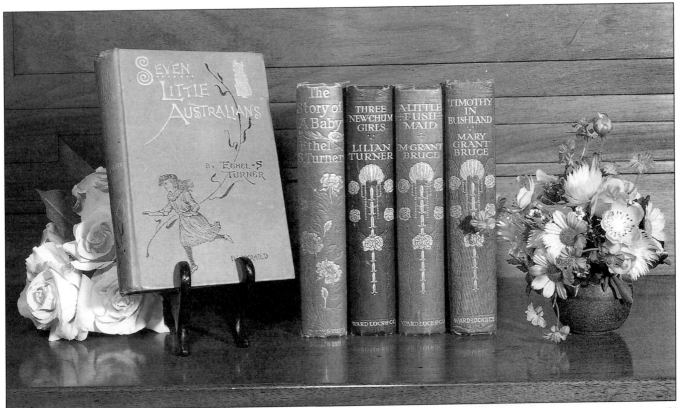

William Steele who joined Ward, Lock & Tyler, London, in 1867. He arrived in Melbourne on 11 July 1884 and founded the Australasian branch of Ward, Lock & Company Limited. He died in 1918.

Ethel Turner, the author of Seven Little Australians.

developing Ward Lock's sales and sound publishing reputation in Australia and New Zealand, but also of discovering literary talent. When Ethel Turner sent her manuscript *Seven Little Australians* to Ward Lock's Melbourne office in 1894, William Steele read it with interest and a growing conviction that he had before him the work of an author of great potential. He sent the manuscript to head office in England and negotiated the terms of contract with Ethel Turner himself.

Ethel Sibyl Turner was born in Doncaster, England, in 1872. Her father died when she was two years old, and six years later she emigrated to Australia with her mother and other children in the family. After her primary schooling, she attended Sydney Girls' High School where her interest in writing was aroused.

When Ethel was seventeen, she initiated a serial titled 'The Dreadful Pickle' in a monthly magazine for girls, the *Parthenon*, which she ran with her sister, Lillian. So commenced Ethel Turner's first story about children as she saw them, and also *for* children, because the serial was featured on the children's page for which Ethel was responsible.

Writing of Ethel Turner in *Australia Through the Looking-Glass*, Brenda Niall states:

Ethel Turner accomplished a double revolution. She took Australian fictional children away from the station home-steads and goldfields of earlier novels. More important, she developed a new literary type in her heroes and heroines, in whom the models from her own reading in English and American juvenile fiction were reshaped and given a sense of authentic life as Australian children, unselfconsciously distinctive in idiom and outlook. (p.81)

In later books, the Australian idiom Ethel Turner used in dialogue, and at times her disregard of generally prohibited topics in children's books, such as divorce, were to cause a few problems between the author and her English publishers, Ward Lock, who were vitally interested in the extremely profitable, but conservative, Sunday-school prize-giving market for their books. On occasions, Ethel Turner was forced to make changes to the text herself or accept editorial alterations. However, in the case of her first book, *Seven Little Australians*, Ward Lock was eager to publish. Coulson Kernahan, the firm's literary adviser in England, hailed Ethel Turner as 'the Louisa Alcott of Australia'.

In *Seven Little Australians*, the heroine, Judy Woolcot, is crushed by a falling tree as she runs to save her young brother. There is many a death-bed scene in children's literature of the Victorian era, but it was usual for the *good* to die, and for some moral to be pointed out by the tragedy. The death scene described by Ethel Turner breaks with this tradition. Judy was far

from being a perfect child because she was so often rebellious; she stays true to character to the end, and no moral is intended by the author.

Many a reader has been reduced to tears by this stage in the book; even William Steele professed himself to be 'deeply moved' by Judy's death, as was recorded in Ethel Turner's diary, which was edited by Philippa Poole, and published in 1979.

18th October:
Morning wrote chapter XX, 7 Australians, killed Judy to slow music. Copied out chapter XIII and XIV. I'll be glad when its done.

20th October:
Finished 7 Little Australians. Hurrah, I thought I'd never get to the end. Now I only have to copy out 7 more chapters and it is ready to hunt for a publisher.

2nd November:
Walked up to the post and sent 7 L. Australians to Ward Lock, Melbourne. It took 18 stamps . . .

9th November:
Had a letter from Ward Lock, I was amazed to get it so soon. They say they have read my MSS and conclude 'I wish to negotiate for the immediate publication of it. That owing to the terrible depression they are using their power of selection

Louise Mack, an author of schoolgirl novels at the turn of the century.

Jacket of the 1925 edition of Teens, designed by Percy Lindsay of the famous Lindsay family; copy in the Dromkeen Collection.

very sparingly but if I will tell them what value I place on the work they will write me further.' Not at all a bad letter to get from my first publisher and within a week. I can't think what value I place on it, I must get advice. (P. Poole, The Diaries of Ethel Turner, pp. 98-99)

Ethel Turner eventually agreed to an offer by Ward Lock of £15 for the copyright of her novel and a royalty of 2½ pence on each copy sold at two shillings and sixpence. She also agreed to supply a sequel by April of the following year.

In 1896, Ethel Turner married Herbert Raine Curlewis, later Judge Curlewis. From that time, until her death in 1958, she lived at Mosman, Sydney, where she brought up her two children, a boy, Adrian, and a girl, Jean, and continued to write novels for young readers. Her daughter also took up writing, but unfortunately she died at the age of thirty-one.

Seven Little Australians has sold more than a million copies and has been translated into ten languages since it was first published. In 1895, it featured as a stage play; as a film in 1939; a television serial in England in 1953; and in 1975, a television

version was made for the Australian Broadcasting Commission. The book is still in print, and is regarded by many as an Australian children's classic.

Louise Mack

A school friend of Ethel and Lillian Turner, Louise Mack, based her first novel on a school theme. This was the book *Teens*, published by Angus and Robertson in 1897.

Louise Mack was born in Hobart in the early 1870s and later spent five years at Sydney Girls' High School, where she became friendly with Ethel Turner.

Teens was based on Louise Mack's own years as a schoolgirl in Sydney. She sold the royalty rights to Angus and Robertson for £25, but refused to accept such a sum for her sequel, *Girls Together*. George Robertson offered her two guineas per 1000 words for her sequel; this totalled £115 for the complete manuscript. Louise did not agree, and on asking her husband, John Creed, for his considered opinion as to the value of the work, he suggested £150. Three weeks later, George Robertson grudg-

Illustration from the first edition copy of Dot and the Kangaroo. *The illustrations were reproduced by the then new photogravure method.*

ingly conceded this amount and purchased the manuscript. Angus and Robertson would not have lost financially on the deal.

Boys' Stories

During the Victorian and Edwardian eras, the separation of male and female roles in society was very apparent. Therefore, publishers adopted the vogue of publishing junior novels specifically for girls, and others for boys, even though it was common knowledge that boys' stories, being generally filled with adventure, were frequently read by girls as well. In general, however, this publishing vogue continued into the late 1930s, when more open-minded social attitudes began to influence trends in junior literature.

Stories for boys by Australian authors usually fell into two main categories: school stories and adventure stories, as they did in junior novels published in Britain. School stories were based on life in boarding-schools and did not have the hold on Australian readers that such stories had on their English counterparts. Two examples of such school stories for boys in the Dromkeen Collection are *Dick* by Mary Grant Bruce, published in 1918, and *The Heart of the School*, by Eustace Boylan, published the following year.

There were also books about the young settler, but in the north of Australia, not the south, such as *Comrades* by Joseph Bowes, published in 1912. Another book by Bowes, *The Young Anzacs*, as its title implies, is centred on young Australians as fighting men in the First World War. It was published in 1917.

Apart from school stories, the Australian boy of twelve to fifteen years of age does not feature in Australian junior fiction of this era because young adult characters were needed to carry the action. There is one notable exception: *The Gold-Stealers* (1901), written by Edward Dyson and set in the Victorian goldfields. The author had personal experience of the life about which he wrote, and his work has a tremendous feeling of immediacy and realism.

The titles mentioned, and many other books written specifically for boys at the turn of the century, are in the Dromkeen Collection.

Ethel Pedley and Dot and the Kangaroo

As well as junior novels, books for younger Australians were also being written at the turn of the century. A fantasy, *Dot and the Kangaroo*, has proved the longest lasting. *Dot and the Kangaroo* was published in London in 1899. The author was Ethel Pedley, an English-born music teacher who had lived in Sydney for some time. While in Australia, the bushland had captured her interest and imagination, and the indiscriminate slaughter of Australian animals for their fur, or for other reasons, had distressed her intensely. The dedication in her book reads:

> *To the Children of Australia, in the hope of enlisting their sympathies for the many beautiful, amiable, and frolicsome creatures of their fair land; whose extinction, through ruthless destruction, is surely being accomplished.*

The story is told directly and simply, and even though the moral pointing out the need for people to show kindness and understanding towards animals comes through strongly, there are many moments of fun.

Dot, the little girl lost in the bush, finds security in the friendship of a female kangaroo who has recently lost her joey and amiably carries Dot in her pouch through the bushland, where the child meets with many adventures involving Australian bush creatures. The kangaroo risks being shot by Dot's father when she insists on returning the little girl safely to her home, and is saved just in time by Dot's intervention. Young children of today identify with Dot and her need for love, care

THE PLATYPUS SINGS OF ANTEDILUVIAN DAYS.

Mary Grant Bruce, author of the Billabong books.

Frontispiece and title page of the first-edition copy of Mates at Billabong, *held at Dromkeen. The illustrator, John Macfarlane, created the visual images of the well-loved characters of the Billabong books.*

Mary Grant Bruce and C. Oakley Lock, a director of Ward Lock, at the centenary celebration of the firm in London in 1954.

and attention, just as readily as their counterparts did almost a century ago.

Ethel Pedley died in England before *Dot and the Kangaroo* was published, but as she had made previous arrangements for the Sydney artist, Frank Mahony, to illustrate the story, the bush scenes and drawings of the animals were authentically Australian.

With his usual discerning eye for the right kind of book to publish, George Robertson of Angus and Robertson secured the publishing rights for *Dot and the Kangaroo* and brought out the next edition in 1906. Many editions have been published since. A first edition copy is in the Dromkeen Collection.

Mary Grant Bruce and the 'Billabong' books

In 1910, a children's novel, *A Little Bush Maid*, written by an Australian author, Mary Grant Bruce, was published in London by Ward Lock after the manuscript had been recommended by William Steele. This book became the first of a series centred around an Australian family, the Lintons, who lived on a grazing property called 'Billabong', situated 'somewhere in northern Victoria'. More idyllic than truly realistic, Mary Grant Bruce's 'Billabong books', as they were affectionately known, gripped the hearts and imagination of several generations of readers. A complete set, comprising fifteen titles, as well as other children's novels by Mary Grant Bruce, are in the Dromkeen Collection.

Mary Grant Bruce was born in 1878 at Sale, a country town in Gippsland in eastern Victoria, where her father was a government land-agent. Holidays spent with the other children in the family on their grandfather's cattle property in Gippsland made a lasting impression on the young Mary Grant Bruce, one which she drew on later for her Billabong books.

At the age of sixteen, Mary Grant Bruce completed her matriculation at Sale Ladies' High School. After winning the annual essay competition organised by the Melbourne Shakespeare Society, for three years in succession, she left Sale to carve a career as a journalist in Melbourne. There she became 'Cinderella', the editor of the children's page of a weekly paper, *The Leader*, which had a readership of mainly country people. Part of her job was to write stories for the children's page. One of the stories that appeared in serial form was 'A Little Bush Maid'.

Like other Australian authors of the time, Mary Grant Bruce was interested in human relationships and the ways in which people handle problems, interests, joys and disappointments. However, in contrast to two of her contemporaries and main rivals for market popularity, Ethel Turner and Louise Mack, who took city settings for their family or school-centred novels, Mary Grant Bruce centred hers in country towns, or on farms

and grazing properties, and she made full use of the type of life she knew and understood so well.

Mary Grant Bruce travelled between Australia and Britain several times during her career. The first occasion was a few years before the First World War, when she went to England to work as a journalist. There she met her second cousin, Major George Bruce, an officer in the Norfolk Regiment. They became engaged and, in 1914, they sailed for Australia to be married. She was thirty-six years of age; he was forty-six.

At the outbreak of war only a few weeks after they arrived, Major Bruce was recalled to his regiment and his wife travelled with him in a troop-ship to England. There Major Bruce was transferred to the Dublin Fusilliers, and Mary Grant Bruce spent most of the war years in Ireland where her two sons, Jonathan

and Patrick, were born. She continued to write novels for Ward Lock, submitting them to the London office.

Tragedy struck Mary Grant Bruce twice in her life — the second mirroring the first in a macabre fashion. When she was seven, her beloved brother, Paddy, was killed in a shooting accident just before his ninth birthday. In Ireland, in 1929, her youngest son, Patrick, then aged twelve, also died in a shooting accident. Grief-stricken after Patrick's death, the Bruce family moved to England. It was several years before Mary Grant Bruce was able to write again.

Although Mary Grant Bruce introduced tragedy, misfortune and poverty into many of her children's novels and numerous short stories in the Billabong series, the lives of the characters who had become so well loved by readers remained stable — not one of the characters in the saga dies, up to, and including, the last book of the series, *Billabong Riders.*

Mary Grant Bruce travelled to London in 1954 to take part in Ward Lock's centenary celebrations and died in England at the age of eighty.

Australian Illustrators Enter the Publishing Scene

At the turn of the century, Australian illustrators of children's books, as well as Australian children's authors, came into prominence. Some have already been mentioned in Chapter 2, but are reintroduced here because their work was of vital importance in the development of Australian books for children.

Ida Rentoul Outhwaite

On 6 August 1903, some small pen sketches appeared in the Melbourne magazine *New Idea* as illustrations for a story 'The Fairies of the Fern Gully'. The magazine editor's introductory comment states:

> *This is the first of a number of purely Australian stories we propose to publish. The nom-de-plume of 'Billabong' is that of a writer whose stories are well known to the Australian public. The illustrations, which are quite remarkable in character, are the work of Miss Ida S. Rentoul, daughter of Professor Rentoul of Melbourne University. Miss Rentoul is only 16 years of age, has had no instruction in drawing, and, though she shows the influence of some masters of line in her drawings, her work is quite original, and we have no hesitation in stating that she has a brilliant future open to her in the artistic world. These are the only examples of Miss Rentoul's work that have appeared in print.*

Prophetic words by the editor! However, Ida would have been only fifteen years of age in 1903, not sixteen as stated.

" Could it be a Fairy-bell . . . swayed by woodland fairy." (*The Bell-bird*)

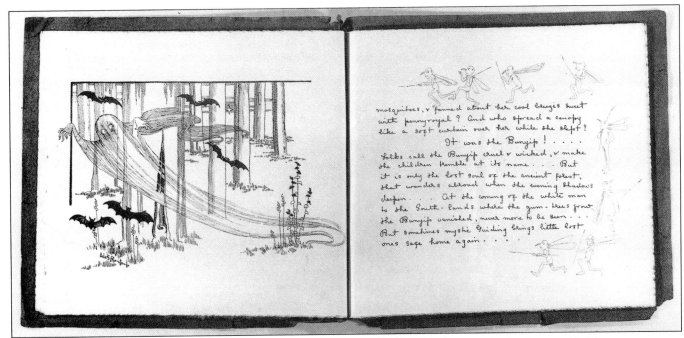

Several books illustrated by Ida Rentoul when she was still a schoolgirl can be found in the Judge's Room at Dromkeen. The earliest, titled *Mollie's Bunyip*, was written by the artist's elder sister, Annie Rattray Rentoul, and published in Melbourne in 1904. It is a slim, soft-covered booklet in a horizontal format, the deckle-edged pages being printed on one side only, and the poems and short tales handwritten not typeset. The drawings are, understandably, immature, but bright little sketches of elves and Australian birds decorate the margins on many pages.

The next book the young Ida Rentoul illustrated was *Mollie's Staircase*, written by her mother, Annie Isobel Rentoul, and published in Melbourne in about 1906. This booklet is of similar format to its predecessor, but this time the text has been typeset. The drawings are more assured and the young artist has tackled interior scenes of Mollie's house.

A book of songs, titled *Australian Songs for Young and Old*, published about 1907, followed. Illustrated by Ida, the verses by Annie were set to music by a friend of the family, Georgette Peterson. This was the first of several Australian song-books produced in the following years by the Rentoul sisters and Georgette Peterson. The lilting tunes were sung in Australian schools for many decades.

Also in the Dromkeen Collection is a first-edition copy of *Gum-Tree Brownie and Other Faerie Folk of the Never Never*, published in 1907. The stories were written by Tarella Quin Daskein (usually known as Tarella Quin) and illustrated by Ida

"Seated on a world no larger than his own . . . sat the two queerest beings he had ever seen."

Rentoul. A natural sense of design and composition is becoming increasingly apparent in Ida Rentoul's work. By the time she had illustrated *The Lady of the Blue Beads*, written by her sister Annie and published in 1908, and *Before the Lamps Are Lit* by Tarella Quin and published in 1911, she had achieved true

Illustration of the Gum-Tree Brownie, from the first edition of Gum-Tree Brownie *in the Dromkeen Collection.*

Title page of Mollie's Staircase; *copy in the Dromkeen Collection.*

Watercolour illustration of the Little Witch by Ida Rentoul Outhwaite from Elves and Fairies. *A certain prettiness accompanied by flowing lines and silhouette effects often discernible in* art nouveau *are noticeable in this illustration.*

Translucent watercolour by another illustrator of fairyland creatures, Harold Gaze. This is an illustration from the first edition copy of The Merry Piper *in the Dromkeen Collection.*

"Sitting on the pannikin."

MOLLIE'S STAIRCASE

By A. I. RENTOUL and I. S. RENTOUL.

Published by
M. L. HUTCHINSON,
Glasgow Book Warehouse,
305-7 LITTLE COLLINS ST., MELBOURNE.

professional status as an illustrator and a wide public following.

After her marriage in 1909, Ida illustrated many stories written by her husband, Arthur Grenbry Outhwaite, who also edited the lavish book referred to earlier, *Elves and Fairies*, which contained poems by Annie Rentoul, illustrated by Ida. The large format of *Elves and Fairies*, its fifteen tipped-in colour plates (ie separately printed colour illustration plates pasted in by hand in the printery) each with a tissue-paper guard, and thirty black-and-white illustrations, all printed on high-quality paper, made this book an exotic production and an expensive acquisition. Virtually a collector's item, it was considered too beautiful a book for children to handle if unsupervised.

Elves and Fairies was financed initially by subscription, and an imposing list of subscribers' names, including that of Dame Nellie Melba, appears at the back of the book. The publication of *Elves and Fairies* in 1916 marked a highlight in Australian book production. There are two first-edition copies at Dromkeen.

The Merry Piper.

First edition copies in the Dromkeen Collection of Boronia Babies, Wattle Babies, Gum Nut Babies, Gum Blossom Babies *and* Flannel Flowers and Other Bush Babies *by May Gibbs.*

May Gibbs working in her studio in Bridge Street, Sydney. On the wall behind her are framed copies of covers which she designed for Sydney magazines.

Among other books illustrated by Ida Rentoul Outhwaite in the Dromkeen Collection are *The Little Green Road to Fairyland*, published in 1922, which has proved to be the most lasting, and a companion volume to *Elves and Fairies*, titled *Fairyland*. Published in Melbourne in 1926, *Fairyland* was just as lavishly produced as its predecessor.

The Great Depression of the late 1920s and through the 1930s brought the publishing of sumptuous books to an end. At the same time, public interest in fairy folk diminished in favour of tales centred around Australian bushland creatures. Although Ida Rentoul Outhwaite changed her subject-matter in order to fulfil these new demands, her work was never to receive the same public acclaim she had enjoyed in her younger days when her illustrations were novel and her imagination inspired. She is best remembered for her delicate, and often impish, illustrations of fairy folk, and the books she illustrated at the height of her fame became cherished possessions of children of her own and later eras.

May Gibbs, Creator of Snugglepot and Cuddlepie

In 1916, George Robertson of Angus and Robertson must have been delighted to be offered two small manuscripts by the well-known Sydney artist May Gibbs, accompanied by her illustrations of the cherubic imps she had created — her Gum Nut Babies and Gum Blossom Babies. Their wide, blue eyes peering over the top of bunches of gum leaves gave them an innocent, yet somewhat startled expression, and a view from the back showed two minute white wings sprouting from between their shoulders.

Apart from the Gum Nuts' snugly-fitting, green caps, they were quite naked, but the Gum Blossom Babies had an added touch: pink gum-blossom stamens fringed their caps and formed their short, ragged skirts. May Gibbs' tiny bushland babies were both appealing and unique, and George Robertson had no hesitation in publishing her work.

Gum Nut Babies and *Gum Blossom Babies* arrived in bookshops in time for the Christmas-buying season that year. They

were beautifully-produced booklets, with a colour plate on the cover, a coloured frontispiece and sepia-tinted drawings inside. The short pieces of fanciful prose that accompanied each illustration were more in the nature of whimsical observations of the way of life of the bushland babies, and the creatures with whom they spent their time, than stories. Both booklets sold out before Christmas.

May Gibbs' vision of her bushland babies did not come about suddenly. All manner of experiences over the years had contributed to their evolution: her intense love of nature, her observation of the ways and interests of children, and the skills developed while earning a living in the fiercely competitive field of commercial art.

Cecilia May Gibbs was born in Surrey, England, in 1877, and emigrated to Australia with her family when she was four. Landing first in South Australia, where an attempt to farm resulted in failure, the family eventually moved to the west and lived in several places outside Perth before settling in the city itself, close enough to the Swan River for occasional boating trips or picnics on the riverbank.

May's father, Herbert Gibbs, was a portrait painter in his spare time. He used to delight in taking his daughter on long rambles through the bushland, where they could observe the plants and animals and make detailed sketches. Under his influence, May developed the love of nature and interest in draftmanship that were later reflected in her work. No bunch of gum leaves she drew was ever leaf-perfect. One can always find evidence of a hungry insect having paused here or there for a bite or two.

May Gibbs made several trips to London between 1900 and 1909. On each occasion, she attended London art schools and, with the exception of her first visit, also worked as a commercial artist. Between trips to London, she worked as a freelance artist

The Gum Blossom Ballet

Snugglepot and Cuddlepie.

A bad banksia man.

in Perth, designing advertisements and drawing cartoons for newspapers. Her quick wit and keen appreciation of the ridiculous or comic had been noticed by her father when she was still a child, and he had encouraged her to make amusing sketches of family and friends, which unfortunately at times resulted in bruised feelings. May's love of satire now found ready expression in her cartoons, and there was the added attraction of being paid for her efforts. In 1913, she moved to Sydney, for there were far more opportunities for a commercial artist in that city.

Even before Federation in 1901, there was strong evidence of developing feelings of nationalism in Australia, and concurrently, a growing awareness of distinctive aspects of the Australian environment. As world tensions prior to the First World War increased, feelings of patriotism heightened. It was in this dramatically altered atmosphere that May Gibbs' bushland babies were first introduced. Small prototypes appeared in her work as early as 1913. By 1914, gumnuts and other bush babies had crept into some of her cover designs for the *Sydney Mail* and *The Lone Hand* and had assumed the characteristics which now are so familiar.

During the war, May Gibbs designed a collection of postcards for sending to Australian troops overseas. There were drawings of kookaburras and other Australian birds, some wearing the slouch hat of the Australian soldier. On other cards, birds or animals were shown as part of a family group, or a knitting or sewing circle, working to fill the Red Cross parcels for the soldiers in the trenches. Each postcard had a humorous caption intended to lift the men's spirits and let them know that those at home were thinking of them. May Gibbs included her gumnut babies in several of these postcards and a few, printed during the First World War, are in the Dromkeen Collection.

It was when she was using her bush babies in commercial designs that May Gibbs began to realise their potential as characters in children's books. Her first venture in this direction was the two booklets published by Angus and Robertson in 1916. These were followed in 1917 by *Boronia Babies* and *Flannel Flowers and Other Bush Babies* and, in 1918, by *Wattle Babies*. Also in 1918, Angus and Robertson published May Gibbs' first full-length children's book about the two gumnut babies, Snugglepot and Cuddlepie, and their friend Little Ragged Blossom. The title page of the book read *Snugglepot and Cuddlepie: Their Adventures Wonderful*, but the book is usually known by its cover title, *Tales of Snugglepot and Cuddlepie*. The book was an immediate success.

It was in her book *Snugglepot and Cuddlepie* that May Gibbs first developed the personalities of her bushland babies and introduced their animal friends and enemies. In the two sequels, *Little Ragged Blossom*, published in 1920, and *Little Obelia*, published in 1921, the author took her small characters beneath the sea.

Norman Lindsay, author and illustrator of The Magic Pudding.

May Gibbs' home Nut Cote, at Neutral Bay, a harbour suburb of Sydney.

In the busy world of Snugglepot and Cuddlepie, life is a continuous round of exciting adventures, drama and suspense as the story of the gumnuts' struggles to outwit their enemies unfolds. And what formidable foes the gumnuts have — Mrs Snake, deceitful and cunning, and her cohorts the bad banksia men, the epitome of wickedness! Violence committed by the evil-doers serves to highlight the warmth and loyalty the gumnuts and their friends feel for one another, and their courage as they go to each other's aid in a crisis, even though terribly afraid themselves. And so the balance of good against evil sways this way and that, until good emerges triumphant.

Many people who read the adventures of Snugglepot and Cuddlepie as children cannot look at a banksia tree even as adults without being reminded of the bad banksia men of May Gibbs' imagination, proof of her ability to create a lasting impression.

Children delight in May Gibbs' use of language and in her inventiveness: " 'Smoke him and burn him,' growled another. 'Drop him and drown him,' snarled another.'' Who else but the bad banksia men would think of such terrible things! Expressions such as 'My Bully Ant!', 'Oh, Gum!' and 'Great Snakes!' proved a magnificent way of getting around forbidden swear words. And there were other wonderful words, too:

> *'Where's the banksia man?' asked Snugglepot. 'Deadibones,' said Cuddlepie.*

When May was visiting her parents in Perth in 1918, she met James Ossoli Kelly, a friend of the family. They were married the following year and settled in Sydney where May continued her work.

After her success with Snugglepot and Cuddlepie, May Gibbs wrote many other children's books, copies of which are in the Dromkeen Collection. She also devised several comic-strips for children, which were published in various newspapers and magazines. The most famous of these was *Bib and Bub*. First published in 1925 in the Sydney paper *Sunday News*, and later in other newspapers throughout Australia, its two gumnut characters, Bib and Bub, made the name of their creator, May Gibbs, familiar to almost every family in the country. *Bib and Bub* continued to be published for over forty years.

But no matter how well known she became, and even taking her sparkling sense of humour and fun into consideration, May Gibbs was never an outward-going, gregarious person. She became even more retiring as she grew older, living quietly in her home, Nut Cote, at Neutral Bay, Sydney, accompanied by her beloved Scottie dogs, and often not wishing her privacy to be disturbed by anyone.

Since 1940, when the three books about Snugglepot and

82

Cuddlepie were combined in one volume, *The Complete Adventures of Snugglepot and Cuddlepie*, over 400,000 copies have been sold.

May Gibbs was awarded the M.B.E. for her contribution to Australian children's literature. She had no children of her own,

but when she died in 1969, she left to the children of Australia a heritage of remarkable and truly Australian stories and illustrations.

Norman Lindsay and The Magic Pudding

A first-edition copy of the Australian children's classic *The Magic Pudding* is in the Red Room at Dromkeen. A completely different kind of fantasy from those of May Gibbs, it also was written during the First World War and published in 1918. This 'rip-roaring', timeless story, with its spontaneous, lampoon-type illustrations of Australian animals, a pudding, and eccentric human characters was the work of the noted and controversial Australian author and artist Norman Lindsay. Born in 1879 at Creswick, a small gold-mining town in Victoria, he is probably the best known of the gifted Lindsay family.

Norman Lindsay was a man of exuberant personality. A master of satire, his dramatic black-and-white work appeared in the Sydney *Bulletin* for many years. Once called an 'acid and iconoclastic critic of man's absurdities', it is not surprising to find that Lindsay uses biting satire with hilarious effect in his first children's book, *The Magic Pudding.*

This fast-moving, magical tale never seems to pause longer than it takes to devour a slice of pudding before rushing on to the next episode. The title page of the book shows the main characters in the story. Below the title are the heroes: Bunyip Bluegum, Bill Barnacle, Sam Sawnoff and, of course, the never-diminished-no-matter-how-much-is-eaten, 'cut-and-come-again' Puddin' called Albert; above the title are the rascally Puddin'-thieves, 'a Possum with one of those sharp, snooting, snouting sort of faces, and . . . a bulbous, boozy-looking Wombat'.

The odd mixture of characters, their nonsensical adventures as the Puddin' is stolen and retrieved many times, and the numerous nonsense verses throughout the story, make amusing reading. For example, from the courtroom scene:

'If,' said the Usher, in a quavering voice —
'If you take a poisoned Puddin'
* And that poisoned Puddin' chew,*
The sensations that you suffer
* I should rather say were due*
To the poison in the Puddin'
* In the act of Poisoning You.*
And I think the fact suffices
* Through this dreadfulest of crimes,*
As you've eaten seven slices
* You've been poisoned seven times.'*

When asked why he chose to write a tale centred around a pudding, Norman Lindsay replied:

Bert Stevens [Bertram Stevens, a freelance editor and adviser with Angus and Robertson] *and I were once discussing popularity motifs in books for children and Bert gave as his opinion that fairies formed its most fascinating subject matter. I gave him mine for food, on the theory that infantile concepts of happiness are based on the belly. In short, nice things to eat. And I added something to the effect that if a kid was offered his choice between food and fairies as delectable reading matter, I was willing to bet he would plump for food.*

* Bert repeated this conversation to George Robertson* [of Angus and Robertson], *who said, 'If you can persuade him to write a story for children, you're on a fiver'. On Bert retelling this remark of G.R.'s to me, and suggesting that I might try the experiment of writing a book for kids, I said the idea was fatuous, and I was quite incapable of such a literary exercise . . . (Reflections,* Reading Time, *Publication No. 3, pp 60-61).*

However, *The Magic Pudding* eventuated several years later, and

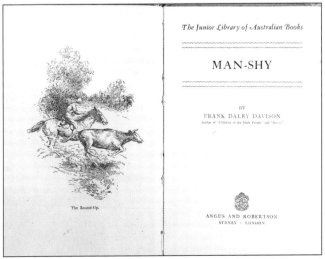

when passing the manuscript to George Robertson, Norman Lindsay stressed that no moral was intended in the story.

George Robertson's acceptance of *The Magic Pudding* again demonstrates his astuteness, for it has been one of his most successful publishing ventures. Now regarded as an Australian children's classic, more than 288,000 copies have been sold. The book is still in print and still selling.

Dorothy Wall

Dorothy Wall, the New Zealand artist who came to Australia in 1914 and spent most of her time in Sydney, is best known for the mischievous koala character she invented — Blinky Bill. Her first book about his adventures, *Blinky Bill: The Quaint Little Australian*, was published in 1933 by Angus and Robertson. This was the same year in which George Robertson died, and it is not known whether he was the one who made the decision to accept Dorothy Wall's manuscript, or if this piece of astute judgement should be attributed to his successor as managing director of Angus and Robertson, Walter Cousins.

Dorothy Wall was a small, neat woman with a strong personality. She was on the staff of the *Sydney Morning Herald* for a short time and much in demand as an illustrator of fashion catalogues and advertisements for retail stores. She appears to have been a tireless worker; in between her usual commercial work, she designed book covers for Angus and Robertson, wrote and illustrated children's books of her own, and also illustrated books for other authors.

"BLINKY BILL", "NUTSY" & "SPLODGE"

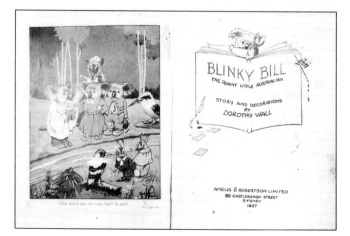

The first children's book Dorothy Wall wrote and illustrated was *Tommy Bear and the Zookies*, published in 1920. The experience she gained from this book resulted in her accomplished illustrations for J. J. Hall's children's book *The Crystal Bowl* which was published the following year. This book established her as an imaginative and competent illustrator, but it was to be twelve years before she produced her first Blinky Bill book. The three years following its publication were her most productive in the field of children's books, for during this period two more Blinky Bill books were published: *Blinky Bill Grows Up* and *Blinky Bill and Nutsy*. Since 1939, when the three books were combined under one title, *The Complete Adventures of Blinky Bill*, over 320,000 copies have been sold. During the early 1930s, Dorothy Wall also illustrated books by other authors — for example, *Jacko, the Broadcasting Kookaburra* (1933) and *The Amazing Adventures of Billy Penguin* (1934) by Brooke Nicholls. It is considered that her illustrations in these books represent some of her best work. Copies of all the books mentioned are in the Dromkeen Collection.

Not long before her sudden death in 1942, Dorothy Wall had been experimenting with ideas for Blinky Bill motifs to be used on ceramic ware for children, on plates, mugs and toothbrush-holders, and on egg-cups. She also drew designs for Blinky Bill

slippers, play-suits and aprons. All were designed with a mass market for Blinky Bill products in mind, but it is not known whether she had interested a manufacturer in her ideas before she died. Many of her original tracings, and both colour and black-and-white sketches for these products, have recently been placed on loan at Dromkeen.

Mary and Elizabeth Durack

A children's book that was unique in several ways was published in Sydney in 1941. The book was titled *The Way of the Whirlwind* and was written by Mary Durack and illustrated by her sister Elizabeth.

The Spider wove her finest silken threads around the wee, wee mite.

Mary and Elizabeth Durack.

Tipped-in colour plate from first edition copy of The Way of the Whirlwind *in the Dromkeen Collection.*

The story is in the folklore tradition — but with a difference, for the hero and heroine are Aboriginal children, Nungaree and Jungaree, who believe their baby brother has been stolen by Here-and-There, the Whirlwind who lives in the 'Nowhere'. The setting is wild, outback Australia, and the spirits and creatures the children encounter on their travels as they try to reclaim their little brother are as Australian as all other aspects of the story.

The Way of the Whirlwind is not an interpretation of an Aboriginal legend, but a fairy story in its own right. It is told with sympathy and understanding by an author who knew the Australian outback and its Aboriginal people well, and was able to portray her young characters quite naturally.

Elizabeth Durack's illustrations in full spirited colour, and also in black and white, lent a feeling of exuberance to the book. In format, the book was large with nine colour plates printed on the conventional shiny art paper.

Published early in the Second World War, the Australianness of *The Way of the Whirlwind* matched the feeling of nationalism prevalent at the time, and it found immediate acceptance with both children and adults. The book was reprinted several times before Angus and Robertson obtained publishing rights and reissued it in a more conventional format.

Mary and Elizabeth Durack are the grandchildren of one of Australia's most colourful pioneers, Patrick Durack, who drove his herds through the unexplored country of north-west Australia last century and founded the huge grazing property he named Argyle Station and several other grazing properties. After their formal schooling in Perth, the two Durack girls spent a great deal of time on these properties, and their droving exploits are well known. Mary became an author, and Elizabeth an artist, and both have portrayed life in the outback in books and magazines.

A first-edition copy of *The Way of the Whirlwind* is at Dromkeen. The early editions of this work, printed and published by Consolidated Press, signalled the end of the publication of children's books with tipped-in colour plates. Some picture-story books printed and published in Australia during, and immediately after, the Second World War were to appear in a completely different format from any that had been published previously in this country.

PART III
Picture-Story Books Galore

In the Dromkeen Collection are some board-covered picture-story books with illustrations in full colour. They are representative of the type of children's picture books that were written, illustrated and produced in Australia during the period 1941 to the early 1960s. *Digit Dick on the Barrier Reef* and *Gecko The Lizard Who Lost His Tail*, both written by Leslie Rees, are two examples of this type of publication. These books, and others of the same era, were printed in tens of thousands during, and for some years after, the Second World War. These 'board books' as they became known, were completely different in design and layout from any children's books with pictures in colour previously produced in Australia.

Imported Picture Books

During the Depression of the 1930s, Australian publishing of children's picture books had declined. This was partly because the Australian market was not large enough to warrant the financial risk of publishing expensive books with illustrations in colour, and partly because Australian publishing houses could not compete with the reasonably priced yet high-quality children's picture books imported from Britain.

Before the Second World War, the distribution of quality children's books in Australia was mostly in the hands of booksellers, who ordered children's books directly from publishing houses in Australia and also imported books from publishing companies overseas. Most imported children's books came from Britain, but some booksellers also brought in children's books from the United States.

A Lack of Picture-Story Books

During the Second World War, the importation of books into Australia was severely restricted and, as a result, there was a death of picture-story books on the market. Referring to those

THE LIZARD WHO LOST HIS TAIL

Gecko

a story by
LESLIE REES

illustrated by
Walter Cunningham

JOHN SANDS PTY. LTD.
SYDNEY, MELBOURNE, BRISBANE, ADELAIDE,
PERTH, HOBART

times, the veteran Australian bookseller and publisher, Frank Cheshire, relates in his autobiography:

> It may not be generally known that during the [Second World] War there were many restrictions on the importation of books. The first essential was to establish a quota which was based on the value of books imported prior to the outbreak of War. The next step was to obtain a license. When the books arrived the invoices were scrutinised by officers of the Customs Department. As there were practically no American school books in use in Victoria at that time, I had a very meagre quota. Under no circumstances could American fiction or children's books be imported. In fact, this regulation lasted for quite a considerable time after the War ceased. (Cheshire, Bookseller Publisher Friend, p. 90).

The governing factor controlling the publication of books in Australia during the war years was the supply of paper. Printing paper was rationed throughout the war and for some years afterwards. Consignments of paper were made to printers, not to publishers, and the size of the allotment was based on the amount of paper a printer had used previously.

Printers were endeavouring to keep their costly colour-printing presses in continual operation, and as they had control of the uses to which their consignment of paper could be put, they quickly capitalised on the demand for low-priced children's picture-story books. The result was quantities of inexpensive, colourful, board-covered children's books mostly with Australian content, printed and published by Australian printing companies during and for some years after the Second World War. A few local publishing companies were also active in the production of children's 'board' books during this time, but most were published by printing companies and distributed through toy-and-gift market wholesalers to department stores, bookshops and newsagents. Unfortunately, a large number of these inexpensive picture-story books were trivial in content and shoddily produced, but on a market starved for children's books, they sold extremely well.

An extra boost was given to sales of children's books with Australian content when America entered the war. American servicemen based in Australia, and those who spent their leave in Australian cities, bought many thousands of children's books featuring Australian animals, birds and plants, and sent them to their families in America.

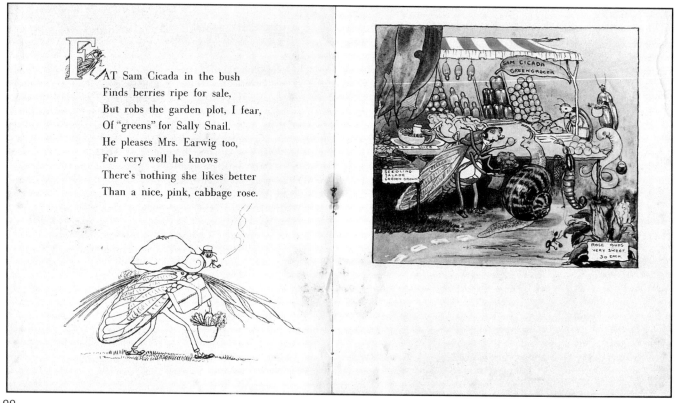

FAT Sam Cicada in the bush
Finds berries ripe for sale,
But robs the garden plot, I fear,
Of "greens" for Sally Snail.
He pleases Mrs. Earwig too,
For very well he knows
There's nothing she likes better
Than a nice, pink, cabbage rose.

Quippy, a John Sands publication, shown here with a dummy of the book prepared by Walter Cunningham.

One other major factor that influenced the development of picture-story books in Australia at this time was the sudden increase in the number of child-care centres and kindergartens.

Kindergartens

The Kindergarten Union of New South Wales was formed in 1895 and the first free kindergarten in Australia was opened in 1896 in the inner Sydney suburb of Woolloomooloo. The kindergarten movement spread to the other states and, by 1916, kindergarten teachers' colleges had been founded in most capital cities.

The expansion of kindergartens was halted during the Depression of the 1930s, but the frightful social conditions of those times led to the first government initiative in the pre-school field. The Commonwealth Department of Health set up Demonstration Centres in each capital city. These Centres were concerned with the nutrition, care and instruction of children between the ages of two to six years. The Governor-General's wife lent her support and the Centres, known to most people as the 'Lady Gowrie Centres', but referred to by many cynics as 'pleasant islands in the slums', took over much of the earlier role of the Kindergarten Unions.

The Second World War had a considerable impact on the role of the kindergarten in Australian society. Due to the urgent demand for labour, women flocked into the labour force in order to increase the output of munitions and to set male workers free to join the military services. The existing kindergartens could not cope with the increased numbers of pre-

school-age children belonging to working mothers. As a result, in 1943, the Federal Minister for Health announced that creches for children of mothers engaged in war work would be established in all states, and that pre-school organisations already in existence would be subsidised by the government.

Books for Kindergartens

The expansion of kindergartens and child-care centres created a need for toys and for books suitable for children in the younger age groups. Australian printing firms allocated certain of their rationed supplies of paper for books for the pre-school market.

A pre-school book titled *Grandpuff and Leafy*, written by Gladys Lister, was printed and published in 1942 by Marchant and Company, printers and stationers of Sydney. It bore the dedication:

> *To Her Excellency, The Lady Gowrie and to every child with a soldier Daddy.*

A copy of this book is on loan to the Dromkeen Collection.

The Sydney printers and stationers John Sands also published books for the pre-school market. One of the best known was *Quippy* by Olive Mason, published in 1946. The book was just the right size for small hands to hold, and Walter Cunningham's illustrations of the appealing duckling, Quippy, were in colour.

John Sands and Company

In the early 1940s, John Sands was among the first printing firms

to become aware of the pressing need for locally produced, reasonably priced picture-story books that reflected the Australian way of life and the Australian environment.

John Sands and Company was founded in Sydney and by the late 1870s, John Sands Chrome Lithographic Works was manufacturing stationery and printing coloured labels and greeting cards. During the early years of the new century, the firm branched into manufacturing family games (for example, Snakes and Ladders) and occasionally printed a few books, which were slotted into the everyday printing schedule, primarily to keep the costly printing machinery continually operating. Among the firm's early book-printing ventures was the Ginger Meggs series of *Sunbeams Annuals*. The first of these was published by Sun Newspapers and printed by Sands in 1924. A copy is in the Dromkeen Collection.

Ginger Meggs, and His Creator, James Bancks

Almost every child in Sydney and Melbourne in the 1920s had heard of Ginger Meggs. Young Ginger, his girl friend Minnie Peters, his rival for her attentions Eddie Coogan, and his sworn

enemy Tiger Kelly, were, with Ginger's mother Sarah Meggs, the main characters in the comic-strip 'Us Fellers'. This unbelievably successful comic-strip was created by the Australian cartoonist James Charles Bancks.

'Us Fellers' first appeared in 'Sunbeams', the children's section of the Sydney *Sunday Sun*, on 13 November 1921, and the following year also in the Saturday editions of the Melbourne *Sun News-Pictorial*. Later, the title was altered from 'Us Fellers' to 'Ginger Meggs'.

From 1924 onwards, Ginger Meggs comic-strips which had been published during the year were collected in book form and issued prior to each Christmas season. This annual publication was titled *The 'Sunbeams' Book/Adventures of Ginger Meggs*. A further popular title *More Adventures of Ginger Meggs* was issued just prior to, and during, the Second World War.

Rees, Cunningham and Cadsky

In 1943, Grahame Sands, grandson of the founder of John Sands and Company, became chairman of directors and he allowed the profitable printing and publishing of children's books by Sands to continue. This decision led to the production of many picture-story books by the author Leslie Rees, illustrated by Sands' staff artist, Walter Cunningham, and guided through the printing and publishing processes by Sands' advertising and publishing manager, Maurice Cadsky. The first children's book involving the trio Rees, Cunningham and Cadsky, *Digit Dick on the Barrier Reef*, had been published in 1942.

Leslie Rees was Deputy Director of Drama for the Australian Broadcasting Commission when he created the tiny character Digit Dick, after a visit to the Whitsunday Islands off the tropical Queensland coast. Diminutive Digit Dick was the size of his mother's big toe. Rees submitted the story to Angus and Robertson, but to his disappointment this publisher showed no interest. Acting upon a suggestion by a friend that the printing company John Sands may be interested in producing a children's book because a new two-colour printing press had recently been installed, Rees contacted Sands and eventually was introduced to Maurice Cadsky, and later to Walter Cunningham. When published, the Digit Dick book was a great success. It was followed by another very popular children's picture-story book, *Gecko, The Lizard Who Lost His Tail*, published in 1944.

In 1924, as a lad of fourteen, Walter Cunningham had emigrated from England to Australia with his family. He was in his twenties when Walt Disney's first full-colour animated cartoons flashed across the silver screens of movie theatres all around the world; as with many young artists of that time, some of his work shows the Disney influence. This is particularly noticeable in the

tiny character Digit Dick, and in many of the animals in this series, but Walter Cunningham's true versatility showed itself in the innovative illustrative styles he used in other picture-story books of the 1940s to the 1960s.

As a staff artist at John Sands, Walter Cunningham worked closely with Maurice Cadsky when designing packaged games, and also on the format and layout of picture-story books. These books, illustrated and designed by Walter Cunningham, constituted a break-through in children's book design in Australia. Perhaps, Walter Cunningham was influenced in his perception of book design by the wide, colourful layouts demanded by the board-games he was accustomed to designing for Sands, but whatever the source of his inspiration, for the first time, children's books produced in Australia had illustrations that spread across one page to the opposite one, uniting the two pages in one complete design. Small illustrations, either full colour or in two colours, appeared frequently in the margins, or at the top or bottom of a page. Some pages were tinted, the tint being used at times as the unifying factor for the small, separate illustrations, at others as an extension of the background colour of the large illustration on the page opposite. Coloured illustrations appeared on page after page throughout Cunningham's books. By the end of the 1940s, Walter Cunningham had gained recognition as one of the leading illustrators of children's books in Australia.

Maurice Cadsky was a Czechoslovakian, born in Prague in 1898. He emigrated to Australia in 1926 and was naturalised the following year. In Australia, he worked first for an advertising

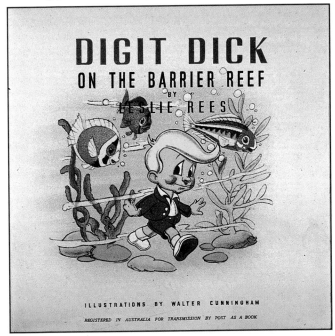

DIGIT DICK
ON THE BARRIER REEF
BY
LESLIE REES

ILLUSTRATIONS BY WALTER CUNNINGHAM
REGISTERED IN AUSTRALIA FOR TRANSMISSION BY POST AS A BOOK

BOOKS for GIRLS and BOYS
Published by
JOHN SANDS PTY. LTD.

	RETAIL PRICE
FOR KINDERGARTEN AND PRE-SCHOOL CHILDREN	
Quippy, by Olive Mason	2 6 each
Squik, by Eve Pownall	2 6 each
CHILDREN'S BOOKS FOR 6-12 AGE GROUP	
Gecko, by Leslie Rees	2 6 each
Digit Dick on the Barrier Reef, by Leslie Rees	3 6 each
Digit Dick and the Tasmanian Devil, by Leslie Rees	3 6 each
Mates of the Kurlalong, by Leslie Rees	8 6 each
Glory Bird, by Veronica Basser	5 6 each
Pamela Finds the Rainbow Castle, by Babs McDonald	4 — each
The Vain Red Fox, by Franklin Moss	4 6 each
Old Man River of Australia, by Leila Pirani	3 6 each
The Rainbow Painter, by Esme E. Bell	4 11 each
Little Brown Piccaninnies, by Jane Ada Fletcher	6 — each
EXCITING NATURE STUDIES ABOUT AUSTRALIAN ANIMALS AND BIRDS	
Shy the Platypus, by Leslie Rees	6 — each
Karrawingi the Emu, by Leslie Rees	6 — each
Silvertail the Lyrebird, by Ina Watson	5 6 each
Sarli the Turtle, by Leslie Rees	5 6 each
Shadow the Rock Wallaby, by Leslie Rees	5 6 each
Kurri Kurri the Kookaburra, by Leslie Rees	6 — each
THRILLING BOOK FOR TEEN-AGE BOYS	
Perils of a Pearl Hunter, by John Gary	5 6 each
DELIGHTFUL BOOKS OF VERSES	
Come Night, Come Ninepence, by Alex. Scott	4 11 each
Sandman Says, by Frank Kauter and Bill Davies	3 3 each
Puppy Days	2 — each
CUT-OUT BOOK	
Locomotive Cut-out	1 11 each
BOOKS FOR ADULTS	
Run O' Waters, by John Fairfax	10 6 each

agency in Melbourne, then moved to Sydney and joined John Sands, where he became manager of the greeting-cards division and, later, manager of the division concerned with the production of games and books.

Maurice Cadsky may have been the first production editor of children's books in Australia, in the sense that he was actually involved in each of the various stages of the production of a children's book, from the commissioning of the manuscript, through the early planning, editing and design stages, to the final printing of the book. He certainly deserves due recognition for the part he played in building the list of children's books printed and published by John Sands from the early 1940s to the 1960s. Cadsky was particularly adroit at maintaining harmonious working relationships between authors and illustrators, and as the number of books being published by Sands increased, authors and artists other than Rees and Cunningham became involved.

Edgar Charles Harris, who initiated the publishing of children's books by Georgian House in the 1940s.

On the left of the photograph is Margareta Webber when she commenced her bookshop in Melbourne in 1931. She is considered to be the first Australian bookseller to specialise in children's books.

Following the success of the first Digit Dick book, Sands suggested to Leslie Rees that a series of nature stories about Australian animals and birds would be a good publishing proposition. The first book in the new series was *The Story of Shy the Platypus*, published in 1944. It was followed two years later by *The Story of Karrawingi the Emu*. Both books were illustrated by Walter Cunningham.

When engaged on a story for a book in the nature series, Leslie Rees researched his subject carefully in libraries, at Taronga Park Zoo and in the bushland of the Blue Mountains, west of Sydney. Sometimes Walter Cunningham accompanied him on these excursions, and they explored gullies, creeks and the rugged bush country, noting and sketching the haunts, characteristics and behaviour of the native animals and birds. There were eventually ten books in this extremely successful series, and they appeared on the market intermittently with new Digit Dick books. Most, but not all, of the books in the nature series were written by Leslie Rees.

Speaking recently of his association with Maurice Cadsky, Leslie Rees remarked:

> *Our working relationship consisted of my calling on him during lunch hour and having a sandwich and a cup of tea, while he would report on the latest progress in the printing of a book of mine, such as getting a roll of paper on to the big machine for colour offset printing. Then we would go to the machine-room and watch the press operating — hundreds of sheets coming off. Editions were exciting in those days — often 20,000 at a time of my stories. For example, [sales of] Shy the Platypus, Digit Dick on the Barrier Reef and Digit Dick and the Tasmanian Devil got up to 105,000 before the first wave of enthusiasm eased off. Of course, it revived again and the total sales of half a dozen Digit Dicks goes beyond 360,000.*

Georgian House, Publishers

One Melbourne publishing company that took a special interest in the production of picture-story books during the 1940s was the newly-formed company, Georgian House. To quote from the firm's catalogue, *Georgian House — The First Two Years, 1944 to 1945:*

> *Georgian House Pty. Ltd. began business on November 1st, 1943, for the purpose of publishing books by Australian authors. The Directors were George Jaboor, Managing Director; E. C. Harris, Manager; and H. K. Cartledge, Secretary.*

Before becoming involved in Georgian House, Edgar Harris had been employed at the Hill of Content bookshop in Bourke

Street, Melbourne. Being well aware that booksellers are cognisant of the type of reading material the market lacks, Harris built a working relationship with Margareta Webber, an astute bookseller who specialised in books for children. Margareta Webber, in turn, recommended to Harris any budding authors who were interested in writing for young children.

During the second half of the 1940s and the early 1950s, Edgar Harris developed a successful publishing programme for Georgian House. Among several books for pre-school children published by the company during this period was *Gee Up Bonny*, written by a South Australian kindergarten teacher, Kathleen Mellor. By 1950, sales of four of her titles had exceeded 200,000 copies — evidence of a strong, local demand! In the Dromkeen Collection are several titles published for the pre-school market by Georgian House in the 1940s. *Billy Caterpillar*, by Elsie M. Hackett, a little book of a factual nature, is one of these.

The Children's Book Council of Australia

The Second World War ended on 15 August 1945. Amid the joy and relief that peace had come at last, the American Chil-

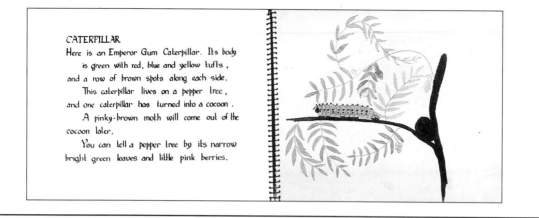

dren's Book Council conceived the idea of making their annual Children's Book Week for 1945 an international one. The theme chosen was 'United Through Books'. This theme typified the feelings of many educators and librarians of that time; they were convinced that the more people understood the way of life of people in other countries through reading about them, the better would be the chance of achieving lasting world peace.

The idea of holding an International Children's Book Week was communicated to other countries. In Australia, the news was received at the United States Information Library in Sydney and the American librarians responded immediately. All wanted to publicise the notion of International Children's Book Week and to include Australian children's books in an exhibition, but there was very little time in which to achieve their aims, since the date set for the Book Week was 12 - 18 November of that year, 1945.

The American librarians arranged a dinner as a 'get-together' of Australian authors, publishers and others who might be interested. To quote Mary Townes Nyland, a librarian from the Information Library, in an article on 'Australia's First Book Week':

> We Americans were amazed, I remember, as the Australians seized upon the idea of Book Week, tossed it back and forth, then were 'off and running'. They formed a committee to meet in Charles Bull's office (at the Australian Broadcasting Commission) within a few days. Enthusiasm spread, more ideas sprang forth, and the principle of Children's Book Week became a warmly accepted fact. (Reading Time, publication no. 4, 1980, p. 3).

It was from the Book Week Committee formed shortly after this 'get-together' in 1945 that the present Children's Book Council of Australia evolved.

In 1945, a group interested in promoting works by Australian authors and illustrators of children's books, the Australian Book Society, was already behind the cause of extending and updating school libraries. After an address to its members by Charles Bull, Chairman of the Book Week Committee, the Society immediately lent its weight to the promotion of Children's Book Week. Two members, Eve Pownall and Nourma Handford, suggested that future Book Weeks should include not only an exhibition of children's books but also an Australian Book of the Year Award, which should be announced at the commencement of Book Week. The Australian Book Society offered to organise the judging of the Book of the Year. The offer was accepted and a panel of judges was convened, comprising one children's librarian from each Australian state.

Before the second International Children's Book Week was held in November 1946, the Book Week Committee had co-opted several other members, including Marie Hurley (US Information Library), Leslie Rees (Australian Broadcasting Commission Drama Department and author), Maurice Cadsky (John Sands, printers) and Eve Pownall (author and committee member of the Australian Book Society).

At the opening of Book Week in 1946, the president of the Australian Book Society announced that the first Australian Book of the Year chosen by the judging panel was *The Story of Karrawingi the Emu*, written by Leslie Rees, illustrated by Walter Cunningham, and published by John Sands and Company. This award was the forerunner of the now much-publicised annual awards for children's books made by the Children's Book Council of Australia.

Before Book Week 1947, the Book Week Committee had changed its name to the Children's Book Council of New South Wales. Children's Book Councils were formed in other states, and in 1959, an inaugural meeting of the Children's Book Council of Australia took place in Sydney, and all state Book Councils combined as a national body.

Elisabeth MacIntyre

Towards the end of the Second World War, the young author/illustrator of children's books, Elisabeth MacIntyre, accepted a commission by Dawfox Productions in Sydney to write and illustrate four books with animal stories. One such book was *The Black Lamb*, published in 1944. An original illustration for this picture-story book is in the Dromkeen Collection.

The Black Lamb was not Elisabeth MacIntyre's first venture into children's books. Her first published work was *Ambrose Kangaroo: A Story That Never Ends* which was published by Consolidated Press in Sydney in 1941, and in New York the following year by the American publisher, Charles Scribner.

For a previously unknown Australian author and illustrator to have a picture-story book published in America in the 1940s was remarkable. Even though many American servicemen were stationed in Australia during the war, and through them unprecedented interest had been aroused in the United States about Australia, this alone would not have prompted an American publishing company to issue a picture-story book that featured Australia and was written and illustrated by an Australian. Elisabeth MacIntyre's clear, but simple text, her uncomplicated line drawings and her original use of colour had captured the attention and approval of the American publisher. When these aspects of *Ambrose Kangaroo* were combined with the sales-market possibilities, Scribners had no hesitation in securing the

Text and illustration from Billy Caterpillar *written and illustrated by Elsie M. Hackett in 1945; copy in the Dromkeen Collection. (Opposite)*

After her discharge from the Land Army, Elisabeth MacIntyre was commissioned by Dawfox Productions to write and illustrate four books for the children's market. One of these small books was The Black Lamb. *(Original artwork)*

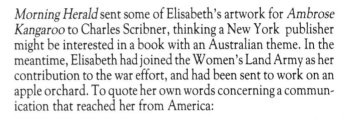

Elisabeth MacIntyre and her daughter, Jane, with Hugh's Zoo, *winner of the Picture Book of the Year in 1965.*

American rights to publish the book. Later, Scribners published other titles by this Australian author and illustrator of children's books.

Elisabeth MacIntyre was born in Sydney in 1916. She spent her childhood in the country and loved the life, loved her assortment of animal pets, and adored horses. When she was fifteen, an accident involving a horse left her acutely deaf and changed her outlook on life. She decided on a career in art and she attended the Julian Ashton Art School in Sydney.

From 1937 until the early years of the Second World War, Elisabeth MacIntyre worked at Lever's Advertising Agency in Sydney, and in her spare time wrote and illustrated *Ambrose Kangaroo*. After the book was published, a friend at the *Sydney Morning Herald* sent some of Elisabeth's artwork for *Ambrose Kangaroo* to Charles Scribner, thinking a New York publisher might be interested in a book with an Australian theme. In the meantime, Elisabeth had joined the Women's Land Army as her contribution to the war effort, and had been sent to work on an apple orchard. To quote her own words concerning a communication that reached her from America:

. . . I will always remember the historic occasion when, away up on a ladder amongst the topmost branches of an apple tree, someone handed me a letter from Alice Dalgliesh at Scribner's, saying they would publish my first book Ambrose Kangaroo, *and suggesting that I should do a picture book*

about what it was like in Australia because so many American children had fathers and brothers in the services stationed in that remote continent 'down under' that nobody seemed to know anything about. It was a mean blustery day, sharp little bullets of sleet stung my face as I trudged down the hillside to the primitive barracks where we were housed; but nothing worried me — my gumboots squelching through mud beat out the rhythm: This-is-young-Susan-who-lives-in-Australia, with-her-toys-and-her-books and her . . . paraphernalia . . . (Something About the Author, *Vol.17, p.164*)

Elisabeth MacIntyre complied with Alice Dalgliesh's wishes and wrote and illustrated *Susan Who Lives in Australia*, which was published by Scribner's in 1944. For Australian publication, the book was re-titled *Katherine* and published by the Australasian Publishing Company in 1946.

Elisabeth MacIntyre has authored many picture-story books and several children's novels since those days, and has made a definite contribution to the development of the Australian picture-story book. In 1965, with her book *Hugh's Zoo*, she won the Picture Book of the Year Award given by the Children's Book Council of Australia. The Dromkeen Collection has recently acquired a piece of artwork for another of her children's books, *Ambrose Kangaroo Delivers the Goods*, published in 1978.

The Fairy Who Wouldn't Fly

On loan to Dromkeen is a first-edition copy of *The Fairy Who Wouldn't Fly*, written and illustrated by Pixie O'Harris and published in 1947 by the Sydney printers Marchant and Company.

The idea for the story came when Pixie O'Harris was in hospital suffering from rheumatic fever and a representative of Marchant, Norman White, visited her and suggested that she write a fairy story, which the company would publish. In a few weeks, the story about the fairy who refused to fly had formed in the author's mind. When Pixie O'Harris was able to work again, she wrote her story and took the manuscript to Norman White

at Marchant and he agreed to publish it. When the author asked to see the publishing contract, he looked somewhat blank and explained that as Marchant was a printing company, they did not have contracts, but if Pixie O'Harris would 'shake hands on it', she would be assured of a ten per cent royalty. Pixie shook hands. *The Fairy Who Wouldn't Fly* was reprinted several times after its publication in 1947 and not once did Marchant falter on their 'gentlemen's agreement'.

Many years later, Angus and Robertson acquired the publishing rights of *The Fairy Who Wouldn't Fly* and the book has been re-issued recently, with new illustrations by its author and illustrator.

Angus and Robertson during the 1940s

During the 1940s, Angus and Robertson continued to republish books by authors of earlier years, with occasional sorties into new fields. While the company endeavoured to maintain its tradition of high-class publication, it also continued to retain the old-style design in children's books — a coloured frontispiece, full-colour plates placed at intervals throughout the book, and line drawings here and there on the pages in between.

Angus and Robertson encouraged a few new authors, but cautiously, preferring those whose work had already met with public acceptance. One publication by a new author was *Pegmen*

Snugglepot and Cuddlepie peered down at Scotty.

Coloured frontispiece and title page from Pegmen Tales, a traditional format maintained by Angus & Robertson during the 1940s.

Tales. The story was written by Ella McFadyen and illustrated by Edwina Bell.

Three old-fashioned, wooden 'dolly' clothes-pegs seem unlikely characters for stories today — many children of the present generation would never have seen such a clothes peg, but earlier this century, children often used to draw a face on the knob at the top of a dolly peg, dress the peg and then play games with the little 'doll'.

Pegmen Tales commenced as a daily serial in the Queensland press; the stories were then dramatised for the Australian Broadcasting Commission before being illustrated and issued as a book. The dedication gives the setting for the stories:

To the children I knew years ago who built Pegmen's Run beside the Macquarie River and grew up and forgot, and to their heirs, the children of today who have greeted every tale of the Pegmen's adventures with the cry of 'Tell us some more!', this book is dedicated.

The author of *Pegmen Tales*, Ella McFadyen, was born in Sydney of Scottish parents. To quote her own words:

Memory goes back to my mother alighting from her bicycle at our playroom door, in her bloomer costume of navy serge and announcing 'The Old Queen's dead'. Our whole world was well over an acre in extent, high fenced, with a gate operated by cables from a winch in the scullery. Visitors rang an electric bell, so did nasty little boys, and ran away. I secretly longed for a portcullis and battle axes, but our fierce dog was armament enough, though so indulgently kind to us that he bit an unpopular governess — the only dog I have ever deeply loved . . .

I had always meant to be a writer and was soon ransacking the dictionary — that delightful playbox of words, for such treasures as anthropophagy and metempsychosis . . . Prescribed reading included archaic moralities by Edgeworth and Aguilar, but the doors of the old red cedar bookcase swung open on father's collection — a world of Scott and Dickens,

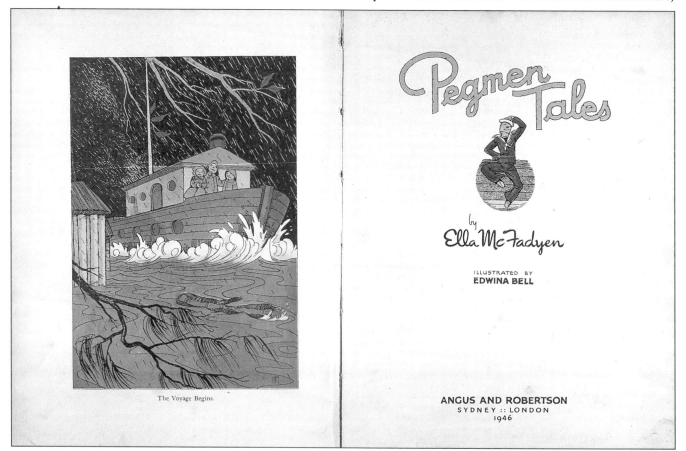

The Voyage Begins.

Pegmen Tales

by
Ella McFadyen

ILLUSTRATED BY
EDWINA BELL

ANGUS AND ROBERTSON
SYDNEY :: LONDON
1946

Margaret Senior (left) and Eve Pownall (right), the artist and the writer who collaborated on books for children.

Cover of The Australia Book, *from the first edition copy at Dromkeen.*

Shakespeare and Kipling . . .

We sold that home and bought Noonan's Point on Brisbane Water. Nature paragraphs and verses began to trickle from my pen to the Sydney weeklies; unexpected half-guineas came back and my weekly eighteen pence was cut in consequence. Then . . . I made a forbidden leap and landed in a newspaper office where I discovered a talent for winning country readers. World War I, overwork and pneumonia, transferred me to a voluntary job . . . The War's end brought an invitation to conduct youth interest on The Sydney Mail, *and so began twenty years of joyous fulfilment. (Anderson,* The Singing Roads, *p. 56)*

Ella McFadyen's determination to escape from the 'fenced-in' type of life, one so commonly expected of women at the beginning of this century, comes out clearly here.

Edwina Bell, who illustrated *Pegmen Tales*, was born at Balmain, Sydney, and after training in art at East Sydney Technical College she worked as an illustrator and commercial artist. Now retired, she and her husband live at Mallacoota Inlet, on the eastern coast of Victoria.

Eve Pownall and Margaret Senior

The demand for Australian picture-story books continued well into the 1950s. In 1952, a children's book printed and published by the House of John Sands was judged Book of the Year by the Children's Book Council of New South Wales. This was *The Australia Book*, written by Eve Pownall and illustrated by Margaret Senior. The book told the history of Australia. In the same year, *The Australia Book* was awarded first prize in the Australian Book Society's manuscript competition. In the following extract, the author explains how *The Australia Book* came to be written:

I was led on to writing a history of Australia for children because my son Gerald was interested in one about the U.S.A. There were things like the first Thanksgiving Dinner, Pony Express Riders . . . Gerald found it fascinating and I used to read it to him when he was about seven as a bed-time story; his brown eyes stayed wide-open while I read, and he studied every detail of the pictures. Inevitably I got to thinking that Australia had as much human interest to offer and so why not a book like the U.S.A. one with pictures? So I began to collect material. (Anderson, The Singing Roads, *p. 86)*

Eve Pownall's intensive research for *The Australia Book* led to another book, *Cousins-come-Lately*, a junior novel set in old Sydney Town at the time of Governor Bourke. Published in 1952, this book was also illustrated by Margaret Senior.

Eve Pownall was born in Sydney, but grew up in country towns in New South Wales. After attending the North Sydney Girls' High School, she became interested in children's literature and eventually was offered the position of Children's Book Editor for the *Australian Book News*. She was closely associated with the Children's Book Council of New South Wales from its inception.

Dromkeen has a first-edition copy of *The Australia Book* and after Eve Pownall visited the homestead several years ago, she sent the original artwork for the cover of *Cousins-come-Lately* and sketches for several illustrations for the book to Dromkeen for display.

Margaret Senior was born in London in 1917 and emigrated to Australia with her husband not long after the Second World War. From the moment the liner sailed into Port Jackson, the couple became entranced with the harbour and its headlands

Final cover artwork for Cousins-come-Lately, *illustrated by Margaret Senior.* (Original artwork)

Two sketches by Margaret Senior for Cousins-come-Lately. (Original artwork)

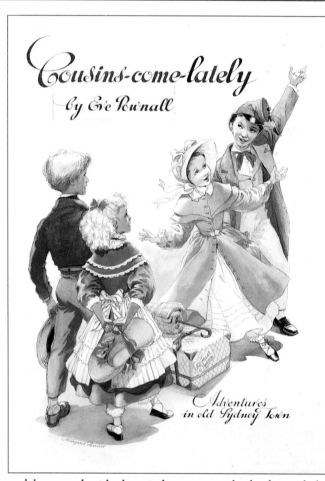

and bays, and with the winding streets, the bridge and the historical background of Sydney. In a letter to the authors Margaret Senior relates:

All my life I have never stopped drawing or designing or making for different purposes, unexpected opportunities, changed circumstances; each time with the sustained concentration that everyone with a job to complete knows very well . . .

There are broadly two kinds of illustrators: those who decorate the facts or credible aspects of life, and those with the enviable gift for fantasy. Artists with a way-out imagination often do best with stories of their own. The art of writing is an inimitable skill in which the writer's own images are never visibly shareable. A good written description, for instance, creates a different image for each reader which can only be approximated by someone else's drawing. It is possible for a writer to feel partly dispossessed by illustrations —as of course by films.

Margaret Senior has illustrated many books and she ranks *The Australia Book* among her favourites. A children's book she wrote and illustrated, *Bush Haven Animals*, was published by John Sands in 1954. A copy is in the Dromkeen Collection.

Margaret Paice

The author and artist Margaret Paice was born in Brisbane in 1920. Most of her childhood was spent in country and outback areas of Queensland, and her experiences in those years were of great use to her later as a writer. She recalls:

Author and illustrator of children's books, Margaret Paice.

Title page from the copy of Mirram *in the Dromkeen Collection.*

Front cover of Bush Haven Animals, *from the copy in the Dromkeen Collection. This book, based on a conservation theme, was written and illustrated by Margaret Senior.*

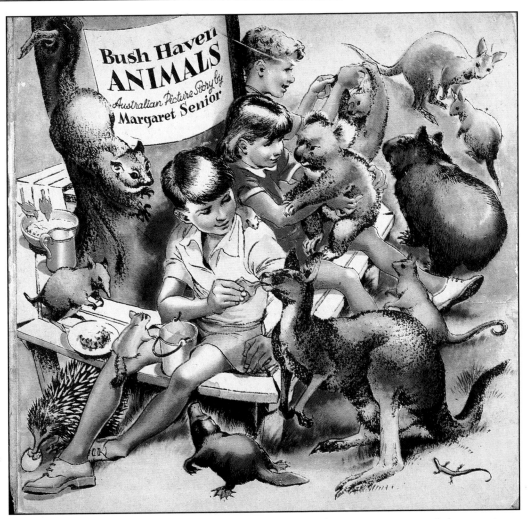

Like so many others, my family was caught up in the Depression. My father had a truck, and with my parents and younger brothers I spent those years wandering through the out-back. I remember a succession of small bush-schools, all much alike, where I acquired a smattering of education, but I was frequently in trouble for scribbling or drawing in my exercise books instead of doing my lessons. I don't think I learned very much. Then came the brief, but exciting Cracow gold rush, which was later to give me my background for The Lucky Fall. *(Anderson,* The Singing Roads, *p. 77)*

For a short time, Margaret was at a boarding-school in Brisbane, but she was glad to return to her family, who were then living on a plateau in Central Queensland, where her father was once again engaged in mining. It was here that she became seriously interested in writing poems and short stories; some were published, but others were returned with rejection slips. However, her drawings were winning prizes at agricultural shows, and she determined that she would one day study art and become an artist.

When the Second World War came, she joined the Women's National Emergency Legion. In 1942, she met Hubert Paice and a short time later, they were married. By 1946, there was a daughter, Jeanette, and a son, Peter, and during the following years the family spent a lot of time in tropical areas in the north of Queensland. In 1955, Hubert Paice died, and Margaret decided to carry out her early ambition and study art. She moved to Sydney, enrolled at the East Sydney Technical College, and a year later obtained a position in a commercial art studio.

In 1955, Angus and Robertson had published a small book which Margaret Paice had written and illustrated, titled *Mirram*. It was a sensitive story about the life of a young Aboriginal girl. A copy is in the Dromkeen Collection. In 1956 a companion book, *Namitja*, was also published by Angus and Robertson.

In 1960, Margaret Paice married Wilfrid Harriss, a secondary school teacher. Since then she has written many children's books, some of which she has illustrated herself; some have been illustrated by other artists. However, it was to writing, not illustrating, that she eventually dedicated herself. At a seminar conducted by the Australian Capital Territory Branch of the Children's Book Council a few years ago, Margaret Paice made the following observations about her work:

> *. . . With each book I became more involved. I know many people do successfully combine writing and illustrating, but for me somehow it wasn't working.*
>
> *I was becoming a compulsive writer. I know this doesn't necessarily make one a good writer, or a happy one; it can be and often is the most frustrating occupation in the world. You lose countless hours of sleep trying to plot. You live with your characters until there's a real love-hate relationship and you find yourself opting out of what most people call normal everyday life until you get the wretched creatures out of your system. On the other hand you have to go on coping with the family and being interested in their affairs — it's not easy. Nor, I suspect, is it easy for a family to put up with a writing mum.*
>
> *I never read my books once they're in print. I know I'd see exactly what I should have done to improve them. As it is I go over the story so many times, rewriting, polishing, repolishing until I can't trust my own judgement any more. Then, thank God, I have a marvellous Editor who will read it, and put her finger on the weak spot, and say there's where you've gone wrong.*
>
> *An author's best friend is a good editor!* (Writing and Illustrating for Children *p. 129*).

A Decline in the Publishing of Australian Picture-Story Books

By the mid 1950s, imported children's picture-story books from the United Kingdom were again making an appearance in Australian bookshops. Australian publishers could not compete in price with these beautiful new style picture books, and interest in publishing picture-story books diminished in favour of junior fiction. Even from the late 1940s, Australian publishing interest had begun to focus upon newly emerging authors of junior novels.

102

PART IV
New Directions in Australian Children's Fiction

Today, scarcely any works of junior fiction by Australian writers whose names were well known to young readers early this century are to be found on library shelves. An exception is Ethel Turner's *Seven Little Australians*, now regarded by most authorities as an Australian children's classic.

Of all Australian junior fiction published before the Second World War, the Billabong books by Mary Grant Bruce lasted longest. They were read into the 1960s, until, at last, they too gave way in favour of the newly emerging junior novels which began to appear during the first two decades following the end of the war. The names of writers, then unknown, who published their early works of junior fiction during this period, are unknown no longer: Nan Chauncy, Joan Phipson, Eleanor Spence, Patricia Wrightson, Mavis Thorpe Clark, Colin Thiele, Hesba Brinsmead and Ivan Southall, to name a few.

The Direction Slowly Changes

In general, children's novels which appeared in the first ten years following the Second World War did not seem dramatically different from those that were written early in the century. There was a portrayal of family life, but mostly of families entrenched in rural areas; city settings tended to be avoided. Families were stable, well-knit and happy, and values held by rural communities were stressed as being infinitely desirable. There were adventures, hardships to be overcome, tests of loyalty and character to be met and passed with honours, and lessons in compassion and integrity to be learned. Although the emphasis of individual authors differed, in the main, these were the themes, settings and values encompassed by Australian children's novels of the late 1940s and 1950s. Post-war Australia had not yet embraced television; Beatlemania had not ruffled the tenure of teenage emotions and thinking; there were no jet planes and man had not yet ventured into space. As technological advances in communications and transport made inroads into Australia's isolation, the influence of teenage sub-cultures from the United States and Britain began to make themselves felt, and the tempo of Australian life quickened.

The children of the post-war 'baby-boom' years were entering their teens and this presented a special phenomenon. Never before in the Western world had there been such a high proportion of young people in the population. The years between childhood and adulthood seemed to be recognised, quite suddenly, by the community as being especially meaningful in terms of personality development, and filled with problems. The very weight of the numbers of young people in the community demanded this recognition. Traditional social values began to be challenged by the young.

Themes and styles of writing in children's novels published overseas, particularly American junior fiction, began to move away from those that had been traditionally accepted for decades, and to reflect the values, morals and mores of a changing society. These trends set shock-waves rippling through the most conservative of all forms of publishing, the area of children's literature — and the most conservative of all markets for children's books, the school libraries. Although these changes in direction came quite gradually, they were challenged at every step.

From the late 1950s, a new emphasis introduced into Australian children's literature, that of realism and the relevance of themes and incidents to the reader, made stories of mostly untroubled families in idyllic rural settings seem outdated. Some authors switched the venue of their family stories to the city and to inner-suburban locations. Families were sometimes portrayed as impoverished and experiencing problems; the relationships of family members, and of members of groups, began to be explored in depth. Child characters tended to become more introspective and their private thoughts and feelings to be made known. Some stories were cheerful, others less so. Writers for children eventually found themselves in competition for the child's leisure time with the new technologies; there was the challenge of fast-moving television programmes, and the preoccupation of young people with 'pop' music. With the 1970s came the added challenges of greater social freedom and of the changing values of a society that was becoming increasingly materialistic in its outlook. These aspects were frequently reflected in the children's novels of the day.

Since the 1960s, the element of adventure in children's novels by Australian authors had shown a movement towards survival themes. Stories sometimes featured children struggling against horrifying odds presented by the environment, weather or social catastrophe, and at times by the inadequacy of adults to control or cope with situations. Some authors resolved the problems of an individual, or a family or group, in an emotional crisis situation, or fighting for survival, and indicated that there was hope for the future of their characters. Others left stories more 'open-ended' and in doing so intimated that the future might be bleak indeed.

Writing of changes in direction that can be observed in the works of leading Australian authors for children over the past three decades, Walter McVitty comments:

> *Literature may or may not mirror its society and times, but the strongest impression one gains from children's literature generally is of the way it reflects prevailing attitudes towards childhood itself, through the assumptions it makes about what is deemed appropriate in the reading matter it produces for its young. The generalisation which most strongly presents itself in modern times is that, within one generation, the cosy, former view of childhood as a state of happy innocence has gradually changed through a somewhat salutary recognition — perhaps remembrance — that life for the young is not always a time of joy and unsullied innocence. Today's established Australian children's authors, like their counterparts elsewhere, seem to have begun by writing uncomplicated songs of innocence but, just as typically, have each made a kind of Blakean transition, gradually but inevitably, towards sober songs of experience.* (McVitty, Innocence and Experience, p. 2)

Having sketched, in general, some changes in direction that have occurred in the choice of themes by authors of junior novels since the end of the Second World War, it is now necessary to return to the early post-war years when new authors in Australia were beginning to submit their first manuscripts of junior fiction to publishers. One publisher who was actively engaged in this sphere in those days was Frank Eyre of Oxford University Press.

Frank Eyre and Australian Children's Fiction

In 1949, Oxford University Press, London, appointed Frank Eyre as Editorial Manager of its Australian branch in Melbourne, Victoria. This appointment was to have far-reaching effects on the publishing of junior fiction by Australian authors. Frank Eyre sought out and encouraged promising new writers and built up an imposing list of Australian junior novels for Oxford University Press. His influence on Australian children's literature continued for over twenty years.

Frank Eyre was born in Manchester, in the north of England. After completing his secondary education, he commenced a law course, but eventually abandoned it in favour of a literary career. Prior to serving in the Second World War, he had published several volumes of poetry, contributed widely to journals and worked freelance for publishers, including Oxford University Press. Having lost several senior editors in the early years of the war, Oxford University Press suggested to Frank Eyre that he join the firm as a staff member once the war was

over. He accepted, and in 1945 he was appointed to the Children's Book Department, but as a production manager, not as an editor as he had expected. However, it was not long before he was appointed Editorial Manager.

In those early post-war years, Oxford University Press had a highly successful list of children's books, and had earned well-merited prestige for their high standard of book production. Manuscripts were arriving from all over the United Kingdom and also from overseas. One of the latter, hand-written on foolscap paper, was from Tasmania and came directly to the notice of Frank Eyre. It was by a then unknown Australian author, Nan Chauncy, and was eventually published in 1948 under the title *They Found a Cave*.

The acceptance of the manuscript of *They Found a Cave* proved to be the beginning of a long association between its author and Frank Eyre — and also, unexpectedly, with the Australian illustrator, Margaret Horder, who was working in England at the time. Delighted to have an experienced illustrator with an Australian background, Eyre commissioned Margaret Horder to illustrate the book.

When Frank Eyre arrived in Melbourne in 1949, it was with the express purpose of reorganising Oxford University Press's Australian publishing list, but although he had a two-year contract with the company, he did not have a mandate to publish children's books locally — the publishing of books was the prerogative of the company's head office in London. Over the next two years, Frank Eyre instigated a comprehensive, forward publishing programme of works by Australian authors for the company's London office, and when the term of his contract expired, he was appointed General Manager of the company in Australia.

Frank Eyre took an intense interest in reading all the Australian manuscripts for children's books that came to his Melbourne office before submitting them to head office, accompanied by his recommendations for publication, or otherwise. He made a conscious effort to seek out new, talented children's writers and to draw them into the Oxford University Press fold. The combination of Frank Eyre's experience in the publishing of children's books, his enthusiasm and the reputation Oxford University Press had for quality production and sales success, attracted potential authors.

Then came a time when the London head office rejected a manuscript which Frank Eyre had strongly recommended for publication, *A Fortune for the Brave*, by the already established author, Nan Chauncy. Believing the rejection to be ill-advised, Eyre 'bent the rules' and published the book in Australia in 1954 under the Oxford University Press imprint. The book was a success.

In 1958 he repeated the procedure when a manuscript by a new author, Eleanor Spence, was rejected by head office. The book, titled *Patterson's Track*, proved successful, and all further novels by Eleanor Spence were published in London. Eyre's rationalisation for taking the stance he did was that valuable authors would be lost to the company if no chance at all were to be taken with a manuscript.

By this time Frank Eyre had become very much involved with a number of activities associated with children's books in Australia. He was a foundation member of the Children's Book Council of Victoria, and was for fourteen years chairman of the committee that produced the first children's book list to cover publications from all countries. Later, in 1957, the committee also produced the first list of Australian titles for children, *Australian Children's Books: A Select List*. A second edition was produced in 1962. Frank Eyre was for some years president of the Children's Book Council of Victoria and, later, president of the Children's Book Council of Australia.

In 1964, Frank Eyre was instrumental in having Hesba Brinsmead's first book, *Pastures of the Blue Crane*, accepted for publication by Oxford University Press in England. It was published with illustrations by Annette Macarthur-Onslow and received the Children's Book Council of Australia Book of the Year Award for 1965. In 1968, Margaret Balderson's manuscript for *When Jays Fly to Barbmo* passed through Frank Eyre's hands before being published in London, and it won the Children's Book Council of Australia Book of the Year Award in 1969.

Frank Eyre retired in 1975, after having furthered the publishing of Australian fiction for children over a period of twenty-six years. During this period, he had enjoyed a friendly association with Joyce and Court Oldmeadow, a friendship that began when the Oldmeadows had a shop in East Ivanhoe, not far from where Frank Eyre and his family lived. When Dromkeen was established, Frank Eyre watched its development and progress with interest and affection. He is still a visitor to the homestead.

Nan Chauncy

Nan Chauncy, author of *They Found a Cave*, which Frank Eyre published in London in 1948, was the first major Australian children's author to emerge in the post-war period.

Nan Chauncy was born in Middlesex, England, in 1900. Her maiden name was Masterman, and her first name in full was Nancen. She had a twin brother, Janson. There was an elder brother, Kay, and eventually two other brothers, and then a sister, Eve, who was the only one of the six children to be born in Tasmania where the family migrated in 1912.

Mastermans are known to have lived in the village of Great Ayton in Yorkshire, England. A Chauncy came to England from Normandy with William the Conqueror and can be traced to Yorkshire. The two families were united when Nan's grandmother, a Chauncy, married Henry Masterman. As Nan was a Masterman, why did she use Chauncy as her surname?

In 1938, Nan Masterman married Helmut Anton Rosenfeld. They had met that year on board ship: Nan on her way home after being in Europe for eight years; Anton on his way from Germany to a new life in Australia. When the Second World War broke out, feelings against Germans ran high at times in Australia, and so the couple took the surname of Chauncy.

When the Masterman family arrived in Tasmania in 1912, Nan's father took up a two-year engineering position in Hobart, and as he intended to become an orchardist when his contract ended, he purchased an area of virgin bushland near Bagdad, then a famous Tasmanian apple-growing district.

Although the property was only 50 kilometres from Hobart, its aura of isolation was incredible. And what a wonderland for children! The rear of the property sloped up into steep hills. In the valley between was a winding creek of crystal-clear water where some platypus lived; tree-ferns, orchids and towering gums grew there; while in the sandstone cliffs were countless caves. The property was christened Chauncy Vale, after the maternal side of the family.

The land was cleared in true pioneering style. Huge trees were felled and then sawn to make timbers for the house. Everyone had a job to do, and eventually some land was ready for cultivation. Nan grew up at Chauncy Vale, loving the life and hating to be torn away at the end of each weekend to lodgings in Hobart, so she could attend the Collegiate School.

Eventually, her eldest brother Kay bought some land adjoining his father's property, and with the help of the family, he built a cottage which he named 'Day Dawn'. This cottage is of particular significance because Kay gave it to his sister, Nan, as a wedding-present. It was there that she spent her married life, brought up her daughter, Heather, and wrote her children's novels.

For her first junior novel, *They Found a Cave*, and some subsequent works, Nan Chauncy drew upon her experiences as a child at Chauncy Vale, and often included incidents that happened to the Masterman children, which she translated to suit the plots and characters of her novels.

In 1958, Nan Chauncy won the Children's Book Council of New South Wales Book of the Year Award with *Tiger in the Bush*, and the following year, its sequel, *Devil's Hill*, shared the award given by the Children's Book Council of Australia. The latter book also won an American award, the Medal of the Boys' Club of USA, which is voted for by children.

With *Tangara*, published in 1960, Nan Chauncy branched into a serious time-travel fantasy. Set in Tasmania, the story involved an imaginative, solitary, twentieth century child, an eight-year-old girl, Lexie Pavemont, in a deep and sensitive friendship with an Aboriginal girl, Merrina, who had lived in Black's Gully with her tribe over a century previously. A shell necklace that had been in Lexie's family for several generations is the magic object which allows her to make frequent transitions between present and past.

Tangara is considered by most critics to be a sensitive and perceptive work in which a difficult theme, the clash of cultures between white settlers and the Aborigines of Tasmania, has been successfully handled. In 1961, *Tangara* won the Children's Book Council of Australia Book of the Year Award, and also a place on the Honours List for the International Hans Christian Andersen Award.

Albert Ullin, a prominent Melbourne bookseller who founded the specialist children's bookshop The Little Bookroom in 1960, remembers Nan Chauncy well. She used to visit his bookshop whenever she was in Melbourne, and was always ready to chat about her books and her life. When Albert Ullin

Mavis Thorpe Clark, Australian children's author.

Albert Ullin, the founder of The Little Bookroom, a specialist children's bookshop in Melbourne, and a foundation member of the Friends of Dromkeen.

visited Nan Chauncy at her cottage in Tasmania, he was amazed at the number of her books that had been translated into other languages.

In an article about Nan Chauncy, Maurice Saxby states:

> . . . it can well be claimed that she established the contemporary realistic novel for children in Australia which has now been extended and developed in style and technique, as well as in content[by later writers]. (Kirkpatrick, Twentieth Century Children's Writers, p. 165)

Nan Chauncy died in 1970. The books she wrote that have been mentioned here, and others, are in the Dromkeen Collection.

Mavis Thorpe Clark

Mavis Thorpe Clark began writing stories when she was eight years of age. A city child, born in Melbourne, these early stories stemmed from her need to express her delight in the Australian

bushland and countryside where she spent many holidays. Her love of the bush, and of Australia and its history, deepened as she grew to adulthood, and these feelings and interests are ever present in her children's novels — family stories set in various places in Australia, some having historical backgrounds, others of a contemporary nature. She has travelled extensively around Australia researching material for her junior novels. Commenting upon her approach to writing she states:

> . . . I think my main objective is still to tell the story that has come to hand, honestly, both from character and detail of background. To be as true as possible in my facts, and to present the truth of the matter as I see it. (McVitty, Innocence and Experience, p. 32)

Mavis Thorpe Clark spent a great deal of time researching the historical background for her children's novel *The Brown Land was Green*, published in 1956. The story was set around Portland in the Western District of Victoria in the 1840s. This was a part of the country the author knew well, for she had often visited an elderly aunt who lived there and whose parents had been pioneers in the district. *The Brown Land was Green* was highly commended by the Children's Book Council of New South Wales, being runner-up for the award in 1957.

The cover artwork for *The Brown Land was Green*, with its separate colour overlays, and one of the black-and-white illustrations by the Melbourne illustrator, Harry Hudson, were on loan to the Dromkeen Collection.

In 1967, Mavis Thorpe Clark won the Children's Book Council of Australia Book of the Year Award with *The Min-Min*, a family story with an unusual setting. The main character is a teenage girl, Sylvie, who lives with her family in one of ten fettlers' cottages at a railway-siding on the flat, barren Nullarbor Plain in South Australia. The railway-line, which fettlers who live in the small, widely-spaced settlements maintain, links the eastern and western parts of the continent, and stretches in an unrelenting straight line past the railway-siding where Sylvie lives and on towards the distant horizon.

Sylvie helps her pregnant mother to look after the younger children, worries about her delinquent brother, Reg, and rebels against her father, who uses liquor as an escape from boredom. The cultural and emotional barrenness and sameness of Sylvie's young life seem an echo of the barren, featureless plain on which she lives. However, irrespective of the story's unusual setting, the fears, doubts, loneliness and longings of adolescent Sylvie would be recognised by teenagers anywhere, even, or perhaps particularly, by those who live in large modern cities.

The min-min is the tiny 'will-o'-the-wisp', a moving dot of brilliant light that sometimes shines at night from somewhere

Colour separation artwork by Harry Hudson for each stage in the printing of the dust jacket for The Brown Land was Green *by Mavis Thorpe Clark.* (Original artwork)

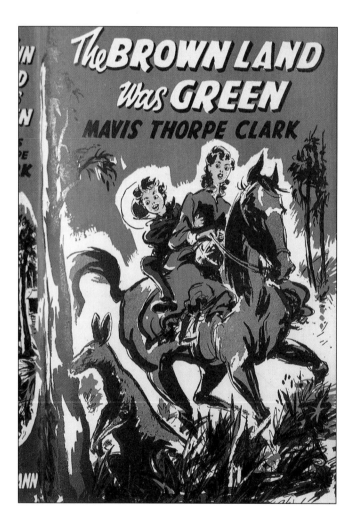

across the unbroken monotony of the vast plain, always intriguing, always beckoning, but never reached.

Of Mavis Thorpe Clark's work, and of *The Min-Min*, Walter McVitty makes the following comments:

> *Mavis Thorpe Clark's historical novels are as good as anything in the field but her present reputation rests more on the contemporary realism of the modern 'problem' novels of her recent period. Of these,* The Min-Min *(1966) is far and away the most accomplished. (McVitty,* Innocence and Experience, *pp. 17-18)*

Joan Phipson

Joan Phipson is represented in the Dromkeen Collection by all the pre-publication material for her historical work *Bennelong*, illustrated by Walter Stackpool.

Joan Phipson was born at Warrawee in New South Wales, and educated at Frensham School in Mittagong. She has worked as a school librarian, as a copy and script-writer, as a telegraphist in the Women's Auxilliary Air Force during the Second World War, and has written many stories and books for children. In 1953, she won the Children's Book Council of New South

Joan Phipson, Australian children's author.

Wales Book of the Year Award with *Good Luck to the Rider* and, ten years later, *The Family Conspiracy* won her the Children's Book Council of Australia Book of the Year Award.

In Joan Phipson's early junior novels, the relationship of family or group members, one to another, was always of importance, and over the years she had delved deeper and deeper into the minds and souls of her characters, expressing the innermost feelings, thoughts and conflicts each individual experiences. Once pre-occupied with contrasting rural lifestyles and values with those of urban dwellers, in recent years she has moved towards stories incurring suspense, intense excitement, survival, and emotional pain and soul-searching.

Writing of Joan Phipson, Walter McVitty has the following to say:

> She is an archetypal Australian children's writer, a gifted storyteller motivated by a desire to share her artistic vision and her affinity for her country with her readers. Without being patronising, condescending or chauvinistic, she pursues universal themes relentlessly in Australian stories which range from the humorous and adventurous to the mystical and profound. (McVitty, Innocence and Experience, p. 61)

Eleanor Spence, Australian children's author.

Eleanor Spence

In 1958 the junior novel *Patterson's Track* was published. Set in the bushland, it was a family story, a theme its author, Eleanor Spence, has continued to pursue in subsequent books, progressing from the more stable and happy family situations to those which present problems and conflict.

Eleanor Spence grew up in the New South Wales coastal town of Erina. Books were an essential part of the home, but although she was scribbling her own stories at an early age, it was not until after she was married and had spent some years as a librarian in England that she began to write in earnest. Her interest in mystery and love of Australian history is reflected in many of her earlier junior novels.

In 1964, Eleanor Spence won the Children's Book Council of Australia Book of the Year Award with *The Green Laurel* — a story portraying an itinerant family (the father owns a miniature train which he drives at fairs and carnivals) and an introspective twelve-year-old child, Lesley, who feels a desperate need to settle in a permanent home.

In 1977, Eleanor Spence won the Children's Book Council of Australia Book of the Year Award again, with *The October Child*. There were indications in *The Green Laurel* that the author was moving away from depicting the stable, rural family and taking on the challenge of portraying contemporary urban lifestyles with teenage characters struggling to cope with family and social pressures and inner conflict. *The October Child* proved that such was the case: in the years between her two awards Eleanor Spence's writing had altered course dramatically.

The October Child presents the personal problems that each member of the Mariner family experiences in adjusting to the unpredictable behaviour of the youngest member, Carl, an autistic child. In *Innocence and Experience*, Walter McVitty comments on the ending of this book at the stage where the sensitive boy, Douglas, who has patiently borne more than his share of the burden of caring for his little brother, sees the child's condition as it really is, and in stark reality:

> However, there are limits to the patience of even the most willing, and at the book's climax Douglas abandons his brother during a particularly exasperating walk in the local park, at a point where Carl refuses to come home:
>
> Carl went berserk. He hooked his feet in the gaps between the railings and held firmly to the top of the fence with one hand, then began to batter his head with audible force against the iron, shrieking with the concentrated intensity of some caged wild animal. . .
>
> 'Carl, please come!' [Douglas] pleaded. 'Come home with me. Please, Carl!'
>
> He held out his arms. Carl's hair flashed golden in the lamplight as his head swung round, and he fastened his teeth in his brother's wrist, ripping like tissue-paper the worn flannelette of Douglas's shirt.
>
> Douglas stumbled backwards. He stared at the small upraised face of his brother, and could see in the round blue eyes nothing but rage and hate. There was no fear, no remorse — worst of all, there was no recognition. It was the face of a hostile stranger.
>
> 'You're not my brother!' Douglas whispered. 'You never were my brother!'
>
> He turned and ran.

The intensity of this moment and the strength of its depiction typify the new Eleanor Spence — one would hardly have predicted such powerful writing at the time of Patterson's Track. *(McVitty,* Innocence and Experience, *p. 83)*

Patricia Wrightson

Patricia Wrightson's first novel for children, *The Crooked Snake*, published in 1955, was a fairly traditional type of story, but one that demonstrated the depth of the author's insight into the world of the child and her ability to portray excitements, joys and fears from a child's point of view. A realistic story, involving groups of children typical of any Australian town or suburb, *The Crooked Snake* won the Children's Book Council of New South Wales Book of the Year Award in 1956.

Patricia Wrightson was born in Lismore, New South Wales, and grew up in country areas. Always interested in books, she dreamed of becoming a writer, but feeling daunted by the amount of literature that already existed, she almost abandoned the idea, as she explained in a note to her publisher:

> I wasn't sure how to begin, was awed by what had already been built up, and couldn't believe there was any excuse for beginning. Only after I had been married . . . and had two children of my own . . . did I dare to try . . .

Patricia Wrightson continued to write, and in the ensuing years her work moved away from realism to fantasy, as she explored a variety of themes incorporating mystery, magic and myth. In her novel *I Own the Racecourse!*, set in contemporary Sydney, she demonstrated her versatility by viewing happenings through the eyes of a boy whose mental development had not kept pace with that of his friends.

Patricia Wrightson is represented in the Dromkeen Collection by copies of her children's novels and also by several pieces of pre-publication material, including the manuscript of *I Own*

*Patricia Wrightson, Australian children's author; The Nargun and the
Stars book jacket, and a photograph of an Aboriginal ceremonial site
taken some years ago.*

the Racecourse!, the trial cover design for the book and the
redesigned, final cover. In 1970, *I Own the Racecourse!* was
nominated for the Hans Christian Andersen Award Honours
List.

Between the years 1964 and 1975, Patricia Wrightson wrote
at least four children's novels. One of these, *An Older Kind of
Magic* (1972), is a fantasy which explores the notion that in the
rocks, earth and waters beneath the surface soil of the ancient
continent of Australia live the magic creatures of Aboriginal
legend and lore. Taking Sydney as her setting, the author inter-
weaves the mischievous habits of the ancient magic creatures
with the activities of modern children of European descent. At
the end of the novel is an epilogue, 'The Edge of Vision', in
which the author writes:

*We are growing very wise and learned — but still, at the edge
of our knowledge, there are things we only half understand
. . . These are the areas, in mind and in vision, that have
always been haunted by magic . . .*

*Those of us who were bred in the old lands and live in the
new have . . . tried to plant here the magic that our people
knew, and it will not grow. It is time we stopped trying to see
elves and dragons and unicorns in Australia. They have never
belonged here, and no ingenuity can make them real. We
need to look for another kind of magic, a kind that must have
been shaped by the land itself at the edge of Australian vision.*

*So I have tried, in a small way. I have pictured Pot-Koorok,
Nyol and Net-Net, unsuspected in their own water and rock;
creeping from tunnels and drains into our streets; never seen,
but perhaps to spring out at us some day . . .*

Margaret Horder, Australian children's book illustrator.

Final manuscript, book jacket and initial original cover art for Patricia Wrightson's children's novel I Own the Racecourse!

Patricia Wrightson's preoccupation with this 'older kind of magic' was carried further in her novel *The Nargun and the Stars*, with which she won the 1974 Children's Book Council of Australia Book of the Year Award.

Four years later, she won the Award again with *The Ice is Coming*, a novel that was to become the first of a trilogy concerning an Aboriginal hero, Wirrun, a young man of the present day who has been specially selected to aid his people in troubled times. This was not the first time Patricia Wrightson had chosen to write of the Aboriginal people. In 1960, her novel *The Rocks of Honey* featured an Aboriginal boy who had become caught up in the power the past had over him, a supernatural element and part of his racial inheritance.

In 1984, Patricia Wrightson won the Children's Book Council of Australia Book of the Year Award for the fourth time with a novel titled *A Little Fear*.

On being asked by her publishers for a statement explaining how she went about her writing, the author replied:

112

Illustrations by Margaret Horder for Patricia Wrightson's book Down to Earth. (Original artwork)

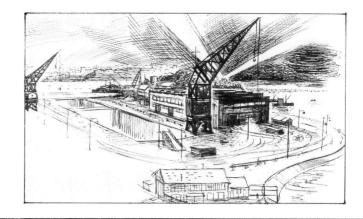

I respond to places and people; plan work carefully before commencing and ignore plans once started when the work itself takes over; work initially in longhand and in notebooks, usually in unconventional positions; reshape and repolish in typing, in a very organised way.

In 1978, Patricia Wrightson was awarded an Order of the British Empire in recognition of her work in Australian children's literature. In 1985, she became the first author to receive the Dromkeen Medal, which is awarded annually to an Australian citizen who has made a significant contribution to the appreciation and development of Australian children's literature.

Margaret Horder — Illustrator

A contemporary of the children's authors Nan Chauncy, Joan Phipson and Patricia Wrightson, the exceptional illustrator Margaret Horder is well represented at Dromkeen by artwork, mainly black-and-white illustrations for books by these authors. Her collaboration with prominent children's authors allowed her access to manuscripts that captured her interest and provided sufficient variety of characters and situations to stimulate her imagination and challenge her illustrative skills. To quote the artist's own words:

An illustrator, it seems to me, needs to be a blend of creator, accompanist, interpreter and book designer. One should also be able to draw in odd spots such as a jeep surrounded by steers [Phipson, Birkin] or in a jostling crowd [Wrightson, I Own the Racecourse!]. Although working to a deadline can be wearing I have nothing but enthusiasm for illustrating as a profession . . . ('Reflections', Reading Time Publication No. 3, p. 83)

Margaret Horder was born in Sydney in 1903, the second of three girls. After studying at the Sydney Art School, she spent a year working for a newspaper before travelling to England with her husband, Arthur Freeman, also an artist. It was in London, not long before the outbreak of the Second World War, that her first illustrations for children's books were accepted by Oxford University Press. More commissions followed throughout the war, and for several years afterwards. When Frank Eyre gave Margaret Horder the manuscript of *They Found a Cave* by Nan Chauncy to illustrate, she found it quite a challenge after so many years away from Australia.

Margaret Horder returned to Australia in 1949 and became completely engrossed in illustrating reading material and books for children. She always worked closely with authors whose books she illustrated and so became thoroughly involved in the particular story to hand. This resulted in illustrations which

captured the mood of the story, complementing and extending the text both visually and emotionally. Margaret Horder also worked as an illustrator with the New South Wales Education Department's *School Magazine*. The variety of subject-matter she encountered in this field — stories, poems, plays and articles — absolutely delighted her. She retired from illustrating in the late 1960s and died in 1978.

Noreen Shelley

Noreen Shelley, former editor of the *School Magazine* of the New South Wales Education Department, was a close friend of Margaret Horder. A children's writer as well as an editor, Noreen Shelley's children's novel *Family at the Lookout*, which involves the growth of a friendship between Dutch migrant children and an Australian family, won the Children's Book Council of Australia Award for Book of the Year in 1973.

In her capacity as editor of the New South Wales *School Magazine* for many years, Noreen Shelley was in the position to encourage illustrators with talent and she gathered 'a clan of artists', as she affectionately termed them, who contributed work regularly to the magazine and helped to maintain the high standard of its illustrations. The 'clan' consisted of Margaret Horder, Walter Cunningham, Noela Young, Elisabeth MacIntyre, Joyce Abbott, Sheila Hawkins, Edwina Bell and Astra Lacis, among others.

Noreen Shelley retired from the editorship of the *School Magazine* a number of years ago. She died in 1985.

Hesba Brinsmead

A variety of themes is found in the work of Hesba Brinsmead, including conservation, the situation of the 'outsider' and stories based on personal experience. Hesba Brinsmead won the Children's Book Council of Australia Book of the Year Award in 1965 with her first full-length children's novel, *Pastures of the Blue Crane*, and again in 1972 with *Longtime Passing.*

Hesba Brinsmead has written mainly for teenagers and about teenagers, commencing at a time when her own children, two boys, were in this age group. Lately, inspired by the interests of

her young grandchildren, she has published books for the eight- to nine-year-olds, and the manuscript for one of these, a picture-story book titled *Once There was a Swagman,* illustrated by Noela Young, is in the Dromkeen Collection.

Some years ago, Hesba Brinsmead gave a talk to the Children's Book Council of Australia in Canberra, titled 'Why I Write for Teenagers; or, Something to Give'. The content reflects the author's background, experiences and philosophy. Speaking of when, at the age of about seven, she decided to become a writer, Hesba Brinsmead said:

> When I remarked to my parents, while bagging turnips in a black frost in the Blue Mountains, that I would grow up into a writer, they cried 'Indeed you won't! That's no way to make a living!' These days the wording, and the nuance would be quite different. These days possibly (but not probably) there may be parents who tell their offspring — 'That's no way to Make Money!' When I became one more mouth to feed in a thread-bare world [the time of the Great Depression], money was an abstract thing. There were lots of folk who hadn't seen it for years and years. They hardly knew what it looked like. But a 'living' was something else again. That meant working for the bare necessities of life. In fact, staying alive. Some did. Writers, as far as my parents knew, didn't.
>
> Also, I began life with what I've since discovered is an occupational disease, the other side of every writer's coin. It's a lack of self confidence, coupled with a lack of determination . . . Certainly, writing is a business that takes an inordinate amount of concentration; and it's strange how the whole world seems to lay traps for writers. Life itself is a kind of bear trap, set to make prisoners of us.

Then, speaking of the time in the early 1960s when she decided to do something about becoming a writer:

> . . . I embarked on a correspondence course in Journalism. As the [advertising] blurb promised, I was selling articles to pay for the course before it was finished. Actually — and this was significant — I had to! The course cost £52. This would represent years of surreptitious saving from the housekeeping . . . So I bought the course on the never-never, knowing that I must sell my work, or go to debtors prison. With what desperate determination now, did I keep out of the bear trap! . . . There was nothing for it but to write.
>
> . . . The course taught me that if an editor returns a piece of work, the solution is not to abuse the editor and put the piece in the incinerator. The solution is to read it again, pin-point its deficiencies, try again and buy another stamp. Sooner or later, if one keeps doing this, the homing article

Two pieces of experimental cover artwork for Josh *designed by Astra Lacis.* (Original artwork)

will be replaced with a cheque, which will refund the stamp money and leave a margin of profit.

For four years or so I delighted in this simple law of cause and effect. I wrote short stories, feature articles, travel pieces and above all, radio talks. Here I must say that I owe everything to the ABC. When they told me, very nicely, not to send anything more for six months as they were afraid they had been using too much 'Pixie Hungerford' [her pseudonym] *material, I bent my brain to finding another outlet.*

Right on cue — a story tapped me on the shoulder. It was The Blue Crane [*later published as* Pastures of the Blue Crane] . . . *(Brinsmead, 'Why I Write . . .', pp. 87-89)*

The ironic humour apparent in Hesba Brinsmead's address to the Children's Book Council is discernible in her children's novels.

Ivan Southall

The jacket for Ivan Southall's junior novel *Josh* was designed by Astra Lacis and two of her design roughs are in the Dromkeen Collection. In an interview, Astra Lacis said that she preferred an emotional challenge in the illustrative needs of a book — she certainly found such a challenge with *Josh*. Her final, evocative jacket design is well suited to the mood set by Ivan Southall in what is probably the most controversial of his works of junior fiction.

Ivan Southall is one of the best-known Australian authors of junior fiction, both at home and overseas. His work always provokes attention, interest and comment. Born in the Melbourne suburb of Canterbury in 1921, he attended primary schools in the area and, later, Box Hill Grammar School. When he was fourteen, his father died and Southall had to leave school to find work. He joined the Melbourne *Herald*, where he was apprenticed to the process engraving department, and wrote

Max Fatchen, Australian children's author, is represented in the Dromkeen Collection by his manuscript for The River Kings.

Final book jacket for Josh *designed by Astra Lacis.*

Ivan Southall, Australian children's author, reading a copy of his novel Ash Road.

articles and short stories in his spare time. He was sixteen when his work first appeared in print.

During the Second World War, Ivan Southall served in the Royal Australian Air Force, piloting a Sunderland flying-boat on reconnaisance flights, and later he drew upon his experience as a pilot in his first junior novel, *Meet Simon Black*, published in 1950. This book became the forerunner of a whole series featuring Simon Black, an intrepid pilot and agent. There was little that could be termed controversial in these extremely popular, fast-moving adventure stories, but with *Hills End*, published in 1962, Ivan Southall branched into a different type of children's novel altogether — one that bared the private thoughts and feelings of the child characters in an intimate and intense manner.

At first Southall's publishers, Angus and Robertson, were concerned about the author's sudden plunge into material that veered so strongly away from what was traditionally accepted in Australia as children's literature. It was almost two years before they made the decision to publish *Hills End*.

In his work concerning contemporary Australian children's writers, Walter McVitty writes:

> Hills End *turned to the tensions and conflict going on in the minds of the child protagonists — the action was . . . internal or introspective. Instead of merely diverting the young reader, it involved him in the personal problems of particular children very much like himself, and did it in a way that made no concessions, taking the reader into his [the author's] trust and addressing him as an intellectual equal. Above all, it [the style] did it with an intensity which provoked strong emotional responses of one kind or another. And that has been true of all of Ivan Southall's novels since* Hills End. *(McVitty,* Innocence and Experience, *p. 237)*

It is indeed so of *Josh*. Speaking of *Josh* in *A Journey of Discovery: Writing for Children*, Ivan Southall relates:

> *I suppose* Josh *was the book I had written for myself, that I felt then could, and probably would, leave the rest of the world unmoved or confused, yet I believed it to be the only*

Experimental cover art by Astra Lacis for Ruth Park's children's novel
Playing Beatie Bow. (Original artwork)

book I had written that was totally enclosed inside a shell of calm resistance to anything anyone could say about it . . . [but] Josh was not inside a shell. Josh was more naked than the others. (Southall, A Journey of Discovery, *p. 27)*

Ivan Southall has won the Children's Book Council of Australia Book of the Year Award four times; the Picture Book of the Year Award once; and with *Josh*, he was awarded the Carnegie Medal of the British Library Association in 1971. His novels have been translated into many languages.

Ruth Park

Two sample roughs, for the jacket of the children's novel *Playing Beatie Bow*, written by Ruth Park, are displayed at Dromkeen. These and the final jacket were designed by Astra Lacis.

Playing Beatie Bow was chosen by the Children's Book Council of Australia as the Book of the Year in 1981. In this gripping story, the author has convincingly interwoven contemporary realism and 'travel-through-time' fantasy. The main character, modern, fourteen-year-old Abigail Kirk, is unwittingly drawn back in time to experience life in the Rocks area of Sydney as it was in 1873. Vigorous prose and strong characterisation bring a sense of immediacy as the mystery of the intertwining of the lives of the families and individuals concerned, past and present, gradually unfolds.

Ruth Park was born in Auckland, New Zealand. A graduate of Auckland University, she worked as an editor with several New Zealand newspapers before moving to Sydney in 1941. A gifted writer and journalist, she has written many adult works and over thirty books for children, ranging from those for the very young to junior novels such as *Playing Beatie Bow*.

In an article by Barbara Ker Wilson in *Twentieth Century*

Joyce Boniwell Saxby, first Australian children's book editor.

Children's Writers, Ruth Park comments on her approach to creating a character for a book:

> *I don't portray real children in stories; I create a fictional child very much as a gipsy makes a blanket . . . a rag here, a tuft of wool there. I pick up a habit of speech, a mannerism, a colour of eye . . . and try to make somebody real out of the bits. I don't always succeed but I do find it a joyful business trying. (Kirkpatrick,* Twentieth Century Children's Writers, *p. 599)*

Children's Book Editors

Prior to 1919, publishers the world over had no special department designated to deal with children's books. This area of publishing had never been considered sufficiently important to warrant special attention; children's books generally were regarded more in the nature of an extension of the interests of women, or as a means of increasing a publisher's list, than worthwhile literature in their own right.

In 1919, the MacMillan Company of New York set a new trend in the publishing of children's books by creating a separate Children's Department. Louise Seaman (later Louise Seaman Bechtel), a young graduate with some teaching experience who had been working in the advertising department of the company, was appointed to supervise the children's publications. She became the first specialised children's book editor.

This specialisation in the publishing of children's books was long overdue. The idea was soon followed by other publishing companies in the United States and, by the end of the 1930s, several London publishers also had appointed children's book editors. However, it was not until 1963 that a children's book department was created by an Australian publishing company. The lead was taken by Angus and Robertson, who appointed Joyce Saxby (then Joyce Boniwell) as the company's first children's book editor.

Joyce Saxby

A Tasmanian and a Carnegie scholar, Joyce Saxby's first professional appointment was to the State Library of Tasmania, where she held the position of librarian of the Lady Clark Memorial Children's Library in Hobart. The aim of this library was to provide books of quality that could be borrowed by Tasmanian children, irrespective of where they lived in the island state. To achieve this aim was not an easy task in Tasmania with its rugged coastline, hosts of small, off-shore islands and many wild, almost inaccessible mountainous areas. With the support of local authorities, the help of schools, the Australian Broadcasting Commission and her own dedication, energy and enthusi-

asm, Joyce Saxby solved the distribution problem with the result that most Tasmanian children had access to the best children's books available at that time.

Following her Tasmanian appointment, Joyce Saxby worked in the schools' section of the New Zealand Library Service, at the Boys' and Girls' House, which is the children's department of the Toronto Public Libraries in Canada, and later, in 1960, as Children's Librarian at the National Library in Canberra. This was a newly-created position, and in her three-year term there, Joyce Saxby built up the collection to 20,000 books.

As children's book editor at Angus and Robertson, Joyce Saxby established the firm's first Children's Department and sought new writers and illustrators, especially of picture-story books, to whom she gave freely her advice and encouragement. Among them was the writer and illustrator Penelope Janic, whose work is represented at Dromkeen.

During her short time with Angus and Robertson, Joyce Saxby was also vice-president of the Children's Book Council of New South Wales. Stricken with a serious illness, Joyce Saxby died in 1964.

Barbara Ker Wilson — Children's Book Editor

Angus and Robertson then appointed Barbara Ker Wilson as

Barbara Ker Wilson, children's book editor at Angus & Robertson, 1965-74.

Nance Donkin whose manuscript for her children's book Margaret Catchpole *is in the Dromkeen Collection.*

their next children's book editor. She was experienced already in this field, having commenced her career in publishing with Oxford University Press in London. From there, she moved to The Bodley Head, later taking up an appointment with William Collins. While working with Collins, she published Michael Bond's first story about that lovable character, Paddington Bear.

Barbara Ker Wilson emigrated to Australia in 1965 and edited children's books for Lansdowne Press for a short time, before securing the position of children's book editor with Angus and Robertson. At that time, Ivan Southall had just submitted his latest manuscript, *Ash Road*, which was to win the Children's Book Council of Australia Book of the Year Award in 1966.

Barbara Ker Wilson was the first Australian children's book editor to exhibit Australian children's books at the Bologna Children's Book Fair in Italy. She had become aware of the possibilities of developing an international list of children's books for Angus and Robertson, and attended the Children's Book Fair at Bologna as the company's representative. On her arrival at the venue, she discovered to her dismay that the Australian children's books to be exhibited had been allotted a small portion of the display area in which children's books published in the United Kingdom were being shown. She insisted that Australian children's books, representing many Australian publishing companies, be allotted a stand of their own.

At international book fairs, such as the Bologna Children's Book Fair, and another, the Book Fair at Frankfurt in Germany, representatives of Australian publishing companies have the opportunity of meeting representatives of publishing companies of other nations. Arrangements for overseas firms to purchase the rights to publish Australian books in their own areas often result from these meetings. Overseas publishing rights are of financial benefit to the Australian publisher, the author and the illustrator.

During her ten years with Angus and Robertson, Barbara Ker Wilson worked steadily to promote authors and illustrators of Australian children's books world-wide. She was also successful in securing rights for Angus and Robertson to publish Australian editions of books by such well-known overseas authors as Emily Neville of the United States, and also the new style of picture-story books that were being published in Scandinavian countries.

Before Barbara Ker Wilson left Angus and Robertson in 1974, she had seen two authors of children's novels published by the company win the Children's Book Council of Australia Book of the Year Award: Ivan Southall, three times (1966, 1968, 1971), and Hesba Brinsmead (1972).

Lloyd O'Neil and Lansdowne Press

Lansdowne Press, who published Mavis Thorpe Clark's *The Min-Min*, in 1966, was then a fairly new Melbourne-based publishing company which had been formed in 1960 by Lloyd O'Neil, a publisher with an entrepreneurial flair. At first, Lansdowne published only adult books involving a variety of topics — sport, travel and natural history, among others. These books required full-colour illustrations, either photographs or artwork, and this led O'Neil to investigate the possibilities of using 'off-shore printing' as a means of cutting down production costs.

The Australian market is very small and, therefore, only a limited number of any title is usually required to satisfy market demand. The costs of printing quality books with full-colour illustrations in Australia, and mainly for the Australian market, meant that books had to be sold at a price higher than most people were willing to pay. Lloyd O'Neil came to the conclusion that a viable profit margin for such books could be obtained by printing overseas, and he was the first Australian publisher to experiment with 'off-shore printing', using printing companies in South-east Asia. Since the late 1960s, many Australian publishers have taken advantage of the economic viability of printing children's picture-story books 'off-shore'.

PART V
A Picture-Story Book Culture

George Ferguson, a former managing director of Angus and Robertson, when speaking on 'Publishing in Australia' at Writers' Week in Adelaide, in 1970, said ruefully:

Only now are we beginning in this country to treat publishing for children with the respect it deserves. It is of such vital importance that it seems odd that so few publishers, authors or critics have been prepared to devote themselves seriously to it . . . (Australian Book Review, April 1970)

Modern four-colour offset printing-press, showing four colours being printed simultaneously.

Illustration by Galina Herbert for An Australian Christmas. *(Original artwork)*

It was a timely statement, for the publishing of children's books in Australia during the next ten years was to be taken very seriously by many publishers. One important area of children's books, that of the picture-story book, which had shown a marked decline since the mid-1950s, burst into full, colourful array in the following decade.

During the 1970s, there was an increase in the number of children's books published each year in many countries. This was particularly so of picture-story books, and there are many reasons for the special interest in this genre. The rapid acceleration in the development of colour-printing technology allowed illustrators unprecedented scope for creativity. Correspondingly, the interest of many authors was aroused by the possibility of presenting quite sophisticated ideas to young children by means of well-designed picture-story books with illustrations that aroused the imagination and curiosity of young readers. Such illustrations not only complemented the text but also extended the written information through the addition of further ideas in the details within each drawing or painting. The number of children's libraries increased steadily during the 1970s, and librarians drew children's attention to the picture-story books available, while the media made known newly published titles to the public. All these factors, and others, have contributed to the emergence of what has almost become a picture-story book culture, world-wide.

Of importance in this upsurge of activity in the publishing of picture-story books was the issuing of children's books in paperback format as an alternative to the traditional hardback for the purchasing public. Paperbacks were less expensive and therefore reached a wider audience.

Of even greater importance to Australian publishing was the incentive offered by 'off-shore' printing. Due to the reduced costs of printing books in South-east Asia, picture-story books produced by Australian publishing companies could be marketed at a price that placed them in fair competition with the reasonably-priced, well-produced and colourful picture-story books that had been flowing into Australia from the United Kingdom and the United States since the early 1950s.

Australian Picture-Story Books in the 1960s

The production of Australian picture-story books, which had escalated during the 1940s, had declined in the following decade because Australian publishers could not compete financially with the books imported mainly from the United Kingdom. Although, in general, this situation continued until the late 1960s, there were a few Australian publishers who were prepared to take a risk. One of these was Thomas Lothian of

Melbourne, and several pieces of artwork prepared for picture-story books published by Lothian in the early 1960s are in the Dromkeen Collection.

In order to produce a picture-story book with an Australian flavour for Christmas 1961, Lothian published *An Australian Christmas*, written by Helen Gibson and illustrated by Galina Herbert. The following year, another book by Helen Gibson, *Buster the Fire Truck*, proved tremendously popular.

The lack of picture-story books published in Australia during this period was reflected in the lack of awards given by the Children's Book Council — no awards for picture-story books were made between 1959 and 1964.

During the late 1960s, Lloyd O'Neil's publishing company, Lansdowne Press, was incorporated with the Melbourne publishing company, F. W. Cheshire. Considering Lloyd O'Neil's pioneering work in the use of 'off-shore' printing, it is not surprising that one of his first projects became the publication of a new picture-story book series, the 'Authors and Artists Series for Australian Children'. The books were to be printed in Hong Kong.

Proven Australian authors wrote the stories for Cheshire's new series and well-known Australian artists illustrated them. The first title, *On My Island*, written by Geoffrey Dutton and illustrated by John Perceval, was published in 1967. The dummy, complete with black-and-white sketches by John Perceval, is in the Dromkeen Collection.

From the late 1960s onwards, the number of Australian picture-story books published each year and printed in Southeast Asia increased steadily.

Australian Children's Book Awards

Public awareness of standards of quality desirable in the writing, illustration, design and production of children's books has been stimulated by increased media coverage of several types of Australian book awards presented annually. Awards by the Children's Book Council of Australia for children's fiction and picture-story books occur each July during Children's Book Week. Media interest focuses upon the award winners — authors and illustrators. Children's librarians in schools and municipal libraries draw attention to award-winning books of that particular year, and of past years. Award-winning authors and illustrators give talks to children and parents in schools and at libraries, and sign copies of their books in bookshops. Special functions attuned to Children's Book Week are always held at Dromkeen homestead in July of each year.

Off-shore Printing

When Australian publishers were first forced by the economics of publishing to engage in 'off-shore' printing, not all Australian organisations who presented annual book awards recognised books printed outside Australia as being eligible. The Children's Book Council of Australia accepted books printed overseas because they were concerned only with content; the Australian Book Publisher's Association did not accept books printed outside Australia because they wanted to encourage Australian book design and printing.

British-based publishing companies had been publishing works by Australian authors since colonial days and the books were usually printed overseas in Britain. Since its inauguration, the Australian Children's Book Council had accepted books printed in Britain as being eligible for its children's book awards, so the fact, that since the late 1960s, many Australian children's books were being printed in South-east Asian countries, had no relevance to their awards. In 1969, the picture-story book *Sly Old Wardrobe*, published by F. W. Cheshire of Melbourne, and printed in Hong Kong, won the Children's Book Council of Australia Picture Book of the Year Award. It was the first Australian picture-story book printed in South-east Asia to do so.

Sly Old Wardrobe was the third book in F. W. Cheshire's 'Authors and Artists Series for Australian Children'. It was written by the children's novelist Ivan Southall and illustrated by the artist Ted Greenwood. The design and style of illustration constituted a breakthrough from traditional Australian illustrative modes in this genre, being more in keeping with contemporary illustrative work in children's books in the United Kingdom and the United States.

In 1952, the Australian Book Publishers Association had inaugurated a Book Design Award for which only books designed and printed in Australia were eligible. By the late 1960s, there was a marked decline in both the quality and quantity of books entered for this award, and the Judge's Report for the period 1969-70 had the following to say concerning book design in Australia:

> Entries . . . this year were disappointingly few, perhaps because so many well-designed books are now printed out of Australia and are therefore ineligible.

However, the rules for eligibility for the Book Design Award eventually had to yield to economic forces, and for the period 1970-71, the award in the children's category went to Ted Greenwood for *Obstreperous*, a picture-story book he had both written and illustrated. Published by Angus and Robertson, it had been printed in South-east Asia.

Changes in Australian Publishing in the 1970s

The early 1970s heralded a great change in Australian publishing houses. During this period, there were many takeovers of traditional Australian publishing companies by large publishing corporations in the United Kingdom and the United States. In some cases, the overseas companies allowed their Australian subsidiaries to publish for the Australian market as they saw fit. In other cases, restrictions were placed on Australian in-house editors with regard to their choice of manuscripts for publication.

123

Original artwork by Annette Macarthur-Onslow for her book Uhu.

As a result, small Australian-owned publishing companies mushroomed. Their owners were prepared to take considered economic risks in order to remain autonomous, and to have the right to publish innovative and exploratory material for the Australian market. Those companies publishing books for children investigated all avenues for making their publications known outside Australia, with the hope of selling overseas publishing rights.

The Co-edition

The selling of rights to overseas publishing companies for the publishing and distribution of children's novels by Australian authors had been established during the 1950s and 1960s. By the 1970s, a new era in publishing had commenced — that of the co-edition.

Australian publishing companies had instigated the procedure of having picture-story books printed in Asia because this made a publishing venture economically viable. When overseas rights to one of these picture-story books was sold, the new edition was also printed in Asia. The ensuing orders were shipped simultaneously from the Asian printing firm to the Australian publishing company involved, and to the overseas publishing company that had procured publishing and distribution rights for a certain area. By this means, the number of copies printed at one time (the print-run) was extended, thus reducing the cost of an individual book. That the printing costs were spread over several editions meant that the individual cost of each book was reduced further. In this way, the retail price of the book in the bookshop was considerably less than it would otherwise have been.

The Australian children's picture-book *Uhu*, by Annette Macarthur-Onslow, serves as an example of the co-edition as applied to 'off-shore' printing. Printed in Hong Kong, *Uhu* was published simultaneously in 1969, by Ure Smith of Sydney, and Rapp and Whiting of London.

Annette Macarthur-Onslow

In a piece of artwork on display at Dromkeen, an owlet nestled on the ground among plants and grasses steadfastly gazes out on the world. This is the original of an illustration from the book *Uhu*, written and illustrated by Annette Macarthur-Onslow. *Uhu* is a book filled with delight for the reader in many ways — for the liveliness of the pencil drawings, the sensivity of the subtle watercolour sketches, and for the beautifully-handled story describing the behaviour of a baby owl in the home of those who try so desperately to rear it, and the love and care it receives during its unfortunately short life. The story is not set in Australia, but in the rolling Cotswold hills of England where Annette Macarthur-Onslow lived for some time. She found the baby owl while she was wandering through the woods. In her own words:

> There he was on the ground, having fallen out of his nest in the pine tree . . . a defiant white ball of fluff with enormous blackcurrant eyes and tiny beak clicking a warning to anyone daring to enter his territory among the roots and pine needles.

Annette Macarthur-Onslow is a descendant of the Macarthur family, graziers of New South Wales, who featured prominently in the early history of the colony. As a child, Annette was always drawing, compiling stories and fashioning small books for herself. Born in Sydney, she spent most of her childhood in the country town of Camden in New South Wales. It was here that her interest in animals developed, and she began to observe and to draw them. She is now well-known for her illustrations of animals and birds, for her ability to suggest movement, liveliness and speed, and to capture the mood of a work she is illustrating, whether it be in black and white, or in subtle colour.

In 1970, the year after it was published, *Uhu* won the Children's Book Council of Australia Book of the Year Award.

Ted Greenwood

Having entered the picture-story book arena as both an author and an artist, Ted Greenwood has continued his interest in this genre. Born in Melbourne, Ted Greenwood has been a teacher and a lecturer. Now a full-time illustrator, artist and writer, he works from his studio 'The Cabin' at Ferny Creek in the Dandenong Ranges.

Displayed at Dromkeen is the cover artwork for the paperback edition of Ted Greenwood's picture-story book *V.I.P. (Very Important Plant)*, first published in 1971. The book tells

Anne Bower Ingram, children's book editor for the Australian branch of the publishers William Collins.

Original artwork for Nicholas and the Moon Eggs *written and illustrated by Mark Way.*

the story of the life-cycle of a eucalypt, from the newly-sown seed to the fully-grown tree. Aghast at the devastation caused by bush-fires in the Dandenong Ranges, Ted Greenwood made conservation the theme in *V.I.P.* The illustrations are in pastel, the medium in which he prefers to work.

Anne Bower Ingram — Children's Book Editor

A picture book usually evolves from the combined efforts of author, illustrator, the children's editor in the publishing house concerned, the designer and the printer. Anne Bower Ingram, an Australian children's book editor, recognised the need for the deployment of these varied talents and actively sought out illustrators whose style, she felt, would both complement and extend an author's story.

Anne Ingram has been associated with the Australian book trade since leaving school. She joined the staff of Thompson's Bookshop in Brisbane in 1953, and for the following seven years she specialised in children's books. During those years, she made several trips to London and while there in 1959, she met Grace Hogarth, a respected children's book editor, with whom she corresponded on her return to Australia. In London again in 1964, Anne had the good fortune to work with this famous children's book editor for several months.

In 1970, Anne Ingram moved to Sydney and took over the editorship of *Reading Time*, the official journal of the Children's Book Council of Australia, a position she retained for the next seven years. Late in 1970, while Kaye Webb, the British editor of Penguin Puffin Books, was in Sydney, Anne Ingram submitted a list of Australian titles for consideration for inclu-

sion on the Puffin list. Also in Sydney at this time was the late Sir Billy Collins, of the British publishing house William Collins. Having learned of Anne's interest in the field of children's books, he invited her to join the staff of the Australian branch of William Collins and to develop a list of Australian children's books for the company. She worked for William Collins from 1971 until 1980, and during that time an impressive number of Australian children's picture-story books was published by that company.

While with Collins, Anne Ingram experienced some exciting publishing achievements — for example, in 1978, Mark Way's picture-story book *Nicholas and the Moon Eggs*, which she had guided through the publishing process, won the Critici in Erba Prize. This coveted annual award for children's literature was first given in 1963, and each year the winning book is announced at the Children's Book Fair at Bologna, Italy. The award is judged by a committee of nine children aged between eight and fourteen, who make their choice from several hundred entries.

Jenny Wagner and Ron Brooks

The author Jenny Wagner and the illustrator Ron Brooks are well represented at Dromkeen by manuscripts and original artwork for books on which they have collaborated. The first of these was *The Bunyip of Berkeley's Creek*.

In 1972, a friend handed Jenny Wagner's manuscript of *The Bunyip of Berkeley's Creek* to Ron Brooks, thinking he might like to illustrate it. Ron Brooks was immediately attracted by the idea of drawing a bunyip — the mythical creature of Australian legend and lore.

The Bunyip of Berkeley's Creek was published simultaneously in Australia and the United Kingdom in 1973, and later in the United States. Pegi Williams, a well-known bookseller in Adelaide, recalls the arrival of this book on the market:

> The Bunyip *was so Australian in content and setting that it heralded in a new era in Australian children's picture books, but the first reaction was 'It's dark and frightening — will the children take to it?'*

Experimental design by Ron Brooks for the cover of John Brown, Rose and the Midnight Cat. (Original artwork)

Original artwork by Ron Brooks for John Brown, Rose and the Midnight Cat.

The answer was *yes*, with approval by children everywhere.

Several years later, Wagner and Brooks collaborated on a picture-story book titled *John Brown, Rose and the Midnight Cat*. It is a story with depth, one that can be read and enjoyed at different levels of understanding, as its illustrator discovered when he began to 'feel' his way into the story. In autobiographical notes to his publisher, Ron Brooks said:

> *The challenge for me was to show and extend all these (different) layers, while at the same time retaining hold of the single, central thread, keeping an overall cohesiveness and simplicity to the imagery throughout, so that even quite young children could get something from it.*

It took Ron Brooks two years to come to terms with the illustrative needs of *John Brown, Rose and the Midnight Cat*. In 1978, the book won the Australian Children's Book Council Picture Book of the Year Award, the Visual Arts Board Award and the Australian Book Publishers Association Design Award. The original artwork for a cover design for the book, which the illustrator decided not to use, is among the other pre-publication materials for the book in the Dromkeen Collection.

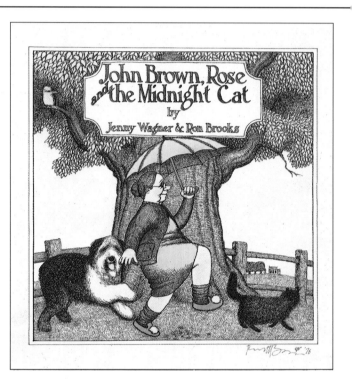

John Brown followed her.

'I'm sure there's no cat,' he said.

The recalcitrant giraffe from The Giraffe in Pepperell Street. (Original artwork)

A Fantasy Set in Suburbia

The Giraffe in Pepperell Street, a picture-story book of fun and fantasy, is another book that can be appreciated at different levels, depending upon the age of the reader. Most people have had the experience of a new puppy or kitten causing havoc in a household; in this book, the disruptive influence is a supercilious, temperamental giraffe. Set in an average Australian home, where Mum and Dad both go out to work, the story is filled with amusing, incongruous, yet immediately recognisable family situations. The narrative is in fast-moving verse:

> *He followed me home from school one day,*
> *Vertical, patterned and neat.*
> *I suppose it was rather irregular —*
> *A giraffe in Pepperell Street.*

> *Mum and Dad weren't home from work,*
> *But the spare key was under the bin.*
> *I unlocked the door and went inside.*
> *The giraffe calmly followed me in.*

The idea for the story came to the author, Robin Klein, as she was waiting for a train at a suburban railway-station, and she wrote it almost immediately. Robin Klein lives in the Dandenong Ranges, not far from Melbourne. In an interview, her thoughts come quickly. She was born in Kempsey, on the northern coast of New South Wales. Descended from a convict family, her maiden name was McMaugh. She is a compulsive writer and feels that she owes this to her mother. When Robin was a child, her mother used to give her a pencil and paper and tell her to, 'go away and write stories', in order to get some peace.

Book jacket for River Murray Mary. *The illustrator, Robert Ingpen, collaborated with the author, Colin Thiele, in the planning and writing of the story.*

In recent years, Robin Klein has won the Mary Grant Bruce Short Story Award for Children's Literature twice, in 1983 and 1984, and has had at least fifteen books for children published. Success has not always come easily; persistence has helped. Robin Klein's children's book *Thing*, which features a pet dinosaur, was rejected by five publishers before being accepted by Oxford University Press in Melbourne. The book was illustrated by Alison Lester and won the Children's Book Council of Australia Junior Book of the Year Award in 1983. A sequel, *Thingnapped!*, was published in 1984. Following the popularity of *Thing*, copies of *Thingnapped!* in Melbourne bookshops sold out in three days.

The Giraffe in Pepperell Street was illustrated by visiting English artist Gill Tomblin, who spent many long hours at Taronga Park Zoo studying the movements of giraffes, and equally as many hours studying the characteristics of Australian suburbia. The illustrations complement the text so well that one might easily suppose that author and artist had worked in close collaboration, but in actual fact they have never met.

All the artwork for *The Giraffe in Pepperell Street* is in the Dromkeen Collection. The book, published in 1978, earned Special Mention at the Children's Book Fair in Italy for the Critici in Erba Prize the following year.

Colin Thiele

All the pre-publication material for the children's picture-story book *River Murray Mary*, written by Colin Thiele and illustrated by Robert Ingpen, is at Dromkeen. The winding Murray River, with its chopped-off billabongs, its banks fringed with red gums and other river trees, had fascinated Colin Thiele and Robert Ingpen for many years.

In the 1920s, Colin Thiele used to visit an aunt who lived at Oxford Landing on the Murray. In those days, paddle-steamers still churned along the river, carrying passengers, towing barges and, at night, showing harsh, bright lights and sounding their hooters. The romantic era of the Murray River paddle-steamers has long passed, but as Colin Thiele had actually experienced something of those times during his boyhood he had the background on which to draw for the story, *River Murray Mary*.

Colin Thiele is one of the best-known Australian writers for children and his work has always been held in high esteem. He was born and brought up in the undulating wheat and sheep country of the Eudunda - Kapunda district of South Australia, and he attended Kapunda High School, then university in Adelaide, followed by Teachers' College. A short time after he graduated, the Second World War engulfed the world and he served with the Royal Australian Air Force in northern Australia and New Guinea.

After the war, he returned to teaching, and it was then that he started to write seriously. He wrote poetry, prose, plays and, especially, material for radio, a great deal of it for children's programmes. His list of published works grew, but it was not until he was on board the *Himalaya* on his way to America to take up a Fulbright Scholarship, that he wrote a book of interest to children. Titled *Sun on the Stubble*, it was published in 1961 and was the forerunner of many children's books by its author, one of the best-known being *Storm Boy*, published in 1963. It was the illustrated *de luxe* edition (1974) of *Storm Boy*, which Robert Ingpen illustrated, that led Thiele and Ingpen to work in collaboration on the picture-story book *River Murray Mary*. This working in 'tandem', to use an expression of Robert Ingpen's, was something both enjoyed, each appreciating the other's particular skills.

River Murray Mary, published in 1979, was commended by the Children's Book Council of Australia in the awards for 1980.

Fantasies Set in Medieval Times

The author and illustrator Judith Crabtree becomes totally absorbed in whatever picture-story book is in her mind and on

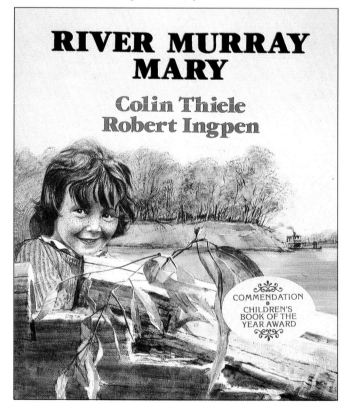

Preliminary sketches by Judith Crabtree for her children's picture-story book Legs. (Original artwork)

her drawing-board. The story she is creating must have sufficient potential for development to hold her interest for the two years it will take her to complete the illustrations.

Her two recent picture-story books, *Legs*, published in 1979, and *The Sparrow's Story at the King's Command*, published in 1983, are fantasies. Although these books are in essence very different from one another, both are set in Europe in medieval times. This is a period of history with which Judith Crabtree has always felt a strong affinity, accentuated by her tireless research.

Legs is a highly original story in which the characters in the book 'come to life'. It begins:

Once upon a time an artist painted a picture. The artist made some sketches too, but some were crumpled into balls and others put aside. Then one day, quite suddenly, the artist went away . . .

The characters in the picture waited for the artist to come back — Lotta, the farm girl, the farmer, and others who were on the way to the market town where the contest to choose 'The Most Beautiful Of Creatures' was to be held. Suddenly, they could wait no longer for the missing artist to return and finish her pictures and the story. They set off to complete the tale themselves:

Lotta left the road.
She ran to the picture's edge and then stepped out.
On the artist's desk she saw, upon a page, a painted thing that stamped and leapt and kicked about and fell down in a feathered heap.
She watched, amazed. 'And what,' she asked politely, 'might you be?'
Between the shining feathers slithered tears. 'I wish I knew,' the something sighed, like wind among the leaves. 'But I suppose I never will, for I'm just half a painting; I'm unfinished. I'm . . . just . . . legs!'

And Lotta took Legs, and a bundle of the artist's brushes and tubes of paint, back into the picture with her.

On loan to Dromkeen are four original illustrations for *The Sparrow's Story at the King's Command*. This book is illustrated in the style of illuminated medieval manuscripts. Detailed illustrations that accompany the small area of text on one page, extend, or illustrate, parts of the story not treated in the large illustration opposite.

The Sparrow's Story at the King's Command is a story within a story — a picture book within a picture book. This is a book to be read many times and its illustrations pored over, for each time one looks, there seems to be something else to notice. The more one gets to know the story, the more meaningful the detail in the illustrations becomes. It is a book to be 'discovered', read and enjoyed.

Judith Crabtree was born in Melbourne, but has lived in several other Australian capital cities, either attending school, studying or working. She has also lived in London, where she studied life drawing at St Martin's Art School and the Polytechnic. She now lives permanently in Melbourne.

Elizabeth Honey

There are several different examples of Elizabeth Honey's many and varied illustrative art styles at Dromkeen. One is a piece of black-and-white artwork for her illustrations for the children's

Detailed black-and-white illustration by Elizabeth Honey for Brave with Ben. *(Original artwork)*

book *Brave with Ben*, written by Christobel Mattingley and published in 1982.

Elizabeth Honey attended Swinburne College of Technology and completed the film and television course. Since then her career has been extremely diverse and has included working with the Australian Broadcasting Commission as a script assistant for the television programme *The Naked Bunyip*, and as art director and television visualiser for a small advertising agency. She has also worked in England.

To quote her own words concerning her work in London:

. . . I worked as continuity girl on the first Barry McKenzie film, which was fun. Continuity, however, is a terrible job; it's like being the memory for the film, everything has got to be recorded and written down. It can be very harrowing if you've got a big scene with lots of special effects and you were wondering whether a particular person should be wearing a white coat, or a blue jumper. (Minding Your Own Business, pp. 16-21)

After she returned to Australia, Elizabeth compiled a folio of imaginative and realistic illustrative material and became a freelance illustrator. This sounds very easy to do, but it is certainly not so in reality. To become a successful freelance illustrator, one has to search for contracts; to learn to sell one's ideas, one's ability, and one's work; and then to live up to all the promises made by delivering the finished goods on time and at an acceptable level of competency, which frequently entails sitting at a desk and drawing, drawing and redrawing, often into the small hours of the morning.

Granny's garden was huge, wild and overgrown. The trees were higher than two-storey houses.
'Brave with Ben'

Elizabeth Honey

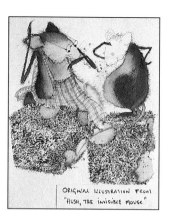

Possum Magic and Omnibus Books

When the pre-publication material for *Possum Magic* arrived at Dromkeen for a short period, an intruder was found among the material — a small invisible mouse, the ghostly ancestor of Hush, the invisible possum in the picture-story book *Possum Magic*. The story of *Possum Magic*, written by Mem Fox and illustrated by Julie Vivas, had evolved from an earlier version in which the main character was a mouse, also called Hush.

After a magic spell had made her invisible, Hush, the mouse, had travelled all around the world, seeking exactly the right kind of food to make her visible again. This she had eventually found in Australia — a vegemite sandwich, a piece of pavlova and a lamington. Hush, the little possum of *Possum Magic*, travels only around Australia accompanied by Grandma Poss, and finds in three different Australian cities one of each of the kinds

of 'people food' that will make her visible: a vegemite sandwich in Darwin, a piece of pavlova in Perth and a lamington in Hobart.

Possum Magic was published by Omnibus Books, an Adelaide publishing company founded in 1980 by two innovative women with a distinct flair for publishing, Sue Williams and Jane Covernton. They met while working for the Adelaide publishing company Rigby. In 1984, *Possum Magic* was highly commended by the Children's Book Council of Australia and won the New South Wales Premier's Award.

Mem Fox and Julie Vivas

Mem Fox, the author of the extremely popular picture-story book *Possum Magic*, was born in Melbourne, but spent much of her early life in Zimbabwe, Africa, followed by some years in

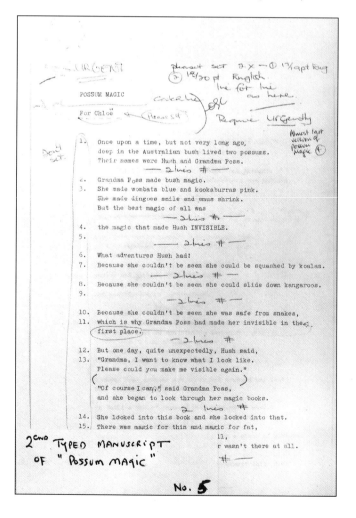

A happy trio — Julie Vivas (illustrator), Mem Fox (author), Jane Covernton (publisher).

Final artwork by Julie Vivas for Possum Magic. *(Original artwork)*

England. On her return to Australia in 1970, she settled in Adelaide and is currently a lecturer in Drama and Language Arts at the South Australian College of Advanced Education.

The illustrator, Julie Vivas, was born in Adelaide, lived briefly in Melbourne, and while still a child, moved with her family to Sydney. She relates that she had a wonderful childhood, always living in houses with large gardens and big trees. In Sydney, the bushland was close by, and she and her friends used to build tree-houses and race billy-carts down dirt tracks. But she liked to be alone, too, and then she would draw. Later, she attended the National Art School in Sydney and after completing a three-year course in interior design, she worked for a while in a veterinary clinic, an experience that deepened her feelings for animals. Since those days she has illustrated several children's books.

The first version of *Possum Magic*, the story about the mouse, Hush, came to her through a friend. The challenge of drawing an 'invisible' animal would have daunted many illustrators, but Julie found a means of solving the problem, and she carried her idea through to *Possum Magic*. Children have happily accepted her solution.

Australian Picture-Story Books — The 1980s

Concerning the future of Australian picture-story books, children's librarian and critic of children's books, Margaret Dunkle made the following apt statement in her article 'The 1985 Children's Book Awards in Retrospect', published in *Australian Book Review, 1985*:

> *Australian picture books are world class, consistently winning recognition at international book fairs; fresh and delightful and innovative, each year's crop with something new to say.*

Australian Children's Books: A Forecast

As a conclusion to this journey into Australian children's literature, the forecast by Anne Ingram, the recipient of the 1986 Dromkeen Medal, merits consideration:

> *Looking at the second half of the 1980s, it's safe to predict that Australian children's books will continue to grow and develop along lines that are original, stimulating and exciting.* (Australian Book Scene, 1984-85)

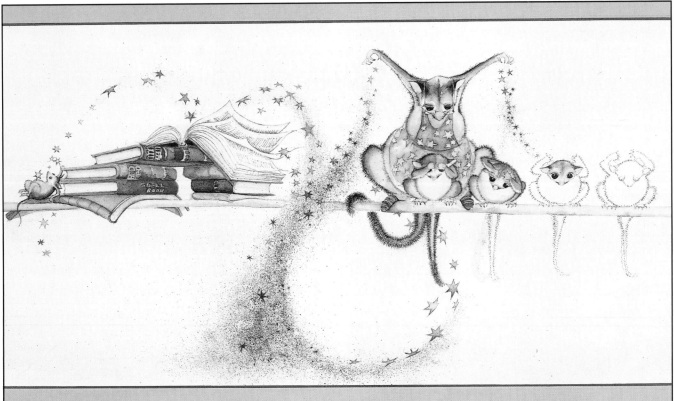

One of the first groups of school children to visit Dromkeen enjoying a story-telling session in the gardens surrounding the homestead.

English author and illustrator Brian Wildsmith visited Dromkeen homestead in 1978. He spoke to a student group and demonstrated his dexterity by drawing a lion simultaneously with both his left and right hands.

Chapter 4
Dromkeen Activities

When Joyce Oldmeadow delivered the acceptance speech on behalf of Court and herself at the presentation of the Eleanor Farjeon Award in England, in 1976, she said:

> *The whole idea about Dromkeen is that it is openly accessible to children. We hope that by visiting Dromkeen they will be helped in their understanding of what a book is, how it is transformed from an author's idea to a book in their school library or on their own shelf, and of the creative work involved in its production. It will also help children to appreciate that the authors whose books they read are real people, people to whom they can talk, people to whom they can write letters. In other words, we like the children who visit Dromkeen to go away feeling that books are living things and the reading of them an enjoyable and vital part of living. (Signal, September 1976)*

The sentiments expressed by Joyce Oldmeadow in her speech summarise the philosophy underlying the educational activities that take place almost every week of the school year at Dromkeen.

After the official opening of the Dromkeen Collection in October 1974, news that the Collection was to be accessible to children spread quickly and attracted the interest of authors, illustrators, editors and publishers of children's books throughout Australia. A glance through the Dromkeen Visitors' Book reveals such names as Mavis Thorpe Clark, Jean Chapman, Eve Pownall and Ron Brooks, among those of other Australian authors and illustrators who visited the homestead in the early days of the Collection.

The names of many well-known overseas authors, illustrators, and editors and critics of children's books also appear in the Visitors' Book, and a few are recorded here: Judy Taylor (1974), William Mayne (1974), William Golding (1975), John Burningham and Helen Oxenbury (1975), Margery Fisher (1975), John Rowe Townsend (1978), Brian Wildsmith (1978), Renate Meyer (1978), Paul Zindel (1980), Shirley Hughes (1982), Mitsumasa Anno (1983), Aidan Chambers (1984), Michael Foreman (1984) and Kit Williams (1984).

Many of the authors and illustrators mentioned entered into

Story-telling session by Virginia Ferguson in progress, in the sunroom at Dromkeen, 1975.

Judith Crabtree, Australian children's author and illustrator, discussing artwork with Jenny Pausacker and Darren Ryan during the Second Pacific Rim Conference on Children's Literature day at Dromkeen in 1979.

American visitors, the McCracken family, and Stella Lees, of Melbourne State College, discuss a piece of artwork at Dromkeen.

activities with groups of children at Dromkeen, sharing freely their experience in illustration and story-telling.

Educational Programmes for School Children

In 1976, a publicity release went out from Dromkeen to primary schools in Victoria, advising them of the organised educational programmes for school children that were to be held at Dromkeen homestead. The information was distributed in order to discover whether schools would be interested in including visits to the Dromkeen Collection as part of their school curriculum. The response was immediate and positive, especially from local primary schools, and within twelve months, the response from primary schools throughout the Melbourne metropolitan area was overwhelming. An idea of the increasing response from schools can be had by looking through the pages of the Dromkeen Diary, which records each visit by a school.

At first, school groups were invited only on the one or two days a week that staff were available to guide them through the Collection; within three years, the educational activities had been extended to five days a week during school terms. Today, Dromkeen is booked out as far ahead as two school terms. Slotted between primary-school group activities are programmes for tertiary students and adult groups.

In 1975, a new member of staff, Darren Ryan, a teacher/librarian with the Victorian Education Department, joined Oldmeadow Booksellers — the business was, at that time, located at Beatrice Avenue, West Heidelberg. Before joining the firm, Darren Ryan had often assisted Joyce and Court Oldmeadow by reviewing recently published children's books and giving talks to groups of teachers. In his new position he became the

buyer of children's fiction and picture-story books for the business.

In 1979, Darren Ryan accepted the position of manager of the bookshop at Dromkeen. For the next four years, he shared with Joyce Oldmeadow the responsibility of devising educational programmes centred around the Collection and graded to suit the various school groups visiting the homestead. Darren Ryan left Dromkeen in 1984.

The scheduled morning group of school children usually arrives at Dromkeen at about half-past ten, either by bus or after having walked from the Riddells Creek railway-station, and the tranquillity of the gardens surrounding the homestead is broken by excited chatter as children move towards the lecture-room. Here, the first stage in the educational programme commences.

The lecture-room was created by excavating an area underneath the wing occupied by the bookshop. This room is also

137

Exhibition of 'pop-up' and moveable books at Dromkeen.

used as a theatre, for puppet-shows, for showing documentary videos and for other events of a similar nature, as well as for preliminary talks to both children and adult groups before they actually view the Collection. The talk is given by a member of the Dromkeen staff.

The style and content of the talk given to children depends upon the general age of those in the group, but it always commences with the history of Dromkeen homestead, Joyce and Court Oldmeadow's reasons for starting a collection of children's literature, and then progresses to 'How a book is made'. The first two items may take only a few minutes, but the discussion concerning 'How a book is made' is central to the children's understanding of the Dromkeen Collection and usually takes about half an hour.

The session is a discussion, not a lecture, and the children are encouraged to participate with questions, and answers to ques-

tions. Pre-publication materials which represent each stage in 'the making of a book' are shown, talked about and compared with the printed page in the published book. The set of pre-publication materials includes the manuscript, edited and 'marked up' with directions for the printer; initial sketches and final artwork by the illustrator; a printer's dummy of the book; and other items of interest, such as the photographs used by the author or artist for reference. The story, or part of the story if it is a long one, is then read aloud to the children from the book.

By the time the children move into the homestead to view the collection of artwork and books, they are aware of the roles played by an author, an illustrator, an editor, a designer, a typesetter, a publisher, and a printer.

School groups commence their tour of the Collection in the Red Room where the exhibits consist mainly of children's books published in the early decades of this century and original

Irena Sibley's illustrations for her book Rainbow *are lino-cuts. The lino block, out of which a design has been gouged, its black-and-white print, and the coloured print of the Lithuanian doll, Rainbow, reproduced here, are in the Dromkeen Collection. The coloured Print of Rainbow is a trial illustration. A second, differently designed illustration of the doll was used in the book. Irene Sibley carried out activities involving lino-cuts with a group of school children visiting Dromkeen homestead.*

pieces of artwork for children's books created during the same period. The children then move through the other rooms of the homestead where work by contemporary authors and illustrators is displayed. As they are conducted from room to room they are encouraged to discuss the wide range of art styles, and the different mediums artists use to achieve a desired effect for an illustration. The depth of discussion is controlled by the average age of the children in a group and influenced by any specific interest they may show in a particular exhibit. Their interest is often stimulated by recognition of artwork from favourite books.

Assignment sheets are handed to the children after they have moved through the main rooms. They are then encouraged to wander from room to room by themselves, filling in the answers to questions on their assignment sheets from the data accompanying each exhibit on the walls, or from memory of the discussion sessions. When the children have completed their assignments, they usually come together as a group and the assignments are corrected. Then they move into the bookshop,

Court Oldmeadow and the English children's author William Mayne in Wensleydale, Yorkshire, in the United Kingdom.

to browse through the books on display and to purchase any if they wish.

Many groups bring a cut lunch or use the barbecue facilities. There is also an area where children can play and generally 'let off steam' before returning home. If the weather is cold and wet, outside shelter is available; in summer, many schools take advantage of the swimming-pool. Teachers and other adults who accompany children to Dromkeen are responsible for their supervision in the homestead grounds.

It is anticipated that some follow-up activity to a Dromkeen visit will occur in the schools. The children take their assignment sheets with them when they leave the homestead, and it is hoped that these are used as a starter to further discussion about children's books by the classroom teacher or librarian.

In a television interview concerning the educational activities organised for school children visiting Dromkeen, Joyce Oldmeadow related:

> *One rewarding experience we had was when a group from St Albans East Primary School visited us. They were so inter-*

ested in how books were made. They went back to school and made their own books, and then nine months later revisited us, bringing two of the books they had made and donating them to the Dromkeen Collection.

Educational activities for school children continue to be a vital component in the Dromkeen programme.

William Mayne as 'Author in Residence' at Dromkeen

Overseas authors and illustrators often take the opportunity to stay for a short period at the homestead in order to write or illustrate a new work. In 1974, the English children's author William Mayne was 'author in residence', and when asked in an interview how ideas for stories came to him and how he actually tackled writing a book, he replied:

> *. . . an idea just happens along — I trip over it and there it is . . . When an idea comes to me I have to put it away, sometimes for years . . . I have to leave it in a sort of pond of*

140

Cover artwork for the children's book Nonsense Places, *written by Michael Dugan and illustrated by Walter Stackpool.*

ideas that I have in my mind and see what it feeds on, what it joins up to; what happens when it's left alone to mature, if that's the word . . . I keep pulling ideas out gently and having a look at them. If they are ready to use, I really get them out on the bench and knock them into shape . . .

When I have done that . . . I have to work at it [the idea] — trimming away — adding pieces on until I can feel the thrill of movement in it, and it's definitely a physical feeling for me — down my neck and spine . . . and at that moment all the ideas that don't belong to that story just . . . drop away — as if the idea has stood up out of the water and taken its first step on dry land . . .

When I have finished the book, well, I have finished. It's nothing more to me . . . All I want after that is a single shining copy for my own shelf. What the rest of the world does with it, I don't mind . . .

During William Mayne's stay in Australia, he wrote *Salt River Times*, a collection of short stories about children living in an Australian inner-city suburb. The book was illustrated by Elizabeth Honey and published in 1980.

'Illustrators in Residence' at Dromkeen

In 1975, two of England's leading illustrators, Helen Oxenbury and John Burningham, spent some time at Dromkeen, working with children from Gisborne Primary School on a giant mural. There is a tape-recording at Dromkeen of John Burningham reading a poem to a group of children during that visit. The poem, 'The Quangle Wangle's Hat', was written many years ago by Edward Lear, and in 1969, republished in picture-story book format with illustrations by Helen Oxenbury.

The Australian illustrator Ron Brooks visited Dromkeen several times. In 1976, guests were invited to a private viewing of his artwork for the books *Annie's Rainbow*, of which he was also the author, and *Aranea*, written by Jenny Wagner. The artwork was for sale, and one piece was donated to the Collection. Since that time, many sales of artwork for children's books have been held at the homestead.

There are several examples of work by the Australian illustrator Walter Stackpool at Dromkeen. On one visit to the homestead, he showed a group of children how his drawings of horses, whether stylised or realistic, depended upon a knowledge of the animal's anatomy.

Dromkeen Open Days

After the formation of the association, the Friends of Dromkeen, in 1981, further activities and programmes centred around the Dromkeen Collection were planned, activities in which members of the 'Friends', the wider fraternity interested in children's literature,and the general public could participate.

Various events organised by the Friends of Dromkeen took place during 1982: the first Dromkeen Open Day was held in July, during Children's Book Week, and attracted over one hundred people. At the Open Day, the visiting English author and illustrator Shirley Hughes gave an interesting and informative talk about her work.

In May 1983, over forty people attended the first workshop at Dromkeen, planned by the Committee of the 'Friends'. The theme was 'Illustrators and Their Craft'. Participants examined and explored a variety of artwork for children's books. Guest illustrators Elizabeth Honey, Heather Philpott, Donna Rawlins and Graeme Base spoke about their work.

Over four hundred people attended the second Dromkeen Open Day during Children's Book Week in July, 1983. Guest speakers that day were Pamela Allen and Jeannie Baker. Pamela Allen delighted young children and parents with her readings from her books *Who Sank the Boat?* and *Bertie and the Bear*.

Jeannie Baker displayed the artwork for a children's book she was in the process of writing and illustrating, which eventually was published under the title *Home in the Sky*. The story was about a flock of homing pigeons and she invited children to say what they thought about the work. To quote Jeannie Baker:

This sort of involvement usually helps to give children a better understanding of the creative process underlying the writing and illustrating of children's books.

Jeannie Baker, author and illustrator of children's books.

Relief collage; illustration by Jeannie Baker for her children's book
Grandmother. (Original artwork)

In a later interview, Jeannie Baker explained some of the techniques of her extremely individualistic style of illustration. Her style is a type of collage, which she calls 'relief collage'. It involves the layering of various materials on to the base paper so that parts of the final illustration are raised a centimetre or so from the background. She explained:

The materials I use are mostly natural. Even the greenery is real, although, of course, I have to treat it with chemicals. I bleach it, bathe it in glycerine so that it will feel as if it is 'alive' when touched, and then spray it finely with oil paint to give a permanent colour.

My work is an illusion in perspective. I try to give as great a feeling of depth as possible without making the work three-dimensional, or a model. Various parts are usually flat at the back, but slightly rounded at the front, to give the feeling of

solidarity and depth I want. Shadows also help me to achieve this.

Since the inauguration of the Friends of Dromkeen in 1981, the activities organised by the association and centred on the Dromkeen Collection have been many and varied, and Dromkeen Open Day, held each July during Children's Book Week, has become an established function.

In November 1984, the Friends of Dromkeen held a Story-Telling Fest. It was a beautiful spring day and hundreds of parents and children attended. Story-tellers sat on rugs in the shade of trees in the gardens surrounding the homestead and kept children enraptured with the stories they told.

Jeannie Baker and *Home in the Sky*

Jeannie Baker came from Sydney to be present at the Story-Telling Fest. *Home in the Sky* had been published since she was last at Dromkeen, and on this visit she explained how she came to write the story.

She told her audience that the idea for *Home in the Sky* came

Jeannie Baker, at the Story-Telling Fest at Dromkeen in 1984, talking to students and adults about her book Home in the Sky.

Children captivated by story-teller Nell Bell, at the Story-Telling Fest at Dromkeen in 1984.

The busy bookshop at Dromkeen homestead.

Joyce Oldmeadow, her son John Oldmeadow and the English author and illustrator of children's books Michael Foreman, discussing the preparation of artwork for Panda and the Bunyips *at Dromkeen.*

to her when she was staying in New York in 1981. The buildings seemed to reach up, far into the sky, from the not-very-wide streets, shutting out the sunlight from people below for most of the day. The skyscrapers, the types of public transport, the masses of people seeming to have to struggle all the time for survival, and the New York graffiti, fascinated her.

One day, as she was wandering along a New York street, a flock of pigeons 'burst into the sky' from the top of a burned-out building. She watched the homing pigeons with delight as they circled higher and higher above the tall buildings. It was then that an idea for a book came to her.

She discovered that the pigeons were owned by a man named Mike. Jeannie persuaded him to show her the pigeons which he kept in coops on the flat roof of the burned-out building. The stairs inside the building that led from one floor to the next were exceedingly ricketty. On one floor, half-way up the building, lived Mike's dog. It was there to guard the pigeons from unwelcome interference by intruders and it took its duty as a guard-dog seriously.

If climbing up the stairs inside the building was a little risky, it was nothing to the feeling of unease Jeannie experienced when she had to navigate the old fire-escape attached to the exterior of the building in order to reach the roof. Researching a project in New York had involved facing unusual situations, some risks and many adventures; she found it an extraordinary experience.

Home in the Sky took Jeannie Baker two years to complete. The original 'relief collage' illustrations were shown at Dromkeen homestead, at the Roslyn Oxley Gallery in Paddington, NSW, and at the Forum Gallery in New York.

Book jacket for Panda and the Bunyips *and a set of blue-prints for the book, both in the Dromkeen Collection.*

Original artwork by Michael Foreman for his book War and Peas.

English Author and Illustrator, Michael Foreman

In the summer of 1984, Michael Foreman, English illustrator and author of books for children, stayed at Dromkeen for several days during his working tour of Australia. Michael Foreman is one of the foremost illustrators of children's books in England today. He has won the Kate Greenaway Medal for outstanding children's book illustration and has been runner-up for this award three times. He has also been awarded the Bologna Children's Book Fair Graphic Prize for Youth.

Talking about the way he began illustrating children's books, Michael Foreman said:

> *To get started I had to do my own stories — do the whole book myself and have fairly finished drawings before a publisher could be sure of the final product. Those were the early days . . . once you begin to get a track record, publishers start to imagine how you would treat illustrations for a manuscript they have received. That is when they start sending you other people's texts to work on.*

> *Part of the enjoyment of being in Australia is suddenly being given the chance to illustrate a story which I would not otherwise have imagined or invented. And that's a challenge. By doing research for the story, I learn more about a particular subject and that, in turn, gives me other ideas for books.*

Michael Foreman has travelled overseas often, and almost every children's book he has written is the result of a journey he has made somewhere in the world. While staying at Dromkeen during his Australian tour, Michael Foreman took the opportunity to commence the illustrations for his book *Panda and the Bunyips*. To watch him flood vibrant watercolour on white paper for what eventually turned out to be a painting of Ayres Rock in Central Australia was a fascinating experience for those present.

Judy Taylor, a children's book editor from the United Kingdom and a frequent visitor to Dromkeen homestead.

A reproduction from the brochure announcing the exhibition of the works by Beatrix Potter held at Dromkeen in 1985. (© Frederick Warne)

Exhibition of Artwork by Beatrix Potter

Once upon a time there were four little Rabbits, and their names were — Flopsy, Mopsy, Cotton-tail, and Peter.

The opening sentence of *The Tale of Peter Rabbit* by the English author and illustrator, Beatrix Potter, must surely be one of the best-known and best-loved in children's literature. It is hard to believe that there would be many children in English-speaking countries who have not heard of the adventures of Peter Rabbit in Mr McGregor's garden, nor looked with wonder and delight at the exquisite illustrations.

The Tale of Peter Rabbit was Beatrix Potter's first book for children and evolved from a story she wrote in 1893 in a letter to a young friend. Several years later, Beatrix Potter published the story herself, with illustrations in black and white. The little book proved so popular that the publishers Frederick Warne of London published a new edition in 1902 with watercolour illustrations by Beatrix Potter. Eventually, Beatrix Potter completed twenty-three stories for children about animals — all are recognised now as children's classics, and most have been translated into other languages.

When Joyce and Court Oldmeadow visited Beatrix Potter's cottage in the Lake District in England in 1971 and saw many of her original sketches and paintings on public view, they thought how wonderful it would be if a selection of her work could be brought to Australia and exhibited. It seemed an impossible dream at the time. However, after the opening of the Dromkeen Collection in 1974, the realisation of this dream became a possibility.

In February 1985, after years of patient negotiation between Joyce Oldmeadow and the custodians of the Leslie Linden Collection in England, a selection of Beatrix Potter's original drawings and paintings was flown from England and displayed at Dromkeen. This was the first time any of Beatrix Potter's artwork held in a collection had been allowed to leave the United Kingdom. It was a tremendous achievement by Joyce Oldmeadow, and during the twelve weeks of the exhibition over sixteen thousand Australians visited the homestead to see Beatrix Potter's work.

At the opening of the exhibition on Friday, 1 February 1985, Judy Taylor, children's book editor and an authority on Beatrix Potter's work, spoke to the gathering. It seemed appropriate that Judy Taylor should be at Dromkeen on such a momentous occasion because, in 1974, she had been the first overseas visitor to the homestead. At that time, Dromkeen homestead was Joyce and Court Oldmeadow's private residence; the wing now occupied by the Dromkeen bookshop was Oldmeadow Booksellers bulk book and freight store; and the first few pieces of artwork that formed the nucleus of the Dromkeen Collection had not yet been purchased.

Appraising the Dromkeen Collection as it exists today, Judy Taylor has commented that in her opinion, Dromkeen, as a home for children's literature where children and their books are brought together, is unique.

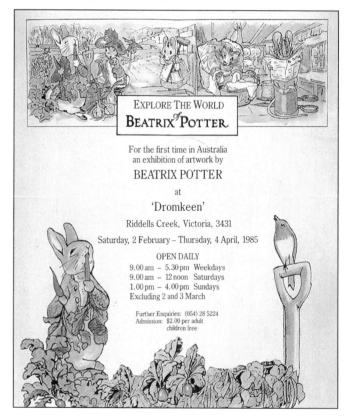

EXPLORE THE WORLD *of* BEATRIX POTTER

For the first time in Australia
an exhibition of artwork by
BEATRIX POTTER
at
'Dromkeen'
Riddells Creek, Victoria, 3431
Saturday, 2 February – Thursday, 4 April, 1985

OPEN DAILY
9.00 am – 5.30 pm   Weekdays
9.00 am – 12 noon   Saturdays
1.00 pm – 4.00 pm   Sundays
Excluding 2 and 3 March

Further Enquiries: (054) 28 5224
Admission: $2.00 per adult
children free

Chapter 5
Recognition and Response

The Eleanor Farjeon Award

Early in 1976, Joyce and Court Oldmeadow received a cable from London informing them that they had been jointly awarded the prestigious Eleanor Farjeon Award for 1975-76 by the Children's Book Circle of the United Kingdom. Never had they thought of receiving such an honour, and never before had the Award been made outside Great Britain. The Oldmeadows made plans to travel to England to receive the Award in person.

The Eleanor Farjeon Award perpetuates the memory of the well-loved children's author Eleanor Farjeon, and is granted 'for distinguished services to children's books'.

Eleanor Farjeon was born in London in 1881. The daughter of the novelist Benjamin Leopold Farjeon, sister of the writers Herbert and Joseph Jefferson Farjeon, Eleanor Farjeon was a prolific writer herself: over seventy books for children — prose, verse and non-fiction. She was also a playwright, a poet, an author of adult novels, and an editor. For her contribution to children's literature, she received the Hans Christian Andersen International Medal in 1956, the Library Association Carnegie Medal in the same year, and the Catholic Library Association Regina Medal in 1958. She died on 5 June 1965, at the age of eighty-four.

The Eleanor Farjeon Award was first given in 1966 by the Children's Book Circle, a group of British editors of books for children. In its designation, it is free of any national or professional restrictions.

When Joyce and Court Oldmeadow received the Eleanor Farjeon Award in 1976, the Dromkeen Collection assumed world status and renown. The following account of the presentation of the Award to Joyce and Court Oldmeadow is quoted from the British trade magazine *The Bookseller* of 5 June 1976:

THE ELEANOR FARJEON AWARD
The 1975 Eleanor Farjeon Award for distinguished services to children's books was presented by the Children's Book Circle on 19th May [1976] at a reception at the Orangery, Holland Park. This year for the first time the Award went outside the U.K., and also for the first time to booksellers,

147

Original Illustration by Edward Ardizzone for
THE LITTLE BOOKROOM by Eleanor Farjeon
(Oxford University Press, 1955)
Page 184, in the story entitled "The Connemara Donkey"

the Australians Joyce and Court Oldmeadow, who were there to accept the presentation in person. The Oldmeadows, children's booksellers and founders of the Australian Centre for Children's Literature, must be rare in the breadth of their concern, not only for the selling of children's books, but also for the dissemination of information about them; they . . . are devoted to the spreading of knowledge about, and interest in, children's books in the widest and most international sense. The new chairman of the Children's Book Circle, Tony Lacy, introduced last year's winner Naomi Lewis to welcome the Oldmeadows and make the Award. The special gift to the Oldmeadows was an original Ardizzone illustration, appropriately from The Little Bookroom *by Eleanor Farjeon . . .*

The Courtney Oldmeadow Children's Literature Foundation

Joyce and Court Oldmeadow took up residence at Dromkeen homestead on Boxing Day, 1973. During 1974, they acquired some pieces of original artwork prepared for children's books, which they displayed for the enjoyment of children and teachers visiting the homestead. The Collection grew.

On 12 October 1974, the Collection was officially opened and named the Dromkeen Collection of Australian Children's Literature, and from that time onwards, the Collection expanded rapidly. A year later, in October 1975, Joyce and Court Oldmeadow established the Dromkeen Trust, to help administer, preserve and develop the Dromkeen Collection. The Trustees were: Joyce and Court Oldmeadow (who had personally

148

financed the Dromkeen Collection); Michael Dugan, author; Ray Hellier, publishing representative; Anne Bower Ingram, children's book editor; and Darren Ryan, teacher/librarian.

The 'Declaration of Trust' document stated that:

The Trustees are of the opinion that it is essential that the said Collection should be both preserved and expanded in order to:
1 *Preserve in a readily accessible form and location a collection of valuable Australian books, manuscripts, tapes and works of art.*
2 *Enable its use for the purposes of research and education.*
3 *Foster an awareness of Australian literature and in particular, Australian children's literature and its development.*
In order to best carry out the objectives referred to above, the Trustees have unanimously resolved to form themselves into an association known as the Dromkeen Children's Literature Foundation.

The 'Declaration of Trust' document laid down the original guidelines that eventually were incorporated in the Courtney Oldmeadow Children's Literature Foundation, as follows:

1 *To retain same* [the Collection] *intact at Dromkeen.*
2 *To exhibit same in such place at Dromkeen to which the public has access.*
3 *To authorise such persons as the Trustees think fit to have access thereto for the purposes of research, provided always that no item or items constituting part of the said Collection shall be removed by such persons from Dromkeen.*
4 *To return to the owners thereof all items which they have donated to the said Collection in the event that:*
   (a) *The said Collection cannot be maintained as a single entity either at Dromkeen or such other place as the Trustees in their discretion think fit.*
   (b) *In the case of items donated to the said Collection by way of temporary loan, the specified loan period has expired.*
   (c) *In the case of items by way of permanent loan, a request in writing to return an item or items lent to the said Collection has been received by the Trustees to the owner thereof.*

The original (1975) Declaration of Trust document achieved its aims in giving the Dromkeen Collection an identity separate from that of Oldmeadow Booksellers, in providing a permanent home for the growing Collection, and in giving credence to the

Australian author Colin Thiele who delivered the second Courtney Oldmeadow Memorial Lecture in 1983.

Joan Zahnleiter, who delivered the third Courtney Oldmeadow Memorial Lecture in 1984.

Collection's unique underlying philosophy, that of *open access* to the public.

In 1979, two years after the death of Court Oldmeadow; Joyce Oldmeadow sold Oldmeadow Booksellers to Ashton Scholastic Proprietary Limited. She was then able to concentrate on furthering all aspects of the Dromkeen Collection.

Inevitably, the pressures and the expense of running and maintaining the growing Collection became impossible for Joyce Oldmeadow to meet. The costs of the displays, the preservation of artwork and the insurance were borne then by Ashton Scholastic, as previously they had been borne by Oldmeadow Booksellers.

In the meantime, the Dromkeen Collection had increased appreciably in size, in value and, especially, in esteem, both in Australia and internationally. In order to ensure the continuance of the Dromkeen Collection, Joyce Oldmeadow made a bequest of her *personal* collection of children's literature (which was an essential component of the Collection) to Ashton Scholastic, on the understanding that they would set up a new foundation, to be named the Courtney Oldmeadow Children's Literature Foundation, and that they would continue to maintain the Foundation, the Collection and the educational activities associated with Dromkeen. All other manuscripts, artwork, books and other pre-publication materials were to pass into the care of the Foundation.

The 'Declaration of Trust' for the Courtney Oldmeadow Children's Literature Foundation was signed on 26 February, 1982, and registered in Victoria under the Hospitals and Charities Act. The 1982 Trust document incorporates all the senti-

ments and guidelines expressed in the initial Trust document of 1975.

In 1982, a Board of Governors was appointed to administer the Courtney Oldmeadow Children's Literature Foundation.

Those on the Board were: Joyce Oldmeadow; her son, John Oldmeadow; Ken Jolly of Ashton Scholastic; and Michael Sinclair, Chairperson.

Honorary Governors, whose special expertise was seen as being of particular advantage to the Foundation, were also appointed. The first Honorary Governors were: historian Professor Geoffrey Blainey, Barry Sheen (Library Branch of the Victorian Education Department) and illustrator Robert Ingpen.

Ashton Scholastic continue to carry out the terms of the Trust, to maintain and further the Dromkeen Collection and all its associated activities.

The Friends of Dromkeen

In the mid-1970s, when the Dromkeen Collection started to

expand, there were many discussions between Joyce and Court Oldmeadow and their friends concerning the future of the Collection and of practical ways in which interested people could help in its preservation and continuance. However, it was not until 1981 that a working paper was prepared concerning the structure of a proposed auxilliary organisation to the Dromkeen Foundation: the 'Friends of Dromkeen'. An inaugural dinner was planned for September 1981, and a guest-list of possible interested persons drawn up.

As a result of this dinner, an inaugural committee of the Friends of Dromkeen was formed; the members of the committee were: John Ward, chairperson; June Huggins, secretary; Darren Ryan, treasurer; and Albert Ullin, Dinny Cullican and Myra Lee. Ex-officio members of the committee were: Joyce Oldmeadow, John Oldmeadow, Ken Jolly and other Governors of the Foundation.

It is through the Friends of Dromkeen that individuals and organisations are able to participate in the on-going activities at Dromkeen homestead. The purposes of the Friends of Dromkeen are as follows:

> *to promote Australian children's literature;*
> *to heighten interest and arouse public awareness of the Dromkeen Foundation;*
> *to initiate support for Dromkeen programmes;*
> *to 'staff' activities at Dromkeen; and*
> *to raise funds for Dromkeen.*

Since the formation of the Friends, a range of activities in which members can participate has developed around the Dromkeen Collection. The main official function is the Annual General Meeting, which is held each February and at which the Drom-

keen Medal is awarded and the Courtney Oldmeadow Memorial Lecture is delivered by a guest-speaker.

The Courtney Oldmeadow Memorial Lecture was initiated by the Friends of Dromkeen. The main criterion is that the subject-matter involves some aspect of children's literature. The inaugural Memorial Lecture, 'On the Side of the Angels', was delivered by Maurice Saxby in 1982.

Many activities which members and the general public can attend are organised throughout the year by the Friends. Dromkeen Open Day is held during Children's Book Week each July, and those who come to view the Collection can meet authors and illustrators of children's books. On other occasions, there may be an exhibition of artwork for a new children's book, a sale of original artwork, a new title may be launched or a workshop conducted where illustrators discuss and demonstrate their craft. These are only a few examples of the activities organised by the Friends of Dromkeen.

Several times a year, the Friends of Dromkeen circulate a Newsletter, which keeps members informed of various events that have taken place recently and activities that have been planned for the following months.

The Dromkeen Medal

The Dromkeen Medal is an annual award, and was initiated by the Governors of the Courtney Oldmeadow Children's Literature Foundation in 1982. The presentation is made in the month of February to commemorate the late Court Oldmeadow's birthday, and takes place during the Annual General Meeting of the Friends of Dromkeen. The recipient must be an Australian citizen who has made a significant contribution to the appreciation and development of children's literature and is chosen each year by a panel of judges. The Dromkeen Medal was designed by Robert Ingpen.

The panel first met on 24 November 1982, and agreed unanimously to recommend to the Governors that the first Dromkeen Medal be awarded to Lu Rees, a prominent figure in the world of children's literature. Sadly, Lu Rees died several weeks before the presentation of the Medal and the award was accepted on her behalf by her son, John Rees, in February 1983.

Lu Rees, daughter of James and Jeanette Waugh, married Wilfred Rees in 1925. She was appointed manager of the Canberra branch of the booksellers and publishers, F. W. Cheshire in 1955, a position she held until her retirement in 1968. Lu Rees became the first president of the Canberra branch of the Children's Book Council in 1957, and later wrote its history, *The Children's Book Council of Canberra*. In 1964, Lu Rees was awarded the M.B.E. for her services to literature. The 'Lu Rees Archives Collection' at the Canberra College of Advanced

Education is named in her honour, because she was responsible for much of the College's children's book and manuscript collection.

Prior to the presentation of the first Dromkeen Medal to Lu Rees at the Annual General Meeting of the Friends of Dromkeen in February 1983, Joyce Oldmeadow read the following citation:

Mrs Rees has worked vigorously and with great dedication and determination to promote an appreciation of children's literature and the provision of good books for children for over thirty years.

During the 1950s, Lu Rees began to voice concern over the lack of children's libraries in Canberra and the general apathy towards quality in children's books. She also felt the need to promote worthwhile Australian books. So she was instrumental in establishing the Children's Book Council in the A.C.T. in 1957 and has been an office-bearer or committee member ever since. At that time, she initiated and organised weekly reviews of children's books in the Canberra Times. When the C.B.C. became a national body, Mrs Rees cam-

paigned for financial aid from the Literature Board and the Visual Arts Board of the Australia Council. It was largely through her personal representations that such grants were forthcoming.

At the same time, Lu Rees was working in a number of related areas:

(a) She instituted and organised seminars on writing and illustrating for children. These weekend seminars have now become part of Canberra's image, and on many occasions Lu Rees has been the gracious and generous hostess to visiting speakers and participants from around Australia and overseas.

(b) She inaugurated a Christmas Book Gift for needy children to whom 'a book with a personal greeting would mean something'.

(c) She began to compile archival files on Australian authors and illustrators. Whilst engaged on this task, she made personal contact with many writers, artists, critics, teachers, librarians and interested parents. Her generosity in sharing her personal knowledge and her resources has become legend. But a legend which is factual, for in 1979 she was instrumental in gaining a grant of $1000 from the International Year of the Child funds to buy Ivan Southall's personal collection of Australian children's works and biographical records for the Canberra C.A.E. for study and research purposes. That College now publishes the Lu Rees Archives: Notes, Books and Authors and distributes each issue to interested people.

Perhaps overriding all these activities is the dynamic force of this lady's personality, her large and generous spirit, the wide-ranging nature of her contribution. For Lu Rees is a well-known name internationally and is associated always with enthusiasm and integrity. Always her name excites admiration and a warm response. She could well be thought of as the godmother who brought an appreciation of children's literature to Canberra, an appreciation which she has helped spread across Australia and which has linked Australia to the rest of the world.

The recipient of the Dromkeen Medal for 1983 was Maurice Saxby. His contributions to children's literature in Australia and overseas are apparent in the citation read by Joyce Oldmeadow at the presentation of the Medal:

In years to come, when writers reflect on the history of Australian children's literature during its rapid expansion from 1950 into the 1980s, they will necessarily give detailed attention to the work of Maurice Saxby.

His has been a seminal influence. As an historian himself, he has given us a sense of continuity with earlier Australians who were similarly concerned with the quality of the culture in which their children were growing. His analysis of the achievements and deficiencies of earlier Australian children's literature was pioneering and built a perspective which continues to influence contemporary practice.

As a teacher, Maurice Saxby has, through his uncompromising excellence in scholarship, been influential in establishing the legitimacy of children's literature as an academic field in Australia. He has tactfully overcome prejudice in designing new courses in children's literature for the colleges in which he has taught and readily given assistance, as consultant and referee, to the development of courses in other institutions. The high standards he has always set for himself have been productively set for others through his role as a judge for the Children's Book Council of Australia awards and as an examiner of Library Association papers and postgraduate theses.

Australian teachers and librarians for many years have

indicated their debt to his teaching. His encyclopaedic knowledge of text, his critical sensitivity, his personal warmth and his evocative readings have worked to inspire enthusiasm and sustained, innovative work by others in this field.

In promoting children's literature in newspapers, on radio and in public lectures, Maurice Saxby has drawn the attention of the general community to the achievements of Australian authors and illustrators, and at the same time, become a trusted voice for parents in encouraging their children's reading.

From the time he was a schoolteacher, when he established one of the early primary-school libraries in New South Wales to his current role as an international judge of children's literature, Maurice Saxby has worked single-mindedly for children's enjoyment of story. That children's literature is now more highly respected and widely taught in Australia than at any other time is part of his personal achievement.

In 1984, Patricia Wrightson became the first author to receive the Dromkeen Medal. The citation read by Joyce Oldmeadow follows:

The third annual Dromkeen Medal, awarded for significant contribution to the appreciation and development of children's literature in Australia, honours and is honoured by Patricia Wrightson's thirty-year dedication to the field.

Since 1955, when her first novel appeared, young readers have shared a number of her concerns. Amongst these are first, a tolerance and understanding of others' points of view, those less gifted mentally, those older in years, those outside the known world; second, the awesome majesty and mystery of the old south land; and third, the complex nature of reality. These personal concerns mark for their author different directions and tentative explorations, but equally they speak to a wider population of universal concerns.

Amplifying these universal concerns is a master storyteller's art, which ensures the attention of her audience. Here abound characters with youthful perspective and familiar dialogue, story with astute pacing and emotional satisfaction, incidents of gentle humour and themes of piercing irony, language of simple directness for the naive reader and language of poetic imagery for the sophisticated reader.

Not surprisingly, her works receive wide critical acclaim. Nine of her thirteen novels have been honoured in the Children's Book Council of Australia Book of the Year Awards, four of these novels chosen as the prestigious Book of the Year. Recognition comes from afar as well. Her books have been honoured as notable by the American Library Association, featured as fanfare by the venerable Horn Book Magazine, commended in the Book World Children's Spring Book Festival and most recently in 1984, presented the Boston Globe-Horn Book Award for Fiction. In England, her work received a Guardian honour award, while on the international scene, two of her novels joined the esteemed company of the Hans Christian Andersen honour books. These numerous honours recognise the enduring quality of Patricia Wrightson's novels and their translation into seven foreign languages ensures such quality is available to a world-wide audience.

It is not only awards and translations which extend Patricia Wrightson's audience world-wide. The author herself eloquently articulates the inspiration and development of her own art. Her speeches invariably draw a respectful hush, then a resounding appreciation from the audience. Likewise, her written deliberations, particularly those exploring fantasy, offer the reader new insights and increased sensitivity.

What lies behind the invariable deep response to her novels and her spoken and written contemplations? Those experiencing the art of Patricia Wrightson sense her sincerity and thus understand her convictions and endorse her concerns, which convince not by overt didacticism but by their compelling clear vision.

Yet Patricia Wrightson's contribution to Australian children's literature extends even further. For eleven years, from 1964 to 1975, she worked as assistant editor and ultimately editor of the New South Wales Department of Education's School Magazine, reaching an audience of some five hundred thousand young people. In this capacity, she raised the artistic and literary standards of countless young people who received her enticing smorgasbord of new and established creators of story. Many a contributor to the School Magazine can attest to her generous encouragement of their creative efforts. Her two edited anthologies of stories and poems reflect again her desire to offer the best to children and encouragement to other creative artists. For all these efforts over the years, Patricia Wrightson was awarded the O.B.E. in 1978 for services to literature, an honour well deserved.

It is fitting that the Dromkeen Medal now joins the many honours for this author. Yet Patricia Wrightson's ability to touch the intellect and the heart will ensure a continuing stream of honours awarded by her many readers and followers.

Chapter 6
Current and Future Developments

The Dromkeen Collection has experienced tremendous growth since its inception in 1974, and ideas concerning its function in the world of children's literature have matured. This growth and development have resulted in many changes in the administration and organisation of the Collection, as well as to Dromkeen homestead itself.

The total concept of the Courtney Oldmeadow Children's Literature Foundation embraces not only a priceless collection of manuscripts, artwork and books, but also a wide range of educational activities in which children play an active role. It is this unique concept, translated into reality at Dromkeen homestead, that has won such overwhelming acclaim from those connected with children's literature both in Australia and overseas.

Today, the Foundation enjoys the support of many people, in particular the authors, illustrators and publishers of children's books who have placed on loan or donated the host of invaluable pre-publication materials that form the Collection. Initially, the Dromkeen Collection and Dromkeen homestead were financed solely by Joyce and Court Oldmeadow; today, the Foundation is fully supported by the publishing company Ashton Scholastic, which bears the main costs associated with the upkeep of the Collection and the homestead.

Recently, several important developments have taken place at Dromkeen. A complete register of every item in the Collection has been compiled, ready to be entered on computer. Apart from the obvious need for such a register, the aim was to have a computer printout listing materials in the Collection so that any item would then be readily available to persons engaged in research.

Methods of preserving materials in the Collection and of storing them at the homestead also have been up-dated. Assistance for this important task came from the Victorian Ministry

of the Arts, which provided a qualified person to undertake the work. Artwork and other materials are now kept in acid-free covers, which ensures their preservation, and the place of storage of each item has been catalogued in detail.

Both the compilation of the Dromkeen Register and the detailed cataloguing of the Dromkeen Collection have facilitated the pinpointing of items in the Collection for persons wishing to view them.

Further Plans For Dromkeen

How does Joyce Oldmeadow foresee the future development of the Dromkeen Collection? Has she formed any further plans for the Collection? Does she have any dreams concerning this 'living collection' of children's literature that are as yet unrealised? Indeed she has.

Joyce Oldmeadow visualises Dromkeen as a centre for children's literature, where authors and illustrators can stay in residence for days or even weeks, working at their particular creative pursuits, exchanging ideas with one another and with groups of visiting children and adults. She feels that small cottages situated here and there in the gardens surrounding the homestead would provide ideal accommodation, and she suggests that it might be possible for the cottages to be supported financially by grants from individuals, from businesses and from government.

The cherished dream of creating a 'living collection' of childrens literature, long nurtured by Joyce and Court Oldmeadow, became a reality only a few years after the first pieces of original artwork for children's books were displayed at Dromkeen homestead. Will Dromkeen see yet another dream realised — one that could involve children even more closely in the creative work of writers and illustrators? Only time will tell.

Bibliography of Children's Books in the Text

Allen, Pamela
Who Sank the Boat?
Nelson, Melbourne, 1982

Allen, Pamela
Bertie and the Bear
Nelson, Melbourne, 1983

Anon. (attrib. Tandy, Sophia)
The Children in the Scrub:
A Story of Tasmania
Religious Tract Society, London,
n.d. [1878]

Anon.
The Life of Captain James Cook
C. F. Cock, London, 1835

Baker, Jeannie
Grandmother
Deutsch, London, 1979

Baker, Jeannie
Home in the Sky
Julia MacRae Books, London,
1984

Balderson, Margaret
(Ambrus, Victor C.)
When Jays Fly to Barbmo
Oxford University Press, London,
1968

Bancks, James C.
The 'Sunbeams' Book:
Adventures of Ginger Meggs
Sun Newspapers, Sydney, 1924

[Barton, Charlotte]
A Mother's Offering to Her
Children: By a Lady Long Resident
in New South Wales
Gazette Office, Sydney, 1841
Jacaranda Press, Brisbane, 1979

Boardman, Alan
(Harvey, Roland)
The First Fleet
Five Mile Press, Melbourne, 1982

Bowes, Joseph
Comrades: A Story of the
Australian Bush
Henry Frowde/Hodder &
Stoughton, London, 1912

Bowes, Joseph
The Young Anzacs
Oxford University Press, London,
1917

Bowman, Anne
The Kangaroo Hunters
Routledge, London, 1860

Boyland, Eustace
The Heart of the School:
An Australian School Story
Roy Stevens, Knox Place, Vic.,
n.d. [1919]

Brinsmead, Hesba F.
(Macarthur-Onslow, Annette)
Pastures of the Blue Crane
Oxford University Press, London,
1964

Brinsmead, Hesba F.
Longtime Passing
Angus & Robertson, Sydney,
1971

Brinsmead, Hesba F.
(Young, Noela)
Once There was a Swagman
Oxford University Press,
Melbourne, 1979

Brooks, Ron
Annie's Rainbow
William Collins, Sydney, 1975

Bruce, Mary Grant
A Little Bush Maid
Ward, Lock, London, 1910

Bruce, Mary Grant
Mates at Billabong
Ward, Lock, London, 1911

Bruce, Mary Grant
Dick
Ward, Lock, London, 1918

Bruce, Mary Grant
Billabong Riders
Ward, Lock, London, 1942

Carter, Angela
(Todd, Justin)
Moonshadow
Gollancz, London, 1982

Chapman, Jean
(Lacis, Astra)
Moon-Eyes
Hodder & Stoughton, London,
1978

Chauncy, Nan
(Horder, Margaret)
They Found a Cave
Oxford University Press, London,
1948

Chauncy, Nan
(Horder, Margaret)
A Fortune for the Brave
Oxford University Press,
Melbourne, 1954

Chauncy, Nan
(Horder, Margaret)
Tiger in the Bush
Oxford University Press, London,
1957

Chauncy, Nan
(Spence, Geraldine)
Devil's Hill
Oxford University Press, London,
1958

Chauncy, Nan
(Wildsmith, Brian)
Tangara
Oxford University Press, London,
1960

Clark, Mavis Thorpe
(Hudson, Harry)
The Brown Land was Green
Heinemann, London, 1956

Clark, Mavis Thorpe
(Melrose, Genevieve)
The Min-Min
Lansdowne Press, Melbourne,
1966

Clark, Mavis Thorpe
(Rowe, Jean H.)
Pony from Tarella
Lansdowne, Melbourne, 1969

Cole E. W.
Cole's Funny Picture Book
Cole, Melbourne, n.d. [1879]

Cole E. W.
Cole's Funny Picture Book No. 2
Cole, Melbourne, n.d. [1918]

Cole E. W.
Cole's Funny Picture Book No. 3
(ed. Cole Turnley)
E. W. Cole Publishing House,
Melbourne, 1951

Crabtree, Judith
Legs
Kestrel Books, Harmondsworth,
1979

Crabtree, Judith
The Sparrow's Story at the King's
Command
Oxford University Press,
Melbourne, 1983

Crane, Walter
The Baby's Opera
Routledge, London, 1877

Daskein, Tarella Quin
(Rentoul, Ida S.)
Gum-Tree Brownie and other
Faerie Folk of the Never Never
George Robertson, Melbourne,
n.d. [1907]

Daskein, Tarella Quin
(Outhwaite, Ida Rentoul)
Before the Lamps Are Lit
George Robertson, Melbourne,
n.d. [1911]

Davison, Frank Dalby
Man-Shy
Angus & Robertson, Sydney,
1932

Donkin, Nance
Margaret Catchpole
Williams Collins, Sydney, 1974

Dugan, Michael
(Stackpool, Walter)
Nonsense Places: An Absurd
Australian Alphabet
William Collins, Sydney, 1976

Durack, Mary
(Durack, Elizabeth)
The Way of the Whirlwind
Consolidated Press, Sydney, 1941

Dutton, Geoffrey
(Perceval, John)
On My Island
Cheshire, Melbourne, 1967

Dyson, Edward
The Gold-Stealers
Longmans, Green, London, 1901

Eden, Charles Henry
The Fortunes of the Fletchers:
A Story of Life in Canada and
Australia
Pott, Young & Co., New York,
n.d. [?1873]

Ewing, Juliana Horatia
(Caldecott, Randolph)
Jackanapes
Society for Promoting Christian
Knowledge, London, n.d. [1879]

Farjeon, Eleanor
(Ardizzone, Edward)
The Little Bookroom
Oxford University Press, London,
1955

Fatchen, Max
The River Kings
Hicks Smith, Sydney, 1970

Fishers' Juvenile Scrap-Book
Fisher, Son & Co., London, 1844

Fitzgerald, Mary Anne
King Bungaree's Pyalla
Edwards, Dunlop & Co., Sydney,
1891

Flack, Marjorie
(Wiese, Kurt)
The Story About Ping
Viking Press, New York, 1933

Foreman, Michael
War and Peas
Hamish Hamilton, London, 1974

Foreman, Michael
Panda and the Bunyips
Nelson, Melbourne, 1984

Fox, Mem
(Vivas, Julie)
Possum Magic
Omnibus Books, Adelaide, 1983

Gaze, Harold
The Merry Piper
Longmans, Green & Co., London,
1925

Generowicz, Witold
The Train
Kestrel Books, Harmondsworth,
1982

George, Jean Craighead
(Shimin, Symeon)
The Wentletrap Trap
Dutton, New York, 1978

Gibbs, May
Gum Nut Babies
Angus & Robertson, Sydney, n.d.
[1916]

Gibbs, May
Gum Blossom Babies
Angus & Robertson, Sydney, n.d.
[1916]

Gibbs, May
Boronia Babies
Angus & Robertson, Sydney, n.d.
[1917]

Gibbs, May
Flannel Flowers and other Bush Babies
Angus & Robertson, Sydney, n.d.
[1917]

Gibbs, May
*Snugglepot and Cuddlepie:
Their Adventures Wonderful*
Angus & Robertson, Sydney, n.d.
[1918]

Gibbs, May
Wattle Babies
Angus & Robertson, Sydney, n.d.
[1918]

Gibbs, May
Little Ragged Blossom
Angus & Robertson, Sydney, n.d.
[1920]

Gibbs, May
Little Obelia
Angus & Robertson, Sydney, n.d.
[1921]

Gibbs, May
*Bib and Bub:
Their Adventures*
Cornstalk Publishing Company,
Sydney, 1925

Gibbs, May
*The Complete Adventures of
Snugglepot and Cuddlepie*
Angus & Robertson, Sydney,
1940

Gibbs, May
Scotty in Gumnut Land
Angus & Robertson, Sydney,
1941

Gibson, Helen
(Herbert, Galina)
An Australian Christmas
Lothian, Melbourne, 1961

Gibson, Helen
(Herbert, Galina)
Buster the Fire Truck
Lothian, Melbourne, 1962

Giles, Barbara
(Greenhatch, Betty)
Jack in the Bush
Penguin, Ringwood, Vic., 1983

Glusac, R., et al.
(Rawlins, Donna)
Time for a Number Rhyme
Nelson, Melbourne, 1983

Goodrich, Samuel Grimswold
see 'Parley, Peter'

Greenwood, Ted
Obstreperous
Angus & Robertson, Sydney,
1970

Greenwood, Ted
*V.I.P.
(Very Important Plant)*
Angus & Robertson, Sydney,
1971

Gunn, Jeannie
*The Little Black Princess:
A True Tale of Life in the
Never-Neverland*
Alexander Moring, London, 1905
Melville & Mullen, Melbourne,
1905

Hackett, Elsie M.
Billy Caterpillar
Georgian House, Melbourne, 1945

Hall, J. J.
(Wall, Dorothy)
*The Crystal Bowl:
Australian Nature Stories*
Whitcombe & Tombs,
Melbourne, n.d. [1921]

Hodgetts, J. F.
*Tom's Nuggett: A Story of the
Australian Gold Fields*
Sunday School Union, London,
n.d. [1888]

Howitt, William
*A Boy's Adventures in the Wilds
of Australia; or, Herbert's
Note-Book*
Arthur Hall, London, 1854

The Infant's Magazine
vol. XII, 1877
Seeley, Jackson & Halliday,
London

Ingpen, Robert
The Voyage of the Poppykettle
Rigby, Adelaide, 1980

Kennedy, E. B.
*Blacks and Bushrangers:
Adventures in Queensland*
Sampson, Low, London, 1889

Kerr, Judith
The Tiger Who Came to Tea
William Collins, London, 1968

Kingston, William H. G.
*The Gilpins and Their Fortunes:
An Australian Tale*
Society for Promoting Christian
Knowledge, London, n.d. [1865]

Kingston, William H. G.
Australian Adventures
George Routledge, London, n.d.
[1884]

Klein, Robin
(Tomblin, Gill)
The Giraffe in Pepperell Street
Hodder & Stoughton, Sydney,
1978

Klein, Robin
(Lester, Alison)
Thing
Oxford University Press,
Melbourne, 1982

Klein, Robin
(Lester, Alison)
Thingnapped!
Oxford University Press,
Melbourne, 1984

Lear, Edward
(Oxenbury, Helen)
The Quangle Wangle's Hat
Heinemann, London, 1969

Lindsay, Norman
The Magic Pudding
Angus & Robertson, Sydney,
1918

Lister, Gladys
(Abbott, Joyce)
Grandpuff and Leafy
Marchant, Sydney, 1942

Liston, Maud Renner
(O'Harris, Pixie)
*Cinderella's Party:
A Fairy Story*
Rigby, Adelaide, n.d. [1923]

Low, Joseph
The Christmas Grump
Atheneum, New York, 1977

Macarthur-Onslow, Annette
Uhu
Ure Smith, Sydney, 1969
Rapp & Whiting, London, 1969

McFadyen, Ella
(Bell, Edwina)
Pegmen Tales
Angus & Robertson, Sydney,
1946

MacIntyre, Elisabeth
*Ambrose Kangaroo:
A Story That Never Ends*
Consolidated Press, Sydney, n.d.
[1941]
Scribners, New York, 1942

MacIntyre, Elisabeth
The Black Lamb
Dawfox Productions, Sydney, n.d.
[1944]

MacIntyre, Elisabeth
Susan Who Lives in Australia
Scribners, New York, 1944

MacIntyre, Elisabeth
Katherine
Australasian Publishing Co.,
Sydney, 1946

MacIntyre, Elisabeth
Hugh's Zoo
Angus & Robertson, Sydney,
1964

MacIntyre, Elisabeth
*Ambrose Kangaroo Delivers the
Goods*
Angus & Robertson, Sydney,
1978

Mack, Louise
(Mahony, Frank P.)
*Teens: A Story of Australian
Schoolgirls*
Angus & Robertson, Sydney,
1897
(illus. Karna Birmingham)
Cornstalk Publishing Co., Sydney,
1925

Mack, Louise
(Lambert, George W.)
Girls Together
Angus & Robertson, Sydney,
1898

Maltby, Peg
Peg's Fairy Book
Murfett, Melbourne, n.d. [1944]

Maltby, Peg
Ben and Bella and The Apple Tree
Murfett, Melbourne, 1949

Mason, Cyrus
The Australian Christmas Story
George Robertson, Melbourne,
1871
Book

Mason, Olive L.
(Cunningham, Walter)
Quippy
John Sands, Sydney, n.d. [1946]

Mattingley, Christobel
(Mullins, Patricia)
Rummage
Angus & Robertson, Sydney,
1981

Mattingley, Christobel
(Honey, Elizabeth)
Brave with Ben
Nelson, Melbourne, 1982

Mattingley, Christobel
(Lacis, Astra)
The Angel With a Mouth-Organ
Hodder & Stoughton, Sydney,
1984

Mayne, William
(Honey, Elizabeth)
Salt River Times
Nelson, Melbourne, 1980

Mellor, Kathleen
Gee Up Bonny
(Made for the children at the Lady
Gowrie Child Centre, Adelaide)
Georgian House, Melbourne, n.d.
[1945]

Meredith, Louisa Anne
*Loved, and Lost!
The True Story of a Short Life
Told in Gossip Verse, and
Illustrated*
George Robertson, Melbourne &
Sydney/W. C. Rigby,
Adelaide/Walch & Sons, Hobart
& Launceston, n.d. [1860]

My New Book
Religious Tract Society, London,
n.d. [1877]

Nicholls, Brooke
(Wall, Dorothy)
Jacko, the Broadcasting Kookaburra
Angus & Robertson, Sydney, 1933

Nicholls, Brooke
(Wall, Dorothy)
Adventures of Billy Penguin
Angus & Robertson, Sydney, 1934

O'Harris, Pixie
The Fairy Who Wouldn't Fly
Marchant, Syndey, n.d. [1947]

Outhwaite, Arthur Grenbry
see Rentoul, Annie Rattray and Outhwaite, Arthur Grenbry (ed.)

Paice, Margaret
Mirram
Angus & Robertson, Sydney, 1955

Paice, Margaret
Namitja
Angus & Robertson, Sydney, 1956

Paice, Margaret
(Stackpool, Walter)
Colour in the Creek
William Collins, Sydney, 1976

Park, Ruth,
(Young, Noela)
The Muddle-headed Wombat
Educational Press, Sydney, 1962

Park, Ruth
Playing Beatie Bow
Nelson, Melbourne, 1980

Parker, K[ate] Langloh
Australian Legendary Tales
Melville, Mullen & Slade, Melbourne, 1896

Parker, K[ate] Langloh
More Australian Legendary Tales
Melville, Mullen & Slade, Melbourne, 1898

'Parley, Peter' (Samuel Grimswold Goodrich)
Tales About America and Australia
Darton & Clark, London, n.d. [1840]

Paterson, A. B.
(Stackpool, Walter)
Banjo Paterson's Horses
(Young Australia Series)
Angus & Robertson, Sydney, 1970

Paterson, A. B.
(Niland, Kilmeny and Niland, Deborah)
Mulga Bill's Bicycle
William Collins, Sydney, 1973

Paterson, A. B.
(Hole, Quentin)
The Man From Ironbark
William Collins, Sydney, 1974

Patz, Nancy
Pumpernickel, Tickle and Mean Green Cheese
Franklin Watts, New York, 1978

Patz, Nancy
Nobody Knows I Have Delicate Toes
Franklin Watts, New York, 1980

Pavey, Peter
One Dragon's Dream
Nelson, Melbourne, 1979

Pavey, Peter
I'm Taggerty Toad
Nelson, Melbourne, 1980

Pedley, Ethel C.
(Mahony, Frank)
Dot and the Kangaroo
Thomas Burleigh, London, 1899
Angus & Robertson, Sydney, 1906

Pender, Lydia
(O'Harris, Pixie)
Marbles in My Pocket
Writers' Press, Sydney, n.d. [1958]

Pender, Lydia
(Cowell, Judy)
Barnaby and the Rocket
William Collins, Sydney, 1972

Phipson, Joan
(Horder, Margaret)
Christmas in the Sun
Angus & Robertson, Sydney, 1951

Phipson, Joan
(Horder, Margaret)
Good Luck to the Rider
Angus & Robertson, Sydney, 1953

Phipson, Joan
(Horder, Margaret)
The Family Conspiracy
Angus & Robertson, Sydney, 1962

Phipson, Joan
(Horder, Margaret)
Birkin
Lothian, Melbourne, 1965

Phipson, Joan
(Stackpool, Walter)
Bennelong
William Collins, Sydney, 1975

Piers, Helen
(Baynes, Pauline)
Grasshopper and Butterfly
McGraw Hill, 1975

Potter, Beatrix
The Tale of Peter Rabbit
Frederick Warne, London, 1902

Pownall, Eve
(Senior, Margaret)
The Australia Book
John Sands, Sydney, n.d. [1952]

Pownall, Eve
(Senior, Margaret)
Cousins-come-Lately: Adventures in Old Sydney Town
Shakespeare Head Press, Sydney, 1952

Pownall, Eve
(Johnson, Raymond)
Squik the Squirrel Possum
John Sands, Sydney, 1955

'Quin, Tarella'
see Daskein, Tarella Quin

Rankine, David
(Hook, Geoffrey)
Kangapossum & Crocoroo
Heinemann, Melbourne, 1969

Rees, Leslie
(Cunningham, Walter)
Digit Dick on the Barrier Reef
John Sands, Sydney, 1942

Rees, Leslie
(Cunningham, Walter)
The Story of Shy the Platypus
John Sands, Sydney, 1944

Rees, Leslie
(Cunningham, Walter)
Gecko/The Lizard Who Lost His Tail
John Sands, Sydney, 1944

Rees, Leslie
(Cunningham, Walter)
The Story of Karrawingi the Emu
John Sands, Sydney, n.d. [1946]

Rees, Leslie
(Cunningham, Walter)
Digit Dick and the Tasmanian Devil
John Sands, Sydney, n.d. [1946]

Rees, Leslie
(Cunningham, Walter)
Digit Dick and the Lost Opals
John Sands, Sydney, 1957

Rentoul, Annie Isobel
(Rentoul, Ida Sherbourne)
Mollie's Staircase
Hutchinson, Melbourne, n.d. [1906]

Rentoul, Annie Rattray
(Rentoul, Ida Sherbourne)
Mollie's Bunyip
The Atlas Press, Melbourne, 1904

Rentoul, Annie Rattray
(Rentoul, Ida Sherbourne)
Australian Songs for Young and Old
George Robertson, Melbourne, n.d. [1907]

Rentoul, Annie Rattray
(Rentoul, Ida Sherbourne)
The Story of the Pantomime Humpty Dumpty
J. C. Williamson, Sydney, n.d. [1907]

Rentoul, Annie Rattray
(Rentoul, Ida Sherbourne)
The Lady of the Blue Beads
George Robertson, Melbourne, n.d. [1908]

Rentoul, Annie Rattray
(Outhwaite, Ida Rentoul)
The Little Green Road to Fairyland
A. & C. Black, London, 1922

Rentoul, Annie Rattray and Outhwaite, Arthur Grenbry (ed.)
(Outhwaite, Ida Rentoul)
Elves and Fairies
Lothian, Melbourne, 1916

Rentoul, Annie Rattray and Outhwaite, Arthur Grenbry
(Outhwaite, Ida Rentoul)
Fairyland
Ramsay Publishing, Melbourne, 1926

Roennfeldt, Robert
Tiddalick: The Frog Who Caused a Flood
Puffin Books, Harmondsworth, 1980

Roughsey, Dick
Rainbow Serpent
William Collins, Sydney, 1975

Roughsey, Dick
Giant Devil-Dingo
William Collins, Sydney, 1976

Senior, Margaret
Bush Haven Animals
John Sands, Sydney, n.d. [1954]

Shelley, Noreen
(Micklewright, Robert)
Family at the Lookout
Oxford University Press, London, 1972

Sibley, Irena
Rainbow
Gryphon Books, South Melbourne, 1980

Southall, Ivan
(Norton, Frank)
Meet Simon Black
Angus & Robertson, Sydney, 1950

Southall, Ivan
Hills End
Angus & Robertson, Sydney, 1962

Southall, Ivan
(Seale, Clem)
Ash Road
Angus & Robertson, Sydney, 1965

Southall, Ivan
(Greenwood, Ted)
Sly Old Wardrobe
Cheshire, Melbourne, 1968

Southall, Ivan
Josh
Angus & Robertson, Sydney, 1971

Spence, Eleanor
(Forbes, Alison)
Patterson's Track
Oxford University Press, Melbourne, 1958

Spence, Eleanor
(Spence, Geraldine)
The Green Laurel
Oxford University Press, London, 1963

Spence, Eleanor
(Green, Malcolm)
The October Child
Oxford University Press, London, 1976

Temple, F.
(Corrigan, M.)
Shopping in Creepyville
Georgian House, Melbourne, 1946

Thiele, Colin
The Sun on the Stubble
Rigby, Adelaide, 1961

Thiele, Colin
(Baily, John)
Storm Boy
Rigby, Adelaide, 1963

(*de luxe* edn, illus. Ingpen, Robert)
Rigby, Adelaide, 1974

Thiele, Colin
(Ingpen, Robert)
River Murray Mary
Rigby, Adelaide, 1979

Timperley, W. H.
Bush Luck: An Australian Story
Religious Tract Society, London, n.d. [1892]

Turner, Ethel S.
Seven Little Australians
Ward, Lock & Bowden, London, 1894

Turner, Ethel
The Family at Misrule
Ward, Lock & Bowden, London, 1895

Uden, Grant
(Baynes, Pauline)
A Dictionary of Chivalry
Longmans, London, 1968

Villiers, Alan J.
Whalers of the Midnight Sun
Geoffrey Bles, London, 1934
Angus & Robertson, Sydney, 1949

Wagner, Jenny
(Brooks, Ron)
The Bunyip of Berkeley's Creek
Kestrel, London, 1973
Longman Young Books/Childerset, Melbourne, 1973

Wagner, Jenny
(Brooks, Ron)
Aranea: A Story About a Spider
Puffin Books, Harmondsworth, 1975

Wagner, Jenny
(Brooks, Ron)
John Brown, Rose and the Midnight Cat
Hodder & Stoughton, Sydney, 1977
Kestrel Books, Harmondsworth, 1977

Wall, Dorothy
Tommy Bear and the Zookies
Triumph Printers, Sydney, n.d. [1920]

Wall, Dorothy
Blinky Bill: The Quaint Little Australian
Angus & Robertson, Sydney, 1933

Wall, Dorothy
Blinky Bill Grows Up
Angus & Robertson, Sydney, 1934

Wall, Dorothy
Blinky Bill and Nutsy: Two Little Australians
Angus & Robertson, Sydney, 1937

Wall, Dorothy
The Complete Adventures of Blinky Bill
Angus & Robertson, Sydney, 1939

Wall, Dorothy
Blinky Bill Dress Up Book
Offset Printing, Sydney, n.d. [1944]

Walsh, Amanda
Egrin and the Painted Wizard
Penguin Books, Ringwood, Vic., 1972

Walsh, Amanda
Egrin and the Wicked Witch
Penguin Books, Ringwood, Vic., 1978

Way, Mark
Nicholas and the Moon Eggs
William Collins, Sydney, 1977

White, Osmar
(Hook, Geoff)
Super Roo of Mungalongaloo
Penguin, Ringwood, Vic., 1979

White, Osmar
(Hook, Geoff)
The Further Adventures of Dr A. A. A. McGurk
Penguin, Ringwood, Vic., 1981

Wrightson, Patricia
(Horder, Margaret)
The Crooked Snake
Angus & Robertson, Sydney, 1955

Wrightson, Patricia
(Horder, Margaret)
The Rocks of Honey
Angus & Robertson, Sydney, 1960

Wrightson, Patricia
(Horder, Margaret)
Down to Earth
Hutchinson, Melbourne, 1965

Wrightson, Patricia
(Horder, Margaret)
I Own the Racecourse!
Hutchinson, London, 1968

Wrightson, Patricia
(Young, Noela)
An Older Kind of Magic
Hutchinson, London, 1972

Wrightson, Patricia
The Nargun and the Stars
Hutchinson, London, 1973

Wrightson, Patricia
The Ice is Coming
Hutchinson, London, 1977

Wrightson, Patricia
A Little Fear
Hutchinson, London, 1983

Yardley, Lynette *et al.*
(O'Harris, Pixie)
The Pixie O'Harris Fairy Book
Rigby, Adelaide, n.d. [1925]

Young, Noela
Flip the Flying Possum
Methuen, London, 1963

Young, Noela
Mrs Pademelon's Joey
Hicks Smith, Sydney/Methuen, London, 1967

Young, Noela
Keep Out
William Collins, Sydney, 1975

Young, Noela
Torty Longneck
William Collins, Sydney, 1977

References

Adams, J. D., 'Australian Children's Literature: A History to 1920', *Victorian Historical Magazine* (Melbourne), February 1967.

Allan, Fran, *The Role of Angus and Robertson in the Development of Australian Children's Literature*, Melbourne State College, Melbourne, 1977.

Anderson, Hugh, (ed.), *The Singing Roads: A Guide to Australian Children's Authors and Illustrators*, Wentworth Books, Sydney, 1965.

(ed.), *The Singing Roads. Part II: A Guide to Australian Children's Authors and Illustrators*, Wentworth Books, Sydney, 1969.

Australian Children's Books: A Select List, Children's Book Council of Victoria, Melbourne, 1957; 2nd edn, 1962.

Book Design Awards 1969-70, Australian Book Publishers Association, Sydney, 1970.

Book Design Awards 1970-71, Australian Book Publishers Association, Sydney, 1971.

Brinsmead, Hesba, 'Why I Write For Teenagers; or, Something to Give', a talk given to the Children's Book Council Seminar in Canberra, published in *Writing and Illustrating for Children*, Children's Book Council, Canberra, 1985.

Caban, Geoffrey, *A Fine Line: A History of Australian Commerical Art*, Hale & Iremonger, Sydney, 1983.

Carpenter, Humphrey, and Pritchard, Mari, *The Oxford Companion to Children's Literature*, Oxford University Press, London, 1984.

Chambers, Aidan, 'Letter From England: A Place of Their Own', *Horn Book Magazine* (Boston), February 1984.

Cheshire, F. W., *Bookseller Publisher Friend*, The National Press Melbourne, 1984.

Children and Their Families, catalogue of an exhibition of books and pictures arranged by the National Library of Australia for the Eleventh Conference of the Australian Pre-School Association, Canberra, National Library of Australia, Canberra, 1967.

Cianciolo, Patricia, *Illustrations in Children's Books*, William C. Brown, Iowa, 1970.

Commire, Anne, *Something About the Author*, Volume 17, Gale Research Book Tower, Detroit USA, 1979.

Dromkeen: A Home for Australian Children's Literature (information booklet), Dromkeen Children's Literature Foundation, Riddells Creek, 1977.

Dromkeen: A Home for Australian Children's Literature (information booklet), Dromkeen, Riddells Creek, 1979.

Dromkeen: A Home for Australian Children's Literature (information booklet), Dromkeen, Riddells Creek, 1982.

Dugan, Michael, 'A Centre for Children's Literature: Dromkeen Homestead,' *Reading Time* (Canberra), October 1974.

'Children's Literature Here', *Overland* (Melbourne), Winter 1973.

'Dromkeen', *Bookseller and Publisher* (Melbourne), May 1977.

(comp.), *The Early Dreaming: Australian Children's Authors on Childhood,* Jacaranda Press, Brisbane, 1980.

Early Australian Booksellers, Australian Booksellers Association, Sydney, 1980.

Eastman, Berenice, *A Biography of a Tasmanian: Nan Chauncy,* Tasmanian Historical Research Association, Hobart, December 1978.

Eyre, Frank, *British Children's Books in the Twentieth Century,* Longman, London, 1971.

Fenwick, Sara Innes, *School and Children's Libraries in Australia,* Cheshire, Melbourne, 1966.

Ferguson, George, *Some Early Australian Bookmen,* Australian National University Press, Canberra, 1978.

Fleming, William, 'Julie Vivas: The New Illustrators,' *Review*, June 1984.

Historical Records of Australia, Vol. 15, Government Printer, Sydney, 1914-1925.

Historical Records of New South Wales, Vol. 5, Government Printer, Sydney, 1987.

Holroyd, John, *George Robertson of Melbourne, 1825-1898: Pioneer Bookseller and Publisher,* Robertson & Mullens, Melbourne, 1968.

Horgan, John, (ed.), *The Golden Years of Ginger Meggs, 1921-1952,* Souvenir Press, Adelaide, 1978.

Ingham, Margaret, 'Young Australia Reads, 1800-1900', *Victorian Historical Journal* (Melbourne), May 1981.

Ingpen, Robert, 'The Promise of Imagination', notes for a talk at the launching dinner for the 'Friends of Dromkeen', *Australian Book Review* (Melbourne), November 1981.

Ingram, Anne Bower, 'The Quiet Achievers: Australian Children's Books', *Australian Book Scene,* (Melbourne), 1984-85.

Kinross, J. and Shaw, S., *Minding Your Own Business,* Cassell, Australia, Sydney, 1981.

Kirkpatrick, D. L., (ed.), *Twentieth Century Children's Writers,* Macmillan, London, 2nd edn, 1983.

Kirsop, Wallace, *Towards A History of the Australian Book Trade,* Wentworth Books, Sydney, 1969.

Klemin, Diana, *The Art of Art for Children's Books: A Contemporary Survey,* Clarkson N. Potter, New York, 1966.

Lees, Stella, (ed.), *A Track to Unknown Water: Proceedings of the Second Pacific Rim Conference on Children's Literature,* Melbourne State College, Melbourne, 1980.

Lindesay, Vane, *The Way We Were: Australian Popular Magazines, 1856-1969,* Oxford University Press, Melbourne, 1983.

Liveing, Edward, *Adventures in Publishing: The House of Ward Lock, 1854-1954,* Ward Lock, London, 1954.

Lowe, Susan J., *The Original Artwork and Manuscripts of Dromkeen,* Griffin Bibliographies, Melbourne State College, Melbourne, 1979.

McColvin, Lionel, *Public Libraries in Australia,* Melbourne University Press, Melbourne, 1947.

McVitty, Walter, 'Australian Children's Literature: Some Thoughts on Two Decades of Change', *Orana,* May 1982.

Innocence and Experience: Essays on Contemporary Australian Children's Writers, Nelson, Melbourne 1981.

Mackaness, G., *Some Letters of Rev. Richard Johnson,* Part II, D. S. Ford Printer, Sydney, 1954.

Masterman, Kay C., 'Nan Chauncy', a talk given to the Children's Book Council Seminar in Canberra, published in *Writing and Illustrating for Children,* Children's Book Council, Canberra, 1985.

Muir, Marcie, *Australian Children's Book Illustrators,* Sun Books, Melbourne, 1977.

A Bibliography of Australian Children's Books, Deutsch, London, 1970.

A Bibliography of Australian Children's Books: Volume 2, Deutsch, London, 1976.

Charlotte Barton: Australia's First Children's Author, Wentworth Books, Sydney, 1980.

A History of Australian Children's Book Illustrations, Oxford University Press, Melbourne, 1982.

Munn, Ralph, and Pitt, Ernest, *Australian Libraries,* Australian Council for Educational Research, Melbourne, 1935.

Nesdale, Ira, *The Little Missus: Mrs Aeneas Gunn,* Lynton Publications, Blackwood, SA, 1977.

Niall Brenda, *Australia Through The Looking-Glass: Children's Fiction, 1830-1980,* Melbourne University Press, Melbourne, 1984.

Seven Little Billabongs: The World of Ethel Turner and Mary Grant Bruce, Melbourne University Press, Melbourne, 1979.

O'Harris, Pixie, *Was It Yesterday?,* Rigby, Adelaide, 1983.

Oldmeadow, John, 'Crystal or Tile? The Dromkeen Collection of Australian Children's Literature', *Australian School Librarian* (Melbourne), 1980.

[Outhwaite, Ida Rentoul], 'A Creator of Fairies', *Melbourne Punch,* February 1921.

Oxford in Australia, 1890-1978, Oxford University Press, Melbourne, 1978.

Poole, Philippa, (ed.), *The Diaries of Ethel Turner,* Ure Smith, Sydney, 1979.

Pownall, Eve, (comp.), 'The Children's Book Council in Australia, 1945-1980', *Reading Time,* (Canberra), No. 4, 1980.

Rees, Leslie, *Hold Fast to Dreams: Fifty Years in Theatre, Radio, Television and Books,* Alternative Publishing Co-Operative, Sydney, 1979.

Rees, Lu, *The Children's Book Council of Canberra 1957 to 1972* a Brief account of the formation and activities of one of the six councils which now form the Children's Book Council of Australia. The Children's Book Council of Canberra, Canberra 1972.

A Brief History of the Canberra Branch of the Children's Council of Australia Part II 1972-1978, The Children's Book Council of Canberra, Canberra, 1978.

'Reflections', *Reading Time* (Canberra), No. 3, 1973.

Saxby, H. M., *A History of Australian Children's Literature, 1841-1941,* Wentworth Books, Sydney, 1969.

A History of Australian Children's Literature, 1941-1970, Wentworth Books, Sydney, 1971.

Southall, Ivan, *A Journey of Discovery: On Writing for Children,* Kestrel Books, Harmondsworth, 1975.

Stevens, Bertram, (ed.), *An Anthology of Australian Verse,* Angus & Robertson, Sydney, 1906.

Taylor, Judy, 'Joyce and Court Oldmeadow: Winners of the Eleanor Farjeon Award', *Signal* (Gloucestershire, UK), September 1976.

Turnley, Cole, *Cole of the Book Arcade: A Pictorial Biography of E. W. Cole,* Cole Publications, Hawthorn, Vic., 1974.

Walker, Maxine, *Writers Alive! Current Australian Authors of Books for Children,* Westbooks, Perth, 1977.

Wighton, Rosemary, *Early Australian Children's Literature,* Casuarina Press, Surrey Hills, Vic., 1979.

APPENDIX 1

Courtney Oldmeadow Children's Literature Foundation: Checklist of Artwork and Pre-publication Material held in the Dromkeen Collection, as at 1 January 1985.

This Checklist was compiled in 1984, by Bronwen Bennett, Junior School Librarian at Carey Baptist Grammar School, in order to record the work of the authors and illustrators represented either in the permanent Collection at Dromkeen or on loan during the writing of this book. Since that date, a detailed *Register*, compiled by the Victorian Ministry of the Arts, has been completed and as such is an extension of this Checklist.

Authors

AESOP
   see Some Fables From Aesop

ALLEN, Pamela
   see Who Sank the Boat?

ANNO, Mitsumasa
   see Anno's Britain
      Anno's Flea Market
   Anno's USA

AXELSON, Stephen
   see Oath of Bad Brown Bill, The

BAKER, Alan
   see Benjamin and the Box
      Benjamin Bounces Back

BAKER, Jeannie
   see Grandmother
      Home in the Sky

BASE, Graeme
   see My Grandma Lived at
      Gooligulch

BATES, Dianne
   see Magician, The

BAYLOR, Bird
   see Coyote Cry

BENEDICTUS, Roger
   see 50 Million Sausages

BIBBY, Violet
   see Tinner's Quest

BLAINE, Marge
   see Terrible Thing That Happened
      at Our House, The

BLAKE, Quentin
   see Mr Magnolia

BLAXELL, Gregory
(with Gordon WINCH)
   see Ant and Grasshopper
      Big Ox, The
      By Horse and Buggy
      Clara Comes to Life
      Dancing Buildings
      Flea, The
      Frog, The
      Frog and the Ox, The
      Grandad
      In the Garden
      Is It Real?
      Off the Beaten Track
      Our First Town
      Pumpkin Paddy
      Read All About It
      Red Five, The
      Snails, Spiders and Things
      Tell Me Your Story
      Town Mouse and Country
      Mouse

      Trojan Horse, The
      Who's Granny Smith?
      Wind, The

BLYTH (BLIGHT), Delma
   see Peter Pebble

BOARDMAN, Alan
   see Eureka Stockade
      First Fleet, The

BOLTON, Barbara
   see Jandy Malone and the Nine
      O'Clock Tiger

BOND, Michael
      Paddington Cleans Up

BREEN, Barry
   see Benambra Ben

BRIERLEY, Ronald Oliver
   see If You Catch an Elephant

BRINSMEAD, Hesba
   see Once there was a Swagman

BROOKS, Ron
   see Annie's Rainbow

BURNINGHAM, John
   see Come Away From the Water,
      Shirley
      Time to Get Out of the Bath,
      Shirley

BYARS, Betsy
   see Lace Snail, The

CARTER, Angela
   see Moonshadow

CHAPMAN, Jean
   see Moon-Eyes

CHARLWOOD, Don
   see All the Green Year

CHAUCER, Geoffrey
   see Chanticleer

CHILDREN'S BOOK COUNCIL
OF AUSTRALIA
(Victorian Branch)
   see Books For Children

CLARK, Mavis Thorpe
   see Pony From Tarella
      Spark of Opal
      Wildfire

CLOUDSLEY-THOMPSON, J. L.
   see Animals of the Desert
      Spiders and Scorpions

CLUNE, Frank
   see Ned Kelly

CONGER, Lesley
   see Three Giant Stories

CONLEY, Enid
   see Gecko Gully
      Lucas and the Kitemen

COX, David
   see Tin Lizzie and Little Nell

CRABTREE, Judith
   see Legs
      Sparrow's Story at the King's
      Command, The

CURTIS, Nancy
   see Little Chimbu

DAUDET, Alphonse
   see Pope's Mule, The

DAVIDSON, Rodney
   see Beechworth Sketchbook

DE FOSSARD, Esta
   see Puffing Billy

DIESTEL-FEDDERSEN, Mary
   see Tari's First Christmas

DODD, Lynley
   see Apple Tree, The
      Hairy Maclary From
      Donaldson's Diary
      Smallest Turtle, The

DOMANSKA, Janina
   see King Krakus and the Dragon

DONKIN, Nance
   see Friend For Petros, A
      Johnny Tremain
      Margaret Catchpole

DOWNING, Brownie
   see Tinka and the Bunyip

DRUMMOND, V. H.
   see Miss Anna Truly's Christmas
      Present

DUGAN, Michael
   see Dingo Boy
      Dragon's Breath
      Grumble of Glot, The
      My Old Dad
      Nonsense Numbers
      Nonsense Places
      Puffin Fun Book, The (ed.)
      Spooks and Spirits (with
      Margaret HAMILTON)
      Stuff and Nonsense
      Weekend

DUTTON, Geoffrey
   see On My Island

EDWARDS, Hazel
   see There's a Hippopotamus on
      Our Roof Eating Cake

EDWARDS, Pat
   see Classroom Teacher's Diary
      1983, The
      Classroom Teacher's Diary
      1984, The (with
      Regina SILBECK)
      Cockatoos and Galahs (with
      Ken LITTLE)

FANSHAWE, Liz
   see Rachel

FARJEON, Eleanor
   see Little Bookroom, The

FATCHEN, Max
   see River Kings, The

FINKEL, George
   see Matthew Flinders

FLANAGAN, Joan
   see Some Buildings Are More
      Tricky Than They Look

FORBES, Ron
   see Sea Waits . . ., The
      When the Wind Comes

FOREMAN, Michael
   see War and Peas

FRASER, Brian
   see Freddie Martin and the
      Inventor's Club

FRENCH, Fiona
   see Blue Bird, The

GALE, Jennifer
   see Neat and Scruffy

GARFIELD, Leon
   see Drummer Boy, The

GEORGE, Jean Craighead
   see Wentletrap Trap, The

GIBSON, Helen
   see Australian Christmas, An
      Buster the Fire Truck

GILES, Barbara
   see Jack in the Bush
      Mission Defeated
      Puffin Fun Book, The

GLUSAC, R
   see Time for a Number Rhyme

GRAHAM, Bob
   see Here Comes John
      Here Comes Theo

Titles

Bunyip of Berkeley's Creek, The
(Wagner/Brooks)
1 photocopied dummy;
1 photocopied typed MS

Bush Bandits, The (Roland/Melrose)
1 original col. layout cover
artwork

Bush Christening, A (Paterson/Hole)
2 b&w dummies; 1 original col.
artwork

Buster the Fire Truck
(Gibson/Herbert)
1 original col. cover artwork;
2 original col. artwork; 1 original
b&w artwork

By Horse and Buggy
(Blaxell/Winch/Richardson)
1 original col. cover artwork

Call Him Muddy (Sammon/Paice)
6 initial b&w artwork; original
typed MS entitled 'Peanuts';
another typed MS entitled 'Call
Him Mudhead'

Captain Pugwash (Ryan)
1 original col. artwork

Chanticleer (Chaucer/Stobbs)
1 col. dummy

Charlotte & Charles
(Tompert/Wallner)
1 col. poster (dedicated)

Chimpanzees (author/illustrator
unknown)
1 col. dummy

Christmas Grump, The (Low)
1 original b&w artwork
(dedicated)

Cicero Queen's Drum Horse
(Unknown/Roberts)
21 original col. layout artwork

Cinderella (Grimm/Le Cain)
1 original b&w artwork

Clara Comes to Life
(Blaxell/Winch/Van Gendt)
1 original col. artwork

Classroom Teacher's Diary 1983,
The (Edwards/Hogan)
25 original col. artwork; 4 original
b&w artwork

Classroom Teacher's Diary 1984,
The (Edwards/Silbeck/Brown)
11 original col. artwork with
layout overlays

Click Go the Shears
(Unknown/Ingpen)
1 col. dummy

Cockatoos and Galahs
(Edwards/Little/Huxley)
1 original col. artwork; 13 original
col. artwork with text overlays

Cole's Funny Picture Book
1 dummy of No. 3; 2 printer's
col. proofs; tokens;
correspondence

Colour in the Creek
(Paice/Stackpool)
1 original col. cover artwork;
1 typed MS with corrections

Come Away From the Water,
Shirley (Burningham)
3 initial col. sketches; 7 initial
b&w sketches

Cousins-come-Lately
(Pownall/Senior)
1 original col. cover artwork;
4 original b&w artwork;
1 original col. layout cover
artwork

Coyote Cry (Baylor/Shimin)
1 original b&w artwork

Creatures with Pockets
(Gray/Coventry)
3 original col. artwork

Dancing Buildings
(Blaxell/Winch/Hayes)
1 original col. artwork

Devilish Mystery of the Flying Mum,
The (Martin/McAllen)
1 original col. cover artwork

Diamond Valley Sketchbook
(McKinlay/Hawley)
1 original b&w artwork

Dingo Boy (Dugan)
1 typed MS with corrections

Disbelief (Macleod)
1 photocopied typed MS

Dolphins Are Different
(Parr/Mullins)
3 original col. artwork

Donovan and the Lost Birthday
(Ord/Janic)
1 original col. title page artwork;
2 original col. artwork; 1 original
col. cover artwork

Down to Earth (Wrightson/Horder)
4 original b&w artwork

Dragon Kite, The (Lewis/Le Cain)
1 original col. cover artwork

Dragon of an Ordinary Family, The
(Mahy/Oxenbury)
1 initial col. artwork

Dragon's Breath (Dugan/Hicks)
3 b&w dummies; 1 original col.
artwork (unpub.)

Drummer Boy, The
(Garfield/Maitland)
1 original b&w artwork

Duffy and the Devil (Zemach)
1 original col. artwork (dedicated)

Egrin and the Painted Wizard
(Walsh)
1 original col. cover artwork;
6 original b&w artwork;
12 original col. artwork; 1 layout
col. title page; 1 b&w dummy

Elements of Danger (Pownall/Lacis)
3 initial col. cover artwork
(unpub.)

Eureka Stockade
(Boardman/Harvey)
1 original col. artwork; 1 initial
col. artwork; 1 publisher's
typescript; 1 col. proof; 1 initial
b&w sketch; 1 initial proof;
14 galley proofs; 1 b&w dummy
with initial printed col. cover

Everlasting Circle (Greenwood)
1 original col. artwork

Feathers, Fur and Frills (Niland)
1 col. dummy

50 Million Sausages (Benedictus)
8 initial col. artwork

First Ever 1982 Calendar Planner
Diary from Ashton Scholastic, The
(Harvey)
3 original col. artwork; 15 original
col. artwork and overlays

First Fleet, The (Boardman/Harvey)
1 original col. cover artwork with
overlay; 1 original col. title page
artwork with overlay; 16 col.
printer's proofs; 11 original col.
artwork with overlays; 6 b&w
photocopies of artwork; 4 b&w
printer's proofs

Flea, The
(Blaxell/Winch/Cooper-Brown)
1 original col. artwork

Flowers for Samantha (Parr/Mullins)
1 col. dummy; 5 sheets initial
b&w artwork; 3 sheets initial col.
artwork

Flying Ship, The (Harris/Le Cain)
1 original col. artwork

Freddie Martin and the Inventor's
Club (Fraser)
1 typed MS with corrections

Freedom for Priscilla (Nicholson)
1 typed MS

Friend for Petros, A (Donkin/Rowe)
15 original b&w artwork

Frog, The (Blaxell/Winch/Moore)
1 original col. cover artwork

Frog and the Ox, The
(Blaxell/Winch)
1 original col. cover artwork
(illustrator unknown)

Frog Band and the Onion Seller, The
(Smith)
1 original col. artwork

Further Adventures of Dr A. A. A.
McGurk, The (White/Hook)
34 original b&w artwork;
3 original b&w artwork
(damaged)

Furze Folk, The
(Marsden/Thompson)
2 original b&w title pages;
9 original col. artwork; 18 original
b&w artwork

Gecko Gully (Conley)
1 galley proof; 13 photocopied
illustrations; 1 typed MS Ch.
2—14

Giant Devil Dingo, The (Roughsey)
1 photocopied typed MS with
corrections; 1 photocopied typed
MS as received by publisher

Giraffe in Pepperell Street, The
(Klein/Tomlin)
1 original col. layout cover
artwork; 4 original col. artwork

Gloop the Bunyip (Thiele/Baily)
1 original col. artwork

Golden Dream, The
(Keesing/Stackpool)
1 original col. cover artwork;
54 original b&w artwork;
1 original b&w artwork for
endpapers

Gone Children (Harry/Honey)
1 original col. cover artwork

Grandad (Blaxell/Winch/Kerr)
1 original col. layout artwork

Grandmother (Baker)
15 original col. collages; 2 collated
col. proofs; 1 original col.
collage used as cover artwork

Grape That Ran Away, The (Stobbs)
1 col. dummy

Grasshopper and Butterfly
(Piers/Baynes)
1 original col. artwork

Grasshopper on the Road (Lobel)
1 prelim. col. artwork

Great Bagpipe Plague, The (Macleod)
1 typed MS with handwritten
corrections; 1 corrected typed MS

Great Icecream Crisis, The (Zwar)
1 typed MS with corrections

Grumble of Glot, The (Dugan)
1 photocopied typed MS

Hairy Maclary from Donaldson's
Dairy (Dodd)
2 original illustrations

Hans Andersen: His Classic Fairy
Tales (Haugaard/Foreman)
1 b&w dummy; 1 col. first print
copy; 5 initial b&w artwork

Helen is Helen (Hogarth)
1 typed MS (unrevised)

Henry Lawson's Favourite Stories
(Stone/Stackpool)
16 original b&w artwork

Here Comes John (Graham)
1 original col. layout cover artwork; 1 initial col. cover artwork with overlay; 27 original col. artwork with overlays; 1 original col. layout title page; 1 initial col. layout title page with overlay; 1 original col. layout half-title page; 2 original b&w layout artwork for endpapers; 15 layout col. printer's proofs

Here Comes Theo (Graham)
1 original col. layout cover artwork; 30 original col. artwork with overlays; 1 original col. layout half-title page artwork; 4 original b&w layout artwork for endpapers; 1 printed col. cover proof

Heroic Adventures of a Space Puffin, The (Muddlepup)
1 photocopied typed MS with corrections

Home in the Sky (Baker)
1 original col. artwork

Human Adventure, The (Oldmeadow/Schoenheimer)
Research notes

Hundred Watermelons, A (Long)
1 typed MS with corrections

Hustler's Gold (Spencer/Melrose)
1 original col. cover artwork

I Am Adopted (Lapsley/Charlton)
2 col. dummies; 1 b&w dummy; 1 original col. cover artwork; 8 col. proofs; 2 sheets initial b&w artwork; 1 typeset MS

I Own the Racecourse! (Wrightson/Horder)
1 typed MS; 1 original col. artwork rejected for cover

If You Catch an Elephant (Brierley)
1 photocopied corrected typed MS

I'm Taggerty Toad (Pavey)
2 col. dummies; 1 b&w dummy (entitled 'I Am Taggerty Toad'); 1 photocopied dummy; 17 printed dyelines; 1 initial col. artwork; 1 initial b&w artwork

Incredible Steam-driven Adventures of Riverboat Bill, The (Green/Axelson)
1 original col. cover artwork; 24 original b&w artwork

In the Garden (Blaxell/Winch/Hooper)
1 original col. artwork

In the Garden of Badthings (Macleod/Thompson)
10 original col. artwork; 1 original col. cover artwork; 1 original col. artwork of back cover with layout overlays; 1 b&w dummy; 1 original b&w artwork for endpapers; 1 b&w layout cover

artwork lettering; 15 col. printer's proofs; 1 b&w layout title page; 15 layout artwork; 1 layout cover

Is It Real? (Blaxell/Winch)
1 original col. artwork (illustrator unknown)

Island of the Skog, The (Kellogg)
1 initial col. artwork (unpub.)

I was Very Shy (Lippman)
1 printed col. cover ('Archibald; Or, I Was Very Shy'); 3 initial b&w artwork; 1 initial b&w cover artwork; 1 b&w dummy

Jacaranda New Primary Atlas
10 col. layout sheets; 29 col. slides; b&w working photos

Jack and the Beanstalk (Jacobs/Gill)
1 col. dummy

Jackey Jackey (Paice/Cunningham)
1 initial col. cover artwork

Jack in the Bush (Giles/Greenhatch)
8 initial cover artwork; 1 typed MS with corrections; 2 sets b&w publisher's proofs; 10 b&w photographs of completed artwork; 2 printed col. covers (not final col.); 4 initial b&w artwork; 4 original b&w artwork

Jack Jouett's Ride (Haley)
1 original col. cover artwork; 2 original col. artwork; 14 original b&w artwork

Jack the Giant Killer (Jacobs/Wegner)
1 b&w dummy

Jacob Two-Two Meets the Hooded Fang (Richler/Wegner)
1 original col. cover artwork

James and the Roman Silver (Maitland)
3 transparencies of cover artwork; 2 b&w transparencies of artwork and text; 1 b&w dummy (entitled 'James and the Roman Coin')

Jandy Malone and the Nine O'Clock Tiger (Bolton/White)
1 original col. cover artwork

John Brown, Rose and the Midnight Cat (Wagner/Brooks)
1 col. dummy; 2 b&w dummies; 1 original col. cover artwork; 1 original col. artwork; 1 initial col. cover artwork (unpub.); 1 initial col. title page (unpub.); 14 initial col. artwork (unpub.)

Johnny-cake (Stobbs)
1 col. dummy

Johnny Tremain (Donkin)
1 typed MS with corrections

Jo-Jo and Mike (Wagner/James)
initial typed MS; 1 photocopy of initial artwork and text; 1 printer's proof with corrections

Josh (Southall/Lacis)
2 initial col. cover artwork; 1 typed MS with corrections

Kali and the Golden Mirror (Wuorio/Ardizzone)
1 original col. cover artwork

Kangapossum & Crocoroo (Rankine/Hook)
2 original co. artwork.

Kangaroo Joey Finds His Shadow (Hewett/Toucher)
1 original col. cover art; 22 original col. artwork

Keep Out (Young)
1 original col. artwork

Kid, The (Durack)
1 col. hand print of original painting; correspondence

King Krakus and the Dragon (Domanska)
1 original col. artwork (dedicated)

King Rhubarb (Him)
1 original col. artwork from TV series

Lace Snail, The (Byars)
2 original col. artwork (dedicated)

Legs (Crabtree)
9 initial b&w artwork; 1 initial col. alphabet; 12 original col. artwork

Lester and Clyde (Reece)
9 original col. artwork; 1 original col. artwork with corrections; 2 initial col. sketches; 4 large printed col. proofs; 18 printed col. proofs; 1 b&w dummy; 15 initial b&w sketches

Let's Have a Pet Show (Madgwick/Janic)
12 original col. artwork with text overlays; 1 original col. artwork for endpapers

Lion in the Garden, A (Seton/Jaques)
1 b&w original artwork

Little Black Princess of the Never-Never, The (Gunn/Crabtree)
4 original b&w artwork

Little Bookroom, The (Farjeon/Ardizzone)
1 original b&w artwork

Little Chimbu (Curtis)
4 original col. sample artwork

Little Que-i (Sammon/Paice)
1 b&w dummy; original dummy, entitled 'The Lucky Stone'; original typed MS, entitled 'The Lucky Stone'

Lizard Log (Mattingley/Sallis)
1 original col. cover artwork

Lucas and the Kitemen (Conley/Olive)
typed MS of Ch. 1 with corrections; list of suggested illustrations; 1 original b&w artwork (unpub.); 1 typed MS with corrections

Lucy and Tom at the Seaside (Hughes)
1 original col. artwork (unpub.); 1 b&w dummy (entitled 'Lucy and Tom's Day at the Seaside') with original col. cover artwork

Machine at the Heart of the World, The (Wagner/Fisher)
13 original col. artwork; 12 col. printer's proofs

Maggy Scraggle Loves the Beautiful Icecream Man (McDonald)
1 folded col. proof; 2 b&w dummies

Magic Balloon, Sleeping Chair (Young/Abrahams)
2 b&w dummies

Magician, The (Bates)
1 typed carbon MS with corrections

Magpie's Nest, The (Jacobs/Stobbs)
1 col. dummy

Man from Ironbark, The (Paterson/Hole)
2 b&w dummies; 1 original col. artwork

Marbles in My Pocket (Pender/O'Harris)
1 b&w dummy (for 'Verses for Judy'); 1 original b&w artwork; 1 letterpress printing block; carbon copy of original MS

Margaret Catchpole (Donkin/Bell)
66 original b&w artwork; 1 original b&w artwork for endpapers, with overlay; 1 original col. layout cover artwork; 1 typed MS with corrections

Marina (Harper/Crabtree)
1 original b&w artwork; 2 original col. artwork

Marty Moves to the Country (Walker/Treloar)
1 col. dummy

Matt and Jo (Southall)
1 typed MS with corrections

Matthew Flinders (Finkel/Hatcher)
1 original col. cover art; 4 original b&w layout artwork

Merchant Campbell (Park/Bell)
1 initial col. cover artwork

Midget Mouse Finds a House (Lindsay/Marenelle)
1 photocopy of typed MS; 6 col. proofs of artwork

Mirage (Macleod)
1 photocopied typed MS

Miss Anna Truly's Christmas Present (Drummond)
1 b&w dummy

Mission Defeated (Giles)
1 typed MS with corrections

Mr and Mrs Pig's Evening Out (Rayner)
1 original col. artwork

Mr Faksimily and the Tiger (Hewett/Broomfield)
1 col. dummy

Mr Knitted and the Family Tree (Meyer)
2 original col. collages

Mr Magnolia (Blake)
3 initial b&w artwork; 2 original b&w artwork (1 dedicated)

Mister P and His Remarkable Flight (Martin/Lacis)
1 original col. cover artwork; 10 original b&w artwork

Mog's Christmas (Kerr)
1 original col. artwork

Mog the Forgetful Cat (Kerr)
1 original col. artwork

Moon-Eyes (Chapman/Lacis)
1 original col. artwork

Moonshadow (Carter/Todd)
4 original col. artwork

More Night (Rukeyser/Shimin)
1 original col. artwork; 1 b&w dummy

Muddle Country (Varday)
1 photocopied typed MS

Mulga Bill's Bicycle (Paterson/Niland)
1 original col. artwork

Mum Knitted, Little Knittle Threadle, Pearly Twill Spool (Meyer)
1 original col. collage

My Family (Sen/Wilkinson)
1 b&w dummy

My Grandma Lived at Gooligulch (Base)
1 sepia dummy; 1 original b&w artwork

My Old Dad (Dugan)
handwritten poems

My Simple Little Brother (Norman)
1 typed MS

Nargun and the Stars, The (Wrightson)
1 typed MS

Naughty Agapanthus (Macfarlane/Lees)
6 original col. artwork; 1 original col. artwork (unpub.); 1 original col. cover artwork

Neat and Scruffy (Gale/Reece)
9 original col. layout artwork; 2 large col. printer's proofs

Neddie Puddin's Book of Things (Moffatt)
2 original col. artwork

Ned Kelly (Clune/Stackpool)
1 original col. artwork

Nicholas and the Moon Eggs (Way)
2 original col. artwork

Nifty, the Sugar Glider (Sammon)
1 original typed MS entitled 'Nifty Ned'

Nimbin, The (Wagner/Moore)
2 original col. artwork

Nobody Knows I Have Delicate Toes (Patz)
1 original col. artwork with overlay; 3 col. layout artwork; 1 initial col. layout artwork; 1 col. dummy; 1 col. printed artwork; 1 original col. artwork; 1 printer's proof; 3 b&w copies of artwork; b&w printed sketches

Nonsense Numbers (Dugan/Newman)
1 original col. cover artwork with overlay; 16 original col. artwork with overlays; 1 original col. title page artwork with overlay; 1 col. printer's cover proof

Nonsense Places (Dugan/Stackpool)
1 original col. dedication page; 1 b&w dummy with col. cover artwork; 1 original col. layout cover artwork; 1 original col. artwork; 1 original col. layout title page; 1 typed MS with corrections

Oath of Bad Brown Bill, The (Axelson)
1 initial col. artwork (unpub.)

Off the Beaten Track (Blaxell/Winch/Dunphy)
1 original col. artwork

Older Kind of Magic, An (Wrightson)
1 typed MS

Old Green Hat Mike Brady Wore, The (Pownall)
1 typed MS with corrections

Once There was a Swagman (Brinsmead/Young)
1 typed MS; 1 b&w dummy; 1 original b&w artwork; 2 printed artwork (one with transparency)

One Dragon's Dream (Pavey)
1 printed cover; 1 original col. artwork

On My Island (Dutton/Perceval)
1 b&w dummy

Oodoolay (Klein/Goodman)
1 original col. cover artwork; 9 original col. artwork

Other Way Round, The (Kerr)
1 handwritten MS

Our First Town (Blaxell/Winch/Naisby)
1 original col. cover artwork

Paddington Cleans Up (Bond/Fortnum)
4 original b&w artwork

Painted Bird, The (McKimmie)
1 original col. cover artwork; initial col. sketches; initial handwritten MSS and portions of MS, all differing from published book

Pandora Valley (King)
1 typed MS

Pearl Pinkie and the Sea Greenie (O'Harris)
1 metal printer's block

Perkins Street (Prior)
6 original col. artwork (illustrator unknown)

Peter Pebble (Blyth)
1 original col. title page artwork; 1 original col. artwork

Petey (Tobias/Shimin)
2 b&w original artwork

Pet for Mrs Arbuckle, A (Smyth/James)
1 col. dummy; 29 col. proofs; 13 initial b&w artwork; 30 initial col. artwork; 4 initial col. cover artwork; 2 initial b&w cover artwork; 2 col. layout artwork; 4 original col. artwork (unpub.); initial b&w sketches; initial col. sketches; 1 initial typed MS; 1 publisher's MS

Pirate Edna of Old Tallangatta (Lloyd/Williams)
6 original col. artwork; 1 original col. cover artwork with layout overlay; 6 original b&w artwork

Pixie O'Harris Treasury of Children's Verse, The (O'Harris)
1 complete dummy with original col. artwork

Playing Beatie Bow (Park/Lacis)
2 initial col. cover artwork (unpub.)

Polar Bear (Moss/Baker)
2 original col. collages

Pony from Tarella (Clark/Melrose)
1 original col. cover artwork

Pope's Mule, The (Daudet/Lawrence)
1 col. dummy

Porcupine (Turner)
1 photocopied typed MS

Printing (Kurth)
1 lino-cut; 1 col. dummy

Puffineering Around Australia (Sheldrake)
1 typed MS with corrections

Puffin Fun Book, The (Dugan/Giles)
1 photocopied typed MS with corrections of introduction by Barbara Giles

Puffing Billy (De Fossard/Mason)
1 col. dummy

Pumpernickle, Tickle and Mean Green Cheese (Patz)
1 initial col. cover artwork; initial col. sketch; 1 col. study; 1 printed col. cover; 1 printed col. title page; 2 printed col. artwork; 3 b&w dummies; 1 printed b&w artwork; 1 b&w title page; 1 initial MS; rough sketches

Pumpkin Paddy (Blaxell/Winch/Macintyre)
1 original col. cover artwork

Quippy (Mason/Cunningham)
1 col. dummy

Rabbit and Pork (Lawrence)
1 hand-coloured print

Rabbit Pie (Rose)
1 col. dummy

Rachel (Fanshawe/Charlton)
2 original col. artwork; 1 initial col. artwork; 35 initial b&w artwork

Rainbow (Sibley)
2 b&w artwork; 3 initial col. prints; 4 printer's blocks; 1 copy of limited edition (enlarged); 1 b&w dummy with col. title page

Rainforest Children, The (Pittaway/Philpott)
2 original col. artwork

Rat Race: The Amazing Adventures of Anton B. Stanton (McNaughton)
1 original col. artwork

Read All About It (Blaxell/Winch/Richardson)
1 original col. cover artwork

Reading Through the Language Arts (Ridsdale)
1 typed MS with corrections; 1 typed MS with corrections and author's rough illustrations

Red Five, The (Blaxell/Winch)
1 original col. artwork (illustrator unknown)

Ring-In, The (Stivens)
1 typed MS

Ring of the Axe, The (Preston/Melrose)
1 original col. cover artwork

Riverboat Crew, The (McLean)
3 original col. cover artwork

River Kings, The (Fatchen)
1 typed MS

River Murray Mary (Thiele/Ingpen)
printed dust jacket; layout dust jacket; 1 sample cover art; 1 initial cover and title art ('Yesterday's 'Ero' by Michael Page and Robert Ingpen); 1 b&w original artwork; 2 initial col. sketches; 3 col. printed proofs; 1 sepia printed proof; 3 b&w initial sketches; 1 initial sketch/title page; 1 publisher's typescript; galley proofs; 1 col. photograph; correspondence

Rolls Royce Called Ark, A (Stobbs)
1 col. dummy

Roma Mercedes and Fred (Ray)
1 typed carbon MS

Rummage (Mattingley/Mullins)
1 original col. layout cover artwork

Rumplestiltskin (Stobbs)
1 col. dummy

Safe as a Wet Paper Bag (Turner)
1 photocopied typed MS

Salinka (Watts)
part of handwritten MS; same part typed; photocopy of same part

Salt River Times (Mayne/Honey)
2 original b&w artwork; 2 initial b&w artwork

Sam Who Never Forgets (Rice)
1 col. artwork

Sarah and the Kelpie (Unknown/Walker)
3 original b&w artwork (illustrations to a series of magazine short stories, illustrator unknown)

Seasons, The (Unknown/Jaques)
1 original b&w title page artwork

Sea Waits . . ., The (Forbes/Forbes)
2 original col. collages

Shadow of Wings (Paice)
1 typed MS with corrections

Sharpur the Carpet Snake (Pender)
1 revised typed MS

Ships and Seafarers of the South Pacific (Hatcher)
2 original col. layout artwork

Shudders and Shakes (Ingram/Lacis)
5 initial col. cover artwork

Singing Wire, The (Pownall/Stackpool)
1 original col. cover artwork; 1 initial col. cover artwork; 35 original b&w artwork; 1 original b&w artwork for endpapers; 1 original col. artwork with printer's notes; 1 typed MS with corrections

Sir Atholbert Faces Authority (Landsdale)
1 typed MS with corrections

Sly Cormorant (Patten/Le Cain)
32 initial layout artwork; 32 b&w photographs of artwork

Smallest Turtle, The (Dodd)
1 b&w dummy; 7 original col. layout artwork; 6 b&w prelim. sketches; 7 original col. artwork; 6 pages prelim. sketches

Snails, Spiders and Things (Blaxell/Winch)
1 original col. artwork (illustrator unknown)

Snow White and the Seven Dwarfs (Grimm/Wegner)
1 original col. artwork; 1 b&w dummy

Some Buildings Are More Tricky Than They Look (Flanagan)
1 typed MS with corrections

Some Fables From Aesop (Aesop/Jones)
1 col. dummy

Spark of Opal (Clark/Melrose)
1 original col. artwork

Sparrow's Story at the King's Command, The (Crabtree)
4 original col. artwork

Special Birthday Present, The (Unknown/Shimin)
1 original col. artwork

Spiders and Scorpions (Cloudsley-Thompson/Bee)
1 col. dummy

Spooks and Spirits (Dugan/Hamilton/Honey/Niland)
1 printed col. cover; 1 b&w artwork (Deborah Niland); 1 b&w artwork (Elizabeth Honey)

Steamtrain Crew, The (McLean)
1 original col. artwork

Stephen's Useless Design (Martin/Draper)
18 original col. artwork with text overlays; 1 original col. cover artwork with title overlay; initial handwritten MS; 2 handwritten drafts; 5 typescripts; 10 initial b&w artwork; col. proofs

Story of Admiral Sneeze, The (Macleod)
1 original col. cover artwork

Story of Admiral Sneeze, The (Macleod)
1 b&w original artwork (pub. poster accompanying book)

Story of Saul the King (Waddell/Roberts)
2 original col. layout artwork

Story of the Pantomime Humpty Dumpty, The (Rentoul/Rentoul)
1 original b&w artwork; 1 printed proof; correspondence

Stuff and Nonsense (Dugan/Niland)
author's proof copy

Stuffed Parrots (Moffatt)
1 original col. cover artwork (unpub.)

Susie's Dolls' Pram (Meyer)
2 original col. artwork

Tall Talk (Wannan)
1 typed MS with corrections

Tari's First Christmas (Diestel-Feddersen/Gynell)
1 original col. cover artwork; 14 original col. artwork; 1 initial b&w cover artwork (unpub.); 1 original b&w artwork for endpapers; 1 original typed printer's MS

Tell Me Your Story (Blaxell/Winch)
1 original col. cover artwork; 1 original col. artwork (illustrators unknown)

Terrible Thing that Happened at Our House, The (Blaine/Wallner)
1 original col. layout artwork

There's a Hippopotamus on Our Roof Eating Cake (Edwards/Niland)
1 col. dummy

Thoughtful Troglodyte, A (Varday)
1 photocopied corrected typed MS

Three Giant Stories (Conger/Fry)
1 original b&w layout cover artwork; 11 original b&w artwork with overlays; 1 original col. artwork with b&w overlay

Through the Mist (Turner)
1 original col. artwork

Tiddalick: The Frog Who Caused a Flood (Roennfeldt)
3 original col. artwork; 1 initial b&w sketch

Tiger Who Came to Tea, The (Kerr)
1 original col. artwork

Time For a Number Rhyme (Glusac/Rawlins/Tanner)
2 original col. artwork (Donna Rawlins); 1 original col. artwork with text overlay (Jane Tanner)

Time for a Rhyme (Gardner/Philpott/Tanner)
1 original col. artwork

Time to Get Out of the Bath, Shirley (Burningham)
1 initial col. cover artwork; 6 initial col. artwork; 5 initial b&w artwork

Tin Can Tortoise, The (Standon/Standon)
1 col. dummy

Tinka and the Bunyip (Downing)
28 original col. artwork

Tin Lizzie and Little Nell (Cox)
1 typed MS; 1 typed biography of author

Tinner's Quest (Bibby)
part of original MS; correspondence

Too True (Ingram)
photocopied and original MSS as collected; titles and individual authors are listed separately

Torty Longneck (Young)
1 original col. artwork

Town Mouse and Country Mouse (Blaxell/Winch/Oliver)
1 original col. cover artwork

Train, The (Generowicz)
20 original col. artwork; 1 original col. title page artwork; 1 original col. cover artwork

Treasury of Australians in History, A (Stackpool)
1 initial col. cover artwork

Trojan Horse, The (Blaxell/Winch/Oliver)
1 original col. artwork

27th Annual African Hippopotamus Race, The (Lurie)
1 original col. layout cover artwork for Penguin

Uhu (Macarthur-Onslow)
1 original col. artwork

Unchosen Land, The (Ingpen)
16 initial col. artwork

Useless Donkeys, The (Pender/Cowell)
2 original col. artwork

Verses for Judy (Pender)
see Marbles in My Pocket

V.I.P. (Very Important Plant) (Greenwood)
1 original col. artwork (cover art for paperback edition); 1 handwritten MS

Voyage of the Poppykettle, The (Ingpen)
1 original b&w artwork; 2 initial col. sketches

Waltzing Disease, The (Macleod)
1 photocopied typed MS

War and Peas (Foremen)
1 original col. artwork

Weather Strike (White)
1 typed MS

Weekend (Dugan)
1 typed MS

Wentletrap Trap, The (George/Shimin)
1 b&w dummy; 2 original b&w artwork

What — a — Mess (Muir/Wright)
1 original col. artwork

When a Goose Meets a Mouse (Scott-Mitchell/Hogan)

When the Wind Comes (Forbes)
1 original col. collage

When Willy Went to the Wedding (Kerr)
1 original col. artwork

While the Bells Ring (Mayne/Rawlins)
1 typed MS with corrections; photocopies of proposed illustrations

Whistle Up the Chimney (Hunt/Smith)
1 original col. artwork

Who Sank the Boat? (Allen)
2 initial col. cover artwork with overlays; 17 b&w layout artwork; 1 printed col. cover proof; 9 col. proofs; 5 sepia col. proofs

Who's Granny Smith? (Blaxell/Winch)
1 original col. artwork (illustrator unknown)

Wildfire (Clark)
page 81 of typed MS with corrections; photocopy of final copy of page 83

Wind, The (Blaxell/Winch/Honey)
1 original col. cover artwork

Wind in the Willows (Grahame)
1 original col. artwork (illustrator unknown)

Wingdingdilly, The (Peet)
1 original col. artwork

Woodcutter's Duck, The (Turska)
1 col. dummy

Wurley and Woomera (Mathews/Stackpool)
1 initial col. cover art (unpub.); 1 original col. cover artwork

Year and a Day, A (Mayne/Turska)
1 publisher's advance proof

Yusuf and Shirin (author/illustrator unknown)
1 original col. artwork

APPENDIX 2
Children's Book Council of Australia: Book of the Year Awards

The Children's Book Council of Australia announces its children's book awards during Children's Book Week in July of each year.

From 1946 to 1949, the awards were made by the Australian Book Society and from 1951 to 1956, by the New South Wales Children's Book Council. A separate Picture Book Award was established in 1952.

In 1957, the New South Wales and Victorian Children's Book Councils agreed that judging should be shared between the two states and in 1959, with the formation of the Australian Children's Book Council, an all-Australian Children's Book of the Year award became possible.

There are now three awards. They are: Class A, The Book of the Year; Class B, Picture Book of the Year; and Class C, Junior Book of the Year, a 'bridge' book for younger readers, which can be chosen from either Class A or Class B entries. The judges are instructed to select at least eight titles from each category (Classes A and B) for the short list.

Only the winners of each section are included in this Appendix.

Australian Children's Book of the Year

Australian Book Society
1946   *Karrawingi the Emu* by Leslie Rees; illustrated by Walter Cunningham (John Sands)

1947   No Award

1948   *Shackleton's Argonauts* by Frank Hurley; photographs by the author (Angus & Robertson)

1949   *Whalers of the Midnight Sun* by Allan Villiers (Angus & Robertson)

1950   No Award

Children's Book Council of New South Wales
1951   *Verity of Sydney Town* by Ruth C. Williams; illustrated by Rhys Williams (Angus & Robertson)

1952   *The Australia Book* by Eve Pownall; illustrated by Margaret Senior (John Sands)

1953   *Good Luck to the Rider* by Joan Phipson; illustrated by Margaret Horder (Angus & Robertson)

Aircraft of To-day and To-morrow by J. H. and W. D. Martin (Angus & Robertson)

1954   *Australian Legendary Tales* by K. Langloh Parker; selected by Henrietta Drake-Brockman and illustrated by Elizabeth Durack (Angus & Robertson)

1955   *The First Walkabout* by Norman B. Tindall and H. A. Lindsay; illustrated by Madeleine Boyce (Longmans Green)

1956   *The Crooked Snake* by Patricia Wrightson; illustrated by Margaret Horder (Angus & Robertson)

Children's Book Councils of New South Wales and Victoria
1957   *The Boomerang Book of Legendary Tales*, edited by Enid Moodie-Heddle; illustrated by Nancy Parker

(Longmans Green)

1958   *Tiger in the Bush* by Nan Chauncy; illustrated by Margaret Horder (Oxford University Press)

Children's Book Council of Australia
1959   *Devil's Hill* by Nan Chauncy; illustrated by Geraldine Spence (Oxford University Press)

Sea Menace by John Gunn; illustrated by Brian Keogh (Constable)

1960   *All the Proud Tribesmen* by Kylie Tennant; illustrated by Clem Seale (Macmillan)

1961   *Tangara* by Nan Chauncy; illustrated by Brian Wildsmith (Oxford University Press)

1962   *The Racketty Street Gang* by L. F. Evers; jacket design by Arthur Horowicz (Hodder & Stoughton)

Rafferty Rides a Winner by Joan Woodberry;

illustrated by the author (Max Parrish)

1963   *The Family Conspiracy* by Joan Phipson; illustrated by Margaret Horder (Angus & Robertson)

1964   *The Green Laurel* by Eleanor Spence; illustrated by Geraldine Spence (Oxford University Press)

1965   *Pastures of the Blue Crane* by Hesba F. Brinsmead; illustrated by Annette Macarthur-Onslow (Oxford University Press)

1966   *Ash Road* by Ivan Southall; illustrated by Clem Seale (Angus & Robertson)

1967   *The Min-Min* by Mavis Thorpe Clark; illustrated by Genevieve Melrose (Lansdowne Press)

1968   *To the Wild Sky* by Ivan Southall; illustrated by Jennifer Tuckwell (Angus & Robertson)

1969   *When Jays Fly to Barbmo* by Margaret Balderson; illustrated by Victor G. Ambrus (Oxford University Press)

1970 *Uhu* by Annette Macarthur-Onslow; illustrated by the author (Ure Smith)

1971 *Bread and Honey* by Ivan Southall; jacket design by Wolfgang Grasse (Angus & Robertson)

1972 *Longtime Passing* by Hesba F. Brinsmead; jacket design by Victor G. Ambrus (Angus & Robertson)

1973 *Family at the Lookout* by Noreen Shelley; illustrated by Robert Micklewright (Oxford University Press)

1974 *The Nargun and the Stars* by Patricia Wrightson; jacket design by Joan Saint (Hutchinson)

1975 No Award

1976 *Fly West* by Ivan Southall; jacket design by Peter Eldridge-Doyle (Angus & Robertson)

1977 *The October Child* by Eleanor Spence;

illustrated by Malcolm Green (Oxford University Press)

1978 *The Ice is Coming* by Patricia Wrightson; jacket design by David Bergen (Hutchinson)

1979 *The Plum Rain Scroll* by Ruth Manley; illustrated by Marianne Yamaguchi (Hodder & Stoughton)

1980 *Displaced Person* by Lee Harding; jacket design by Alan Scholz (Hyland House)

1981 *Playing Beatie Bow* by Ruth Park; jacket design by Astra Lacis (Thomas Nelson)

1982 *The Valley Between* by Colin Thiele; jacket design by Robert Ingpen (Rigby)

1983 *Master of the Grove* by Victor Kelleher; jacket design by Graham Townsend (Penguin)

1984 *A Little Fear* by Patricia Wrightson; jacket design by Martin White (Hutchinson)

Australian Children's Picture Book of the Year

Children's Book Council of New South Wales

1956 *Wish and the Magic Nut* by Peggy Barnard; illustrated by Sheila Hawkins (John Sands)

Children's Book Councils of New South Wales and Victoria

1958 *Piccaninny Walkabout* by Axel Poignant; photographs by the author (Angus & Robertson)

Children's Book Council of Australia

1965 *Hugh's Zoo* by Elisabeth MacIntyre; illustrated by the author (Angus & Robertson)

1969 *Sly Old Wardrobe* by Ivan Southall; illustrated by Ted Greenwood (Cheshire)

1970 *Obstreperous* by Ted Greenwood; illustrated by the author (Angus & Robertson)

1971 *Waltzing Matilda* by A. B. (Banjo) Paterson; illustrated by Desmond Digby (William Collins)

1974 *The Bunyip of Berkeley's Creek* by Jenny Wagner; illustrated by Ron Brooks (Kestrel)

1975 *The Man From Ironbark* by A. B. (Banjo) Paterson; illustrated by Quentin Hole (William Collins)

1976 *The Rainbow Serpent* by Dick Roughsey; illustrated by the author (William Collins)

1977 *ABC of Monsters* by Deborah Niland; illustrated by the author (Hodder & Stoughton)

1978 *John Brown, Rose and the Midnight Cat* by Jenny Wagner; illustrated by Ron Brooks (Hodder & Stoughton)

1979 *The Quinkins* by Dick Roughsey and Percy Trezise; illustrated by Dick Roughsey (William Collins)

1980 *One Dragon's Dream* by Peter Pavey; illustrated by the author (Thomas Nelson)

1981 No Award

1982 *Sunshine* by Jan Ormerod; illustrated by the author (Kestrel)

1983 *Who Sank the Boat?* by Pamela Allen; illustrated by the author (Thomas Nelson)

1984 *Bertie and the Bear* by Pamela Allen; illustrated by the author (Thomas Nelson)

Australian Junior Book of the Year

1983 *Thing* by Robin Klein; illustrated by Alison Lester (Oxford University Press)

1984 *Bernice Knows Best* by Max Dann; illustrated by Ann James (Oxford University Press)

PICTORIAL ACKNOWLEDGEMENTS

The publisher and authors gratefully acknowledge the following individuals and organizations who permitted illustrations under copyright to be reproduced in this book. Every effort has been made to trace the holder of copyright of the illustrative material. The publisher would be pleased to hear from the artist or publisher of any illustrations not suitably acknowledged so that any omission can be rectified.

2 Herald & Weekly Times; 8 Dennis Wisken; 9 Dennis Wisken, Walter Stackpool; 10 Walter Stackpool, Joyce Oldmeadow; 11 Joyce Oldmeadow, Dennis Wisken, William Collins Pty Ltd; 13 Young and Richardson, Joyce Oldmeadow; 14 Joyce Oldmeadow, Dennis Wisken; 15 Elsie Roughsey, Joyce Oldmeadow; 16 Joyce Oldmeadow, Roger Hargreaves/Joyce Oldmeadow; 17 Lydia Pender, Judy Cowell, William Collins Pty Ltd; 18 Ron Brooks, Alan Maltby; 19 Alden L. Berry, Joyce Oldmeadow, Mitsumasa Anno; 20 Dennis Wisken; 21 A. M. Morris (top), Joyce Oldmeadow; 22 A. M. Morris; 23 Donna Rawlins; 24-26 Lady W. Martin; 26, 27 Curtis Brown (Aust) Pty Ltd; 28 Dr Neil & Marion Shand, Curtis Brown (Aust) Pty Ltd; 29 Pixie O'Harris; 30 Alden L. Berry, Rolf Harris; 31 Dennis Wisken; 32 Beryl White, Alan Maltby; 33 Alan Maltby; 34 Angus & Robertson Publishers; 35 Joyce Badgery, Angus & Robertson Publishers; 36 Elizabeth Durack; 37 Dennis Wisken; 38 Geoff Hook; 39 Amanda Walsh; 40 Betty Greenhatch, Witold Generowicz (Penguin Books), Betty Greenhatch; 41 Robert Ingpen, Penguin Books; 42 Thomas Nelson, Australia; 43 Walter Stackpool, William Collins Pty Ltd; 44 Walter Stackpool, Robert Roennfeldt; 45 The Advertiser, Astra Lacis, Patricia Mullins; 46 Angus & Robertson Publishers; 47 Jeff Prentice, Noela Young; 48 Justin Todd, Judith Kerr, Pauline Baynes; 49 Symeon Shimin/Joyce Oldmeadow, Justin Todd, Symeon Shimin/Joyce Oldmeadow; 50 Nancy Patz; 51 Five Mile Press; 52 State Library of Victoria; 53 Jeff Prentice; 54 Five Mile Press; 55 Five Mile Press (bottom); 58 Dennis Wisken (bottom); 63 Dennis Wisken; 64 Routledge & Kegan Paul; 66 State Library of Victoria (bottom); 67 Max Meth; 68-69 F. Cole Turnley; 70 George Ferguson; 71 Dennis Wisken; 72 Jim McQuilten, Phillipa Poole; 73 J. K. Moir Collection (top); 75 J. K. Moir Collection, Ward Lock (bottom); 76-78 Lady W. Martin; 79 Curtis Brown (Aust) Pty Ltd, Dr Neil & Marion Shand; 80-81 Curtis Brown (Aust) Pty Ltd;

INDEX